THE TRAVELER'S
KEY
TO
ANCIENT
GREECE

THE TRAVELER'S
KEY
TO
ANCIENT
GREECE

A GUIDE TO SACRED PLACES

RICHARD G. GELDARD

with photographs and illustrations by
ASTRID FITZGERALD

A publication supported by
THE KERN FOUNDATION

Quest Books
Theosophical Publishing House

Wheaton, Illinois ◆ Chennai (Madras), India

The Theosophical Publishing House
P.O. Box 270
Wheaton, IL 60189-0270

A publication of the Theosophical Publishing House,
a department of the Theosophical Society in America

Grateful acknowledgment is made to the following for
permission to reproduce photographs: Deutsches
Archaologisches Institut, Athens: pages 4, 15, 20, 73, 197, 198,
199, 208, 223, 253, 291, and 295. Alison Frantz: pages 9, 115,
128, 136, and 137. National Archeological Museum, Athens:
page 221.

Library of Congress Cataloging-in-Publication Data

Geldard, Richard G.
The traveler's key to ancient Greece: a guide to sacred places
/ Richard G. Geldard.
       p.   cm.
Includes bibliographical references and index.
ISBN 0-8356-0784-4
1. Greece—Antiquities—Guidebooks. 2. Gods, Greek, in
art—Guidebooks. I. Title.
DF127.G45   2000
914.9504'76—dc21

                       99-059528

5   4   3   2   1   *   00   01   02   03   04   05   06   07

Printed in the United States of America

This book is dedicated to
the memory of my daughter Cynthia.

*. . . and from her head
and her dark eyes
there was a blowing grace,
as if it were from Aphrodite, the golden.*

— Hesiod

CONTENTS

INTRODUCTION

The *story* of ancient Greece begins with the migrations of pre-historic hunter-gatherers and the worship of the Great Goddess, represented in stone statuettes and cave drawings as a human figure of great magnitude and power identified with the earth. She is giver of life, nurturer of the living, and protector after life in her underworld abode. She appears throughout the Eastern Mediterranean in the earliest records of human habitation and, in particular, in Greece in the landscape and the ancient sanctuaries devoted to her power and glory.

The *drama* of ancient Greece begins with the Mycenaean/Achaean invasions during the Bronze Age, when the male-dominated deities of the north entered to rival the dominance of the Great Goddess in the palaces of the earlier Minoan culture. This god-goddess tension informs much of the history and mythology of Greece, and far from being finished business, remains today a continuing spiritual conflict for the human race. As the new millennium commences, we find ourselves once again coming under the influence of the feminine in spiritual matters, a development that makes the study of the ancient Greek culture especially relevant.

The *myths* of ancient Greece begin with the birth of the gods, the Titans of the Golden Age, whose powers correspond to the forces of Nature. In the context of Greek narrative, the word "myth" does not mean fable or some sense of the fictive. For the Greeks, as well as for many of the world's native peoples, a myth (expressed in Greek as *to legomenon*) refers to *the things spoken about* as opposed to *the things acted out*. A myth, then, is a narrative of events. It is always connected in the minds and hearts of the people with actual events or rituals. Imagination and exaggeration play a major role, but this is not reason to doubt the essential truth of the narrative.

The ordinary *history* of ancient Greece begins too late in

the written record to reflect accurately the ancient tension between the Great Goddess and the Olympian gods. This earlier narrative, which follows and celebrates an obscure but growing body of work devoted to the Goddess, takes up the story well before Homeric Greece, that glorious past familiar to lovers of the *Iliad* and the *Odyssey*. The real story of Greece does not belong to Helen and Paris alone, but rather to the Goddess, whose presence stimulated the myths of Helen of Troy. One beautiful myth says that the first pottery cup was molded from one of Helen's perfect breasts; but prior to that first cup, from which the wine of life was sipped, human culture itself was molded from the body of the Great Goddess herself as she reclined in the landscape of Attica and Crete.

Wonderfully for us, that landscape remains intact even as the ancient palaces and temples do not, and we can, with a little imagination and insight, create again the relationship our ancestors had with the Great Goddess as she was once worshiped in Greece. As long as we keep in mind that climatic changes have imposed a dry landscape where once there were forested mountains, rushing streams, and bubbling springs, we will be able to reconstruct much of the ancient environment.

❖   ❖   ❖

The Traveler's Key to Ancient Greece is divided into four sections: "The Background," "The Palace Cultures," "The Temple Cultures," and "The Lesser Palace and Temple Sites." In the

The oldest road in Europe—the Sacred Way, Knossos, Crete

first section the reader will find a general history, a description of ancient Greek religion, and introductions to the sciences of sacred number, geometry, and architecture. The second section is devoted to the palace cultures—those sites in Greece where the ancient Minoans and Mycenaeans established themselves and left for modern pilgrims and inquisitive archaeologists a record of their distinctive cultures. The third section covers the major sacred sites from the Archaic, Classical, and Hellenistic periods of ancient Greek history, and the fourth, the lesser palace and temple sites.

Plato, the great voice of the journey of the human soul, was the first Western writer to speak in more than fragments of the idea of spiritual development, the idea that human beings might lead life in such a way as to awaken within themselves the divine life. The possibility of such a discovery makes Plato's works a psychology, or a study of human behavior in the physical, intellectual, and spiritual sense. Plato was indebted to the voices of his own culture and his predecessors in philosophy, in particular the great Heraclitus, whose fragments from the Archaic past form a living mythology that still has power to transform lives.

Each section in this book devoted to a site contains information on its history, its mythology, and the physical site itself. The ancient pilgrim would have known some of the history of the site and would have been familiar with its mythology—its living narrative. The purpose of a visit or pilgrimage to the site was to purify the body and the mind and to make a sacrifice to the god or goddess of the place in order to invoke his or her presence. In that presence the pilgrim hoped to acquire knowledge, blessing, and good fortune.

This book is designed to emulate the journey of the pilgrim to a sacred site. The reader is presented with mythological and historical information and is then guided onto the site "in a sacred manner." The ancient gods have not totally vacated the holy places of Greece. If there has been any vacating, it is our own "vacation" from the myths of sacredness within ourselves. A sacred place is, after all, a place on the earth that human beings have set aside as a symbol of their own spiritual longing. It is as much internal as it is external. For the ancient Greeks, the aim of spiritual life was to cause their gods to manifest through acts of creativity, devotion, and sacrifice. What we are able to see in Greece today of these attempts at manifestation are the stones, columns, walls, statues, paths, and artifacts of spiritual devotion.

Limitations of space have not permitted a full treatment of a few of the more important sacred sites in Greece, such as the island of Delos and the oracle at Dodona. The final selection of sites to receive full attention was made on the basis of accessibility and historical continuity, that is, the presence of clear evidence of the pattern of development from Minoan and Mycenaean to Classical and Hellenistic times. The text does not include any consideration of Roman remains. My preference has been to remove Roman overlays whenever possible to reveal the Greek past underneath. The serious student of Greek culture will gradually develop an eye that discriminates the Greek original from the frosting of the Roman overlay.

Finally, a note about spelling. For many years all things Greek were sifted through the Roman experience via Latin. Heroes of Greek myths acquired Latin names, such as "Hercules" rather than "Heracles" or "Herakles." Since the Greek alphabet has no "c," the letter "k" is used for the hard sound that in English is represented by both "c" and "k." For this text, as in many others of recent vintage, a compromise position has been selected. Wherever possible the Greek language is transliterated directly into English, without a Latin influence. Exceptions to this general rule include those names that have become established with the Latin influence, such as "Sophocles," "Socrates," "Pericles," and "Aeschylus." Other names and places, such as "Asklepios" and "Epidauros," being less familiar, appear closer to their Greek form. The author makes no claim of immunity from inconsistency. Decisions have been made based on familiarity so as not to startle the eye too much in the reading process. In general, the decisions involve the use of "u" versus "o" or "c" versus "k." Alternative spellings appear in parentheses where the words are first encountered in the text.

1
THE
BACKGROUND

HISTORICAL OVERVIEW

PREHISTORY

Historians and archaeologists have marked out distinct periods in Greek history, beginning about 3000 BC with the start of what we call the Bronze Age, when evidence of human activity first reveals organized settlements and social groupings larger than the clan or tribe. For our purposes, however, the human history prior to that significant change in culture is also very important.

The archaeological record has yet to establish a beginning for the sacred life of human beings. We do know, for example, that we buried our dead in a sacred manner 60,000 years ago, returning loved ones to the body of the Earth Mother. And if we know little or nothing about daily life then, it is because people lived a nomadic existence, constantly moving and following the horned and cloven-footed herds in their seasonal wanderings in search of grazing pastures. Evidence of the existence of humans is found in the charcoal remnants of their fires inside caves.

Much still needs to be learned about this long period of nomadic life, when we lived with few possessions in temporary or natural shelters, hunting, telling stories, fighting to protect our own, and praying to the spirits who dwelled in the caves, gorges, springs, and mountains. To these nomadic peoples, the landscape was full of powers, which gradually acquired names and qualities. Spirits had wings, teeth, horns, claws, and specifically human qualities like mind and emotion. To placate these spirits and to bring human life under the protective shelter of their power, we developed a ceremonial recognition of divinity—in this case a feminine divinity who ruled over all.

Nomadic peoples began to follow sacred paths through places of danger to where game was available. These routes are still followed and still have the touch of spiritual power in them. In addition, the landscape itself was recognized as having divine qualities. The most important belonged to the Earth Mother Goddess, around and within whom the people lived and died. The earliest evidence we have of sculpted figures reveals an overwhelming interest in and devotion to the earth as mother. Artists molded the earth itself into female images, which they perceived in the likeness of life-giving power. Life-bearing hips, the birth canal, and life-sustaining breasts dominate these early figures. What is crucial to an understanding of ancient Greek culture is that these features corresponded to the hills, clefts, and springs of specific land-scape features. As we shall see, the outstanding example of these features remains vivid at Delphi.

Gradually, with the separation of existence into spiritual and material elements, specific places were set aside as more sacred than others. As long as the nomadic peoples regarded the whole of their world as sacred, they were integrated with the world of spirit. As soon as special sanctuaries were marked out, the drawn boundaries indicated separation as well as devotion; in a sense, civilization was born, and so also the need for periodic renewal of contact with the sacred.

Earth Mother or Goddess figurine, Neolithic Period, from Sparta

The sanctuary began either as an area of the landscape set aside for the gods or as an altar around which a sacred precinct gradually developed. The altar was probably a raised stone, perhaps flat or else cupped at the top, placed in a po-sition facing certain features of the sacred landscape. Sacrificial offerings were made on the stone. Rituals of thanks-giving and appeasement were typical of the offerings made after the hunt. In ritual it was recognized that the spirit had left the animal and that its life-giving meat, bone, sinew, and skin were now available to the group. Such a gift required thanks and the hope that the Earth Mother—later replaced by the sky gods—was not offended by the killing. Greek myths are full of accounts of hunters invading precincts sacred to the gods and killing the animals there. The consequences were always terrible.

The Earth Mother was relatively fixed in her places in the landscape, and specific locations were set aside for her worship. Lesser gods and demons (or spirits) were more mobile, appearing here or there, like the wind or the weather. Sanctuaries and rituals were also established to honor as well as to control these powers, to make access to this power more frequent and less destructive. These places and rituals, too, were the foundations of the Greek religion, which in history actually developed with greater consistency than did the political and cultural history of the region.

One brief comment is also needed to amplify an earlier comment on climate in Greek prehistory. Geological evidence, as well as Plato's account in the *Critias,* indicates that prior to 3000 BC Greece had a more fertile and wooded landscape. The hills and mountains were covered with mature forests, and streams and rivers flowed more abundantly. The present harshness is a later development caused by erosion, deforestation, and overdevelopment. The gradual drying drove the herds north or killed them off, and the end of abundant water ended the nomadic life. The Indo-European migrations from the north brought the beginnings of agriculture and the domestication of cattle. By 2000 BC only the vivid memory of the Earth Mother remained, giving form to the civilization despite the changes in the landscape that remained as an image of her protection and power.

The ancient peoples of Greece were also interested in the celestial bodies—the sun, the moon, planets, and stars, as well as astrological events such as comets, eclipses, shooting stars, and the like. But the overriding interest was in the sun, giver of life and power, and the moon, ruler of the night, giver of cycles and dreams. We know from the evidence of Stonehenge and other prehistoric astronomical sites from the same period that people calculated the rising and setting of the sun and established the moon-year based on the cycle of twenty-eight days, further broken down to patterns of seven days, or the week. One of the earliest references to the week occurs in Genesis—first transcribed in 500 BC—in the account of the creation of the world. As we will see later, these early calculations were sacred expressions of the divine power residing in the sun, moon, and stars. The calculations themselves were given expression not in numbers—a relatively late invention—but rather in geometry. The circle represented both sun and moon and came to be the perfect expression of divinity. Within that circle, contained by it and held in its embrace, emerged the cross, emblematic of the cardinal directions. From the cross came the square, the expression of the manifest creation. This geometric language spoke of the Divine, just as light represents the truth in the quest for knowledge and meaning. It is the combination of the sacred landscape and the sophisticated development of geometry that provides the frame for our picture of the sacred places of ancient Greece.

The Lion Gate, Mycenae, as it looked in the nineteenth century

THE BRONZE AGE

Before describing the essential features of the rich and varied period known as the Bronze Age, let us look at a table that sets out the flow of years and shows relationships from culture to culture throughout the Mediterranean.

Key to Bronze Age Periods

BRONZE AGE		HELLADIC	MINOAN	EGYPTIAN
Early	3000 BC	Early Helladic I	Early Minoan I	1st Dynasty
	2800 BC	Early Helladic I	Early Minoan II	4th Dynasy
	2400 BC	Early Helladic II	Early Minoan III	7th-10th "
	2200 BC	Early Helladic III	Middle Minoan I	11th "
Middle	2000 BC	Middle Helladic	Middle Minoan II	12th "
	1800 BC	Middle Helladic	Middle Minoan III	13th-17th "
	1600 BC	Late Helladic I	Late Minoan I	18th "
Late	1500 BC	Late Helladic II	Late Minoan II	
	1400 BC	Late Helladic III	Late Minoan III	
	1100 BC	End of Mycenaean Rule—Dorian Invasions		
		End of the Bronze Age		

These periods correspond to the archaeological record of levels in the various digs as carefully determined by the dating of pottery and lines of foundation walls. For instance, a Late Minoan I piece of pottery is dated 1600 BC and corresponds to the Late Helladic I period on the mainland.

The term "Helladic" refers to civilization on the Greek mainland, which in this period means primarily what is known as the Mycenaean civilization. The Mycenaean priest-kings— later supplanted by the Achaean kings (Agamemnon, Menelaus, and Odysseus)—flourished throughout what is now modern Greece from 1600 BC to 1100 BC during the Late Helladic Period. "Minoan" refers to the Minoan civilization, which takes its name from the legendary King Minos of Crete. This distinctive civilization, characterized by the elaborate and unfortified palaces of Crete and the Cyclades, came into existence soon after 2200 BC and came to a disastrous end in 1450 BC in what many observers believe to have been the great earthquake and tidal waves of the Thera eruption. Thera— now the modern Greek island of Santorini—remains an active volcanic island in the middle of the Mediterranean Sea. Visitors can still see the great crater and smoking dome that remind us of the end of a great civilization. There are even Minoan ruins on the island still under active investigation.

Another significant date in the Bronze Age is the sacking of Troy, central to Homer's story. Archaeological investigation of the many levels of the site of Troy in present-day Turkey places the great battle near 1200 BC, at the close of the Mycenaean/Achaean era.

SETTLEMENT

At the start of the Bronze Age there was no distinguishing of east from west in the Mediterranean. Trade on the sea lanes spread its influence from Egypt in the south across the islands to what is now the Baltic Peninsula and to the western boundaries of the known world. The dominant culture on the islands to the south was Minoan, belonging to a people whose background may have been either Egyptian or Near Eastern in origin.

Between 2000 BC and 1900 BC a herding people of Indo-European stock came from the north and settled in Thessaly and the lands spreading out from Mount Olympus. These Indo-Europeans brought with them a strong tradition of worship centered on the sky gods, chief of whom was Zeus, Bright Consciousness. They also brought with them a spoken language that was a form of archaic Greek. In what is now northern Greece they encountered the indigenous culture, the ancient people whose religious belief and tradition centered on the Earth Mother Goddess. In the Middle Bronze Age, then, began the courtship of the masculine and feminine gods. It was not always a smooth relationship or a peaceful marriage, but there were principles of spiritual law related to nature and human life that made this union a logical and important development in human history.

The major cultural influence in the region at the time of the Indo-European migration was clearly Minoan and was centered on the island of Crete. The Minoans were a peace-loving, creative people who constructed beautiful palaces, most of which can be dated prior to 2000 BC. The Minoans sailed the Mediterranean freely and established trade routes and colonies throughout the Aegean. Their major conflicts seemed to have been with pirates, who raided the trading routes and disrupted the flow of goods. But they apparently had no difficulty protecting their own palaces, since evidence shows them to have been unfortified during the height of the Minoan civilization.

However, by 1500 BC a new dynasty established itself on the mainland of Greece, no doubt supplanting the Minoan colonies in the process. This new civilization, known as the Mycenaean, was characterized by massive hilltop fortresses and aggressive control of subjugated peoples. The evidence suggests that the Mycenaean culture was formed on the model of the Minoan.

MINOAN CIVILIZATION

The great artistic and religious culture called Minoan thrived on the island of Crete between 2200 BC and 1450 BC. Archaeological remains at Knossos reveal evidence of habitation at the site for at least four thousand years before the construction of the first Minoan palace there. The Minoans developed a religion based in great measure on the worship of the Earth Mother and closely associated with the landscape surrounding the palace and with the sea, over which they traveled and which they painted so lovingly in their frescoes.

Where the Minoans came from we can only speculate. Most likely they landed on Crete from the south or east. The history of Egypt indicates that upheavals in the Fourth Dynasty may have stimulated emigration. In any case, these remarkable people settled in Crete, built astounding palaces, developed a sophisticated religion, made pottery and paintings second to none in the world, and died out in violence.

Their contributions to art, however, survived them. In 1967 on the island of Santorini, the Minoan town at Akrotiri was uncovered, revealing a treasure of wall frescoes now on display in the National Archaeological Museum in Athens. The frescoes of the antelope and of the fisherman holding his blue and golden catch show an artistic power unmatched in much later art and reflect a harmony and a vision that are the envy of the world.

The Dolphin Room in the Queen's Megaron, Knossos, a reproduction based on fragments

Detail of female bull leaper from the famous bull-leaping fresco at Knossos (see p. 136)

It is, indeed, the art of the wall frescoes that also reveals something of the later history of the Minoan culture. After 1700 BC and before the final destruction of the great palaces the frescoes begin to show scenes of war and portraits of warriors. Minoan art began to reflect the general level of violence and upheaval typical of the Aegean in those years.

Other scenes of daily life and the evidence of Linear B script give us a picture of Minoan religious and economic practice. The priest-king ruled in the palace, with a hierarchy of officials taking responsibility for the economy, which included grain production and extensive herds of sheep, goats, and pigs. He was responsible for the religious life of the settlement, monitoring a ritualized culture about which we shall have much more to say later. There was also a full range of craftsmen and professionals in fields related to building, farming, and sailing. Women took a very active part of the life of the palace and participated in most aspects of life, including sport and religious ritual. The wall frescoes picturing women reveal a sense of style and grace unsurpassed in later Greek art.

MYCENAEAN CIVILIZATION

Mycenaean culture began on the Greek mainland in 1600 BC, in the Late Helladic I Period. The first evidence of this culture in the archaeological record is the great circle shaft grave at Mycenae, clear evidence of a burial cult. The elaborate grave sites with their rich tomb offerings, gold masks, and ornaments suggest a reverence for the divinely ordained kings who ruled these hilltop citadels.

The characteristics of Mycenaean culture—citadels with their massive walls, beautifully wrought shaft graves, and beehive tombs—are still evident throughout the Aegean, from the western island of Kephallenia, to the north in Thessaly, to the east at Troy and Kolophon, and to the south in Rhodes and Crete. Over two hundred sites have been identified, and there are undoubtedly more to be discovered.

The heritage of the Mycenaeans is reflected not only in the grandeur of their ornate palaces, exhibiting obvious wealth, but also in the legends of their heroes, the flavor of which was captured in the Archaic Era by Homer and passed along as the foundation of Greek culture. These bearded warriors were not merely barbarians, as we might think of the hordes who later invaded Rome from the steppes of Asia. Rather, the Mycenaeans farmed the land, established trade, and developed beautiful pottery and bronzeware of delicate design. They ruled for 800 years.

The reasons for the decline of Mycenaean culture are not clear. However, it seems logical that with the development of trade and modern weapons, the citadel was no longer a viable form of military organization. Also, a social revolution may have occurred—one based on democratic instincts, which certainly emerged after the Dark Age. The invasion of the Dorian peoples from the north clearly played a part as well. After this time, the dead were no longer buried in the same sacred manner. As the cult of the dead declined, cremation became commonplace. The heroic values immortalized by Homer were obliterated in the general atmosphere of disorder and political chaos.

During the Bronze Age, in both the Mycenaean and Minoan cultures, at the apex of the social, economic, and religious pyramid was the *wanax,* or priest-king. The resulting integration of all aspects of life produced a harmony and unity within the culture that was the source of its great strength. This hierarchal system was emulated somewhat by the leaders of Sparta during the Archaic and Classical periods. The inevitable challenges to leadership and the religious corruption that is bound to befall such a mortal structure produced schism and eventually revolution.

Key to Periods of Greek History after the Bronze Age

1100 BC - 800 BC	The Dark Age
776 BC - 480 BC	The Archaic Period
480 BC - 338 BC	The Classical Period
338 BC - 146 BC	The Hellenistic Period

THE DARK AGE (1100 BC - 800 BC)

It is a concession to Romanticism that we refer to the three hundred years from 1100 to 800 BC as the Dark Age. The term has survived in spite of new discoveries in art and architecture during this period because we have so little information about the political and social conditions that characterized the shift from the palace cultures to the city-state *(polis)* cultures. By 776 BC, the date of the first Olympic Games, a new age had dawned in the Aegean, signaled by an entirely new political structure.

One theory about the Dark Age is that the brown-haired Dorians, who spoke a dialect of Greek, swept south into the territory once dotted by the fortified citadels and defeated the priest-kings. Another theory is that unknown nomadic tribes from the north moved south in vast numbers, destroying and wasting the land, only to die out or be absorbed. It may be that in the wake of this chaos the Dorians restored order with a new vision of political and social organization. This theory accounts for the mixture of genetic strains evident in what can now be called Hellas.

In any case, one group did not totally obliterate another. There was a process of assimilation. The former occupants held onto a few centers of culture, such as Athens, where the Mycenaean citadel on the Acropolis remained fairly undisturbed and where the memories of the *wanax* as priest-king lived on, although in greatly altered political form. But for the most part, we suspect that the Dorian migrations produced a period of disruption and change from which the Greek civilization as we know it finally emerged about 776 BC.

In matters of religion, the Dorians furthered the shift of emphasis away from the Earth Goddess as the dominant deity to Zeus, the sky god and ruler of the universe. Male deities began to dominate, as they did in the Middle East. As symbols of the human relationship to the divine, these gods demonstrated a new distance from the powers of nature and

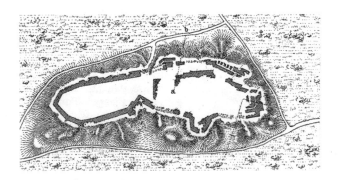

Engraving of the fortress at Tiryns, a port city in the Mycenaean Period

the earth spirits who had prevailed in the prehistoric era. With the Dorians came a fresh intellectual power and a new understanding of human potential. They were a people more at ease with language and expression. Their sense of relationship to the land and to the universe in general expressed itself in new and powerful myths, later written down by Homer, Herodotos (Herodotus), and Hesiod—to name the "three H's" whose work established the Greek culture we have come to know and admire.

Herodotos called all the indigenous peoples living on the mainland prior to the Dorian invasion "Pelasgians," a name that thus referred to the descendants of the Minoans, Mycenaeans, and even the lately arrived Ionians. This assertion by Herodotos, the first great historian of Western culture, made the Dorians the true Greeks, or Hellenes, as he called them. By the time the Dorian and Ionian invasions were complete, the entire eastern coastline of Asia was also "Greek."

According to the distribution pattern of Greek dialects in Classical times, the Doric remained in the southern Peloponnese and Crete, the Ionic dialect dominated Asia and the Cyclades, with the Aeolic near Troy, the Arcadian in the central mountains of the Peloponnese, the Attic in the vicinity of Athens, the Thessalian to the north, and Northwest Greek in Epirus. The presence of so many dialects indicates not only the isolation of populations but also the variety of racial influences over thousands of years.

It is through art and religion that we are able to follow a continuous thread through this labyrinth of history. The two cultural forces of art and religion come together when we realize that both scenes on pottery and religious rituals contain certain elements of design that reflect a given worldview, a coherent sense of place in the universe.

Despite the darkness of this period, we are able to see two major developments. First, the earliest evidence of philosophical thought emerged as religion became public and what had been secrets were shared by a wider spectrum of the population. No longer did the priest-king serve as the exclusive intermediary between the gods and the people. Second, the new political and religious life of the community was organized around what would become the *polis*, or city-state, the most important political and social development in Western history. Thus, as the Dark Age came to an end with the first Olympic Games, the Archaic Period emerged and with it new ideas of government and the relationship of people to their gods and to a more esoteric presence of the Divine within.

THE ARCHAIC PERIOD (776 BC - 480 BC)

Formal Greek history begins in 776 BC with the recording of the victors in the first Olympic Games. We shall say more about the Games in the section on Olympia. The alphabet used to chronicle this event was Phoenician, borrowed through trade from across the Mediterranean. The rapid spread of this alphabet promoted the beginning of written records and thus the true historical record of the Greek civilization.

The Archaic Period lasted until the Persian Wars in 480 BC, the date normally marking the start of the Classical Period. The Archaic Period is characterized by the emergence of the *polis*. With the decline of the priest-king, the battles for authority among warring factions and competing groups went through a period of chaotic experimentation. What generally emerged from the struggle was rule by the successful aristocratic warriors. These victors brought communities together through a combination of leadership, consensus, reason, and force to form a loosely bundled confederacy of families and their retainers in a limited geographic area, usually centered on an acropolis, the "high place" of the city.

The resulting city-state, both small and sovereign, arrived at a middle ground of rule by the few *(aristoi)* for the benefit of the whole *(demos)*, with the many *(hoi polloi)* sharing in the resulting security and wealth. Depending upon the individual *polis*, there was a growing tendency for the landed citizens to have a say in who the rulers would be. In place of the Mycenaean palace, there were erected on the acropolis various temples to the gods of the *polis*. The rest of the community, including the *basileus*, or king, lived nearby but no longer within the sanctuary set aside for the worship and veneration of the gods.

The daily life of the *polis* centered on the *agora,* or marketplace, where business was carried out but, most important, where the affairs of the *polis* were publicly debated. The emphasis on debate and public life as the heart and blood of the *polis* marked a new thing in the civilization of the world. It is in the Archaic Period that political power and religious ritual came out of the darkness of the palace into the light of the marketplace for all citizens to share.

THE LAWS

Late in the Archaic Period, inscribed codes of laws began to appear in the *agora* of many a *polis*. Contrasted with arbitrary laws imposed through military control, these new codes reflected the efforts of an intellectual elite to establish order and justice through consensus, at least to a small degree. Far from democratic in actual practice, these codes set forth for the first time the *nomoi*, or customs and laws, of the state. An example of such a code was discovered on Crete in 1884 in a stream bed at Hagios Deka. These Archaic inscriptions covered walls 30 feet (9.1 m) in length and 6 feet (1.8 m) in height within a circular building. The 600 lines in the code address nearly all phases of life in the *polis* of Gortyn. The rights and duties of citizens and slaves were set forth, as were laws governing inheritance, marriage, and divorce. A good deal of attention was paid to matters of land ownership, which is an indication of the development in the Archaic Period of the relationship between land and power. Indeed, much time seems to have been spent establishing family ties to the heroic past as a basis for authority in the new structures of power in the *polis*.

TERRITORIAL EXPANSION

So successful were these new city-states that wealth and power increased at a rapid rate, as did the desire for expansion. The Greek city-states, particularly Athens, Corinth, Sparta, and Argos, expanded their influence and successfully colonized throughout the Mediterranean. Colonies ranged westward as far as southern Spain and eastward into the Black Sea. While the Persians under Cyrus and Darius were busy conquering Egypt and expanding to the east, the Greeks were establishing profitable trade routes and colonies wherever boats could sail. Even Tyre and Sidon, on what is now the coast of Israel, were under Greek influence early in the eighth century BC.

The most important development during the Archaic Period in the life of the *polis* and its influence was the birth of alliances and regional control as the isolated city-state reached out to extend its base of power. Sparta, for example, expanded within the Peloponnese to control other city-states as far north as Elis (Olympia) and as far east as Megara and

Remains of the Archaic Temple of Apollo in the Agora in Athens

Marble statue called the Almond-Eyed Kore, 500 BC, Acropolis Museum, Athens

Epidauros. Such imperialism was to have devastating effects in the Classical Age, when rivalry between Sparta and Athens broke out into war for the control of Hellas.

ARTS AND LITERATURE

The extraordinary energy of this period was also reflected in the arts and literature. Different ideas and forms typified the sculpture and pottery of each *polis*. The development in these arts in particular was extraordinary. Examples of Archaic *amphorae* and marble and bronze statues have been found throughout northern Europe and Asia Minor. This work shows a vision and a skill unmatched anywhere in the world at that time. Architecture saw the refined development of the temple, as new forms found monumental expression for the first time since the height of Mycenaean brilliance. Although architecture did not see its best work during this period, the principles were being discovered that would later transform the landscape of the Classical Era.

Homer

Homer defines Greek culture in the Archaic Age. The heroic ideal, the standards of conduct, the concepts of excellence, honor, justice, harmony, and moderation—indeed the whole ethos of the Greek people is written out in the *Iliad* and the *Odyssey*. During the late Archaic and early Classical periods school children memorized long passages of these works as the basis for their education. They still do this in Greece today, although the passages are much shorter.

It is probably true that the long epic poems we now have in our possession were not written by a single poet named Homer. None of the history is trustworthy, but it is generally accepted that the poems emerged from bardic tradition and most likely from the island of Chios in the eastern Aegean. The dialect of the poems is Ionian, which places them in the east, and for years Chios boasted a family called the Homeridae, who claimed descent from the poet. As to the dates of the poet's life (or lives) and the composition of the poems, we can only estimate. Some suggest 950 to 900 BC as the time when epic poetry reached perfection. Others place Homer in the eighth century. We do know, however, that by 753 BC both the *Iliad* and the *Odyssey* were firmly ensconced in the Greek culture. We also have, in addition to these two epics, five hymns credited to Homer and twenty-nine shorter poems, all dedicated to various gods. Taken together, these works form the largest and most important source of knowledge about pre-Classical Greece.

Hesiod

The other important epic poet, Hesiod, probably lived in the eighth century BC and came from Boeoba. His life is presented to us as full of turmoil and tragedy and ending in murder. Tradition places him in a position of honor next to Homer for the strength and importance of his work. *Works and Days* is a collection of myths and fables that gives us a good picture of the life and values of the period. It was much cherished for its moral teaching. The *Theogony* (see the section on religion) is an account of the beginning of the universe and of the gods. This poem can be read as a view of the human condition as well as our divine origin and destiny. Although it is not designed as a spiritual guide like, for instance, the Vedic Upanishads, the *Theogony* is nonetheless an excellent mirror of spiritual awareness and conflict.

THE BIRTH OF PHILOSOPHY

Philosophy takes its life from the Far Eastern influences of religious thought (particularly the concepts of unity and being), the development of natural science in the sixth century BC, and the desire of thinkers to reflect upon the new political organization of the *polis* and its effect on the new concept of the individual.

The Milesian Thinkers

The earliest philosophical development centered in the eastern colony of Miletos. The Milesian thinkers, no doubt influenced by Egyptian and Far Eastern theology and philosophy, rejected the simplistic mythologies of polytheism and began a search for first causes and a more philosophic cosmology,

The ideas of unity and being found their Western source in Xenophanes, who lived some time between 570 and 480 BC. He was also the first Westerner to conceive of Mind as not only a cosmic entity but also as the source of being in the universe. Known as the Eleatics, Xenophanes and his fellow philosophers, Parmenides and Zeno, considered the visible world an illusion and infinity the basis of reality.

Heraclitus (Herakleitos) of Ephesus, who lived at the close of the Archaic Period, was in many ways the most modern of the "new" thinkers. He said that "this world, which is the same for all, none of the gods or men has made, but it was ever, is now, and ever shall be an ever-living fire, with measures of it kindling and measures going out." He asserted that divine law (the *logos*) governs the universe and that the law is rational. He conceived of deity as the underlying harmony of the universe and of unity as the supreme lord of all.

In many respects this flowering of scientific and spiritual thought bore fruit with Pythagoras, who lived from 570 to 500 BC and was the most influential among these early thinkers. He founded a school that outlived him and influenced the monumental work of Plato and Aristotle during the next era. Pythagoras traveled widely in Egypt and the East before settling down to teach in what is now Italy.

The foundation of the Pythagorean school was belief in God as the principle of order in one's personal life and in society. The way to achieve this order was through discipline in all aspects of personal life: habits, diet, study, and religious practice. Pythagoras's great discovery was the relationship between number and the divine laws of the universe. Central to these laws are the basic harmonic laws, demonstrable by the ratios and progression of tones produced by lengthening and shortening a vibrating string. The development of the monochord is credited to the Pythagorean school.

THE CLASSICAL PERIOD (480 BC - 338 BC)

Because our sense of time reduces history to qualities instead of chronology, we often affix labels to a span of years and forever regard that era as a name. Classical Greece is simply the period in ancient history usually designated as beginning in 480 BC with the brave defense of the Greek mainland at Thermopylae and ending with the commencement of Alexander the Great's campaign against Persia in 338 BC. Thus, the Classical Period begins with the arrest of Persian ambitions in Greece and ends with invasion of Persia's own lands by Alexander. The significance of Alexander's campaign in terms of Greek culture is that with the successful invasion of Asia Minor, Greek culture once again became orientalized; that is, it was influenced by the grandeur and artistic styles of the East for the first time since Archaic times.

We associate the term "Classical" with highly decorated temple design, epitomized by the Parthenon; more naturalistic marble sculptures of human beings and animals; the development of democratic institutions, characteristic of the years of Pericles in Athens; and the development of philosophy and literature, particularly tragic drama in Athens. These four elements were celebrated in the European Renaissance some two thousand years later and have seen frequent emulations, including the design and planning of Washington, DC. However, neoclassical imitation has blurred the true significance of the period.

THE PERSIAN WARS

A strenuous run of twenty-six miles distance up the coast from Athens is Marathon, the town where in 490 BC a defensive force of 10,000 Greeks, mostly Athenians, overwhelmed a superior Persian force and lost only 192 men. The grave mound erected in their memory still attracts thousands of visitors each year. These "Men of Marathon" represent all that is heroically Greek in the Homeric tradition, and their memory sustains to this day the distinctive Greek sense of independence and freedom.

The victory at Marathon merely delayed further Persian attempts to conquer Greece, and ten years later, a force under the fated leadership of Xerxes made another attempt on Athens. This time huge land and sea forces attacked at Thermopylae and in the Bay of Eleusis, near Salamis. The Persian land force was enormous, some say over a million but probably more like 200,000, and it streamed through a pass known as the Hot Gates toward Athens. The Persians were delayed by a heroic force led by Leonidas, the Spartan king. The defenders all perished, but their defense stood throughout ancient times as the ideal of pride and courage.

At sea, meanwhile, within sight of Xerxes, who sat on a throne carved out of the hillside above the scene, the great Persian fleet sailed out to meet the meager Athenian fleet of 280 ships, which had been sent north to delay the superior Persians. The day was 27 September 480 BC, when the Athenians would otherwise have been celebrating the Eleusinian Mysteries. The site of sacred Eleusis was within a few miles of the Persian invasion force. Athens had been evacuated, and only a small defensive force remained on the Acropolis. Normally, on this day, a huge crowd would have been making

Northwest corner of the Parthenon, Athens

its way up the coast to begin the rituals connected with Eleusis, but now the roads seemed deserted. Such was the scene as described by Herodotos, who also reported the following account of two renegade Greeks in the Persian camp that day.

The two Greeks, the Athenian Dikaios and the banished king of Sparta, Demaratos, were watching from the plain of Thira, through which ran the Sacred Way to Eleusis. Suddenly a great cloud of dust arose in the distance from the direction of Eleusis. The two heard voices shouting "Iakchos! Iakchos!" which was the usual cry in honor of Dionysos (Dionysus). The Spartan asked the Athenian what the dust and the shouting could be. Dikaios replied, "Demaratos, it can only be that the king's army will suffer a great defeat. For this is clear: since all Athens has been abandoned by its inhabitants, those sounds must be a divine host that has come from Eleusis to help the Athenians and their allies. If it makes for the Peloponnese, it will endanger the king and his army on the mainland; if it turns toward the fleet at Salamis, the king is in danger of losing his fleet. For this is the feast that the Athenians celebrate each year in honor of the Mother and the Daughter (Demeter and Kore). At this festival all the Athenians, as well as those other Greeks who so desire, are initiated. The voices you hear are the cries 'Iakchos!' that resound at the feast." The cloud of dust did indeed drift toward Salamis and the two men watching knew that the Persian fleet was doomed.

The victory of the Greek fleet at Salamis will always have this spiritual meaning, validating the belief that the Mysteries were intimately involved with Greek life and destiny. In this way the history of the ancient Greeks is intertwined with images of spiritual presence and divine intervention.

Despite the great victory of the Greek fleet, the Persian land army was successful in overrunning Athens and burning the Acropolis. The sanctuaries were torn apart, the temples gutted, and the treasures of Archaic Athens stolen or destroyed. So devastating was this destruction that the citizens of Athens chose to allow the devastation to remain as a testimony to the bravery of those who died defending Athens and to the constant danger of attack from abroad. It was not until the time of Pericles, thirty years later, that the Acropolis was rebuilt.

A year after the fall of Athens, in 479 BC, the most important victory over the Persians took place, this time at Plataea on the Theban plain. There, an army made up of Spartans, Athenians, and warriors from other allied city-states met the Persian force and destroyed it completely. The Greeks captured Persian treasure far more impressive than anything they had ever seen. Years later, Pericles built the famous Odeion next to the Theater of Dionysos in Athens, using for his design the royal tent of Xerxes captured at the battle.

The Calf-Bearer, 570 BC, Acropolis Museum, Athens

ATHENIAN DEMOCRACY

In the midst of the concerns over foreign invasion and the expansion of cultural and economic influence, city-states such as Athens were also experimenting with a new form of government: democracy. The groundwork for this important experiment in social organization had been laid by Solon, who at the beginning of the century had established the rule of written law in Athens. The combination of a code of law and the decline of the four leading Ionian tribes or clans as a ruling oligarchy eventually led to a new vision of government.

The leader of this change was Cleisthenes. He formalized what had already taken place in the social structure of the *polis*. Under his leadership the ten families whose ownership of the land in and around the growing city constituted districts or *demes* became the center of the political structure. From the ten families emerged an organization from which representatives might be selected to exercise power and to conduct the business of the *polis*.

Cleisthenes also directed the formation of the Council of Five Hundred, a ruling body made up of fifty men from each tribe, chosen by lot from lists drawn up by each *deme*. In addition, in this period a system was developed by which the citizens might control the excesses of a particular individual who was deemed a detriment to the *polis*. Every year on a certain day, citizens could scratch the name of an offending person on a piece of broken pottery (an *ostrakon*) and submit it to an official especially appointed to receive it.

The names were counted, and if 6,000 citizens (out of, say, 30,000 in the fifth century) voted for ostracism, that individual was banished from Athens for ten years.

PERICLEAN ATHENS

After the establishment of democratic principles under the leadership of Cleisthenes, Athens reached its highest level of development between 460 and 430 BC under the leadership of Pericles (Perikles). In the arts of vase painting, sculpture, architecture, drama, and politics, Athens was, as Pericles himself claimed, "the school of Hellas." Actually he need not have limited himself to Greece, since the influence of Athens went beyond the bounds of the Hellenic world into the known world of the fifth century.

Much of this success came about because of two seemingly opposite forces: the impulse to promote and achieve democratic ideals of equality and justice in the *polis*, and the willingness of the aristocracy of Athens to take an active part in the government. Pericles was one such aristocrat, a member of the ancient family known as the Alcmaeonidae, to which Cleisthenes had also belonged.

Pericles served as general, an appointed position corresponding to the chief executive in a representative government. Pericles maintained his power for nearly thirty years through his eloquence, political skill, and firm grasp of principle. Forty times a year, on a regular basis, the Assembly met on the Pnyx, a hillside overlooking the Acropolis where five thousand persons could gather to hear and take part in debate. All major questions of foreign and domestic policy were decided by the Assembly of Five Hundred. On one such occasion, Pericles spoke in praise of those young Athenian men who had died in the conflict with Sparta. It is

Engraving of the Acropolis in Athens, showing a temple-like propylon and a statue of Athena

overtly a political speech, but it also reflects in its finer moments some of the principles that supported the best of the age. Here is an excerpt from that oration:

> Our love of what is beautiful does not lead to extravagance; our love of things of the mind does not make us soft. We regard wealth as something to be properly used, rather than something to boast about. As for poverty, no one need to be ashamed to admit it: the real shame is in not taking practical measures to escape from it. Here in Athens each individual is interested not only in his own affairs but in the affairs of the *polis* as well: even those who are mostly occupied with their own business are extremely well-informed on general politics—this is a peculiarity of ours: we do not say that a man who takes no interest in politics is a man who minds his own business; we say that he has no business here at all. We Athenians, in our own persons, take our decisions on policy or submit them to proper discussion: for we do not think there is an incompatibility between words and deeds; the worst thing is to rush into action before the consequences have been properly debated. And this is another point where we differ from other people. We are capable at the same time of taking risks and of estimating them beforehand. Others are brave out of ignorance; and, when they stop to think, they begin to fear. But the man who can most truly be accounted brave is he who best knows the meaning of what is sweet in life and what is terrible, and then goes out undeterred to meet what is to come.

The first remarkable thing about this address is that it was delivered in public to the assembled citizens of Athens. It is not a private treatise on society. The second is the recognition of the role of debate and conscious understanding as a prelude to action. Knowing "the meaning of what is sweet in life and what is terrible" means recognizing the principle that understanding is the foundation of human action—a characteristic of Athenian society that gives its history a special significance. This sort of self-awareness was one of the qualities that made the Classical Age in Greece unique. It also helps us define the idea of tragedy as it was used in drama and as it reflected the decline of Athenian culture soon afterward.

CLASSICAL DRAMA AND PHILOSOPHY

The origins of drama are much debated among historians and literary critics. The archaeologists and anthropologists have also made their contribution to the discussion, leaving us all with our heads spinning with theories. The traditional view is that a singer of choral odes named Thespis, known as the first actor, first engaged in a dialogue with a lyric chorus in 540 BC. The combination of choral ode and dialogue was developed in Athens, and the form known as tragedy gradually evolved. According to another theory, drama grew out of the

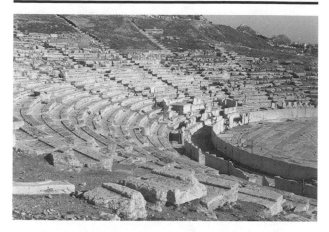

The Theater of Dionysos beneath the Acropolis in Athens

religious ritual and festivals of the cult of Dionysos. More of this religious background will be examined in the section on religion and in the site description of the Theater of Dionysos. It does need to be said here, though, that in the fifth century BC dramatic festivals were state occasions and were competitive. This approach to drama as a mixture of contest, holiday, and religious ritual was surely unique and contributed to the high level achieved in this art form as well as in religious expression.

Aeschylus

The first great tragic poet was Aeschylus (525-456 BC), who was a native Athenian and as a young man had fought in the battle of Marathon. He took for the subject matter of his plays the myths of Homer, the myths of the Olympian gods, and current history. Developing the form inherited from Thespis and adding his own elements, including masks and costumes, Aeschylus was responsible for the development of the tragic form to its maturity.

In the years between 484 and 468 BC, the height of his career, Aeschylus was awarded the first prize thirteen times by the judges of tragedy. For these competitions each poet wrote three plays, usually but not always connected in theme and content. Of the eighty titles left to us of Aeschylus's plays, only seven are extant, the most important of which are the trilogy of the House of Atreus. The *Oresteia* details the story of Agamemnon's return from the Trojan War, his death at the hands of his wife, Clytemnestra, the revenge of that murder by their son Orestes, and the subsequent trial and release from guilt granted to Orestes by Athena and the tribunal at Athens.

When Aeschylus was living and writing in Athens, the *nomoi* were being established. Not merely an artist on the fringes of society, Aeschylus took an active part in politics. Part of his vision of the human relationship to the gods and to justice and fate is articulated in his description of the trial of Orestes. This close connection between drama and civic affairs as well as foreign policy was special to Athens during the Classical Period.

Sophocles

The second great tragic poet of the age was Sophocles (496-406 BC), also a native Athenian. As his birth and death dates show, he lived a long life, and it was a productive and prominent one. Gifted from birth, Sophocles won his first prize in 468 BC with his first entry. Besides a poet, he was also a priest, a general, an ambassador, and at one time a treasurer in Athens. His good friend Pericles said that as a general Sophocles was a good poet—no doubt true enough, but it is still a mark of the age that citizens were able to undertake such contrasting roles at all.

Sophocles wrote well over one hundred plays, of which only seven remain. His major trilogy, written over a long span of his later life, included *Antigone, Oedipus Tyrannus,* and *Oedipus at Colonus,* written in that order. Sophocles did not live to see the final defeat of Athens in the Peloponnesian War but must have understood the drift of the times. His loyalty to Athens and devotion to truth emerge in all his plays. The Sophoclean vision sees human beings aspiring to overcome limitation and to understand their place in the universe. The great hero Oedipus blinds himself from the horror of his fate, wanders in suffering, but then finds the grace to understand and accept his life. The acceptance of fate through suffering was a message that Sophocles meant to leave Athens when he died.

Sophocles was a conservative, that is, one who wished to conserve the values of an earlier time. Some say he was the last of the Archaic thinkers, an assessment too radical but one that reflects the times in which he lived. He always affirmed that the gods worked out reality in their own time, and human beings struggled and suffered to understand that reality. The works of Sophocles may be read as a history of the human spirit during the fifth century BC.

Euripides

It is perhaps significant that Euripides, the third of the great tragic poets, was not an Athenian, but was born on the island of Salamis in 480 BC, on the day of the great battle when the Persian fleet met defeat. Not born to the Athenian inner circle, he looked on from the outside and wrote as an outsider. His revolutionary plays stirred strong feelings of both admiration and animosity. His was a tragic vision of human nature as a destructive force working out its destiny in the face of divine *ananke,* or the necessity of being a flawed, mortal creature. Euripides won the prize only four times and yet was a prolific writer, credited with over one hundred plays, nine-

The fourth-century BC theater at Epidauros, where the classical dramas are performed each summer

teen of which are extant. His best and most famous plays include *The Bacchae, Medea, Electra,* and *The Trojan Women.* A close friend of Socrates (Sokrates), he took issue with the common thought of the day and was a strong critic of the ongoing war with Sparta. In 409 BC, just before the death of Sophocles and the downfall of Athens, Euripides left the city and went north, first to Thessaly and then to Macedonia, where he died in 405 BC at the age of seventy-five.

The plays of Euripides that remain to us show a variety of subject matter and artistic powers. In his works human beings are overcome with their own passions to the point of self-destruction. The gods are indifferent to this suffering and remain aloof. However the hero is still able to rage against this indifference and create new values which transform society, even though he may be destroyed in the process.

Aristophanes

At the same festival where the tragedies were played, comedies were presented on the final day. During the fifth century the comic form evolved as a celebration of the ordinary person's release from *ananke*, the freedom to live like a god or to escape the realities of mundane existence. Aristophanes (444-380 BC), the master comic poet, is known to have written forty-five plays, eleven of which have come down to us. These are the only comedies to have survived, which may be a reflection of the superior quality of Aristophanes' works.

The comic poets were free to mock citizens as well as gods, and to name names in the process. There was little censorship of either language or content, and the plays are graphic in portraying sexual and bodily functions. *Lysistrata*, first performed in 411 BC, was written to protest the conduct of the Peloponnesian War and was, at the same time, a marvelous parody of human nature.

Both Euripides and Socrates were targets of this biting satire, and it was said that Euripides might well have left Athens to avoid further jabs from the comic sword of Aristophanes. Careful study of these plays reveals a genuine concern for the decline of values in Athens toward the end of the fifth century. In that sense Aristophanes was a conservative, even though his inventive genius produced radical plays.

Socrates

It is difficult to measure the influence and effect of the presence in Athens of Socrates. He was born in 469 BC and condemned to death by the Assembly in 399 BC. Trained as a sculptor by his father, Socrates gave up this art in favor of conversation. He was seen almost daily in the *agora* in earnest discussion with the citizens of Athens. His topic was always the truth: What was it? Could one know it? His method was the dialectic, or what Plato later called the science of philosophy.

As we shall see later on in our glimpse of Greek religious thought, Socrates engaged his students, friends, and opponents in dialogue, the purpose of which was to uncover the truth. He believed in the soul, or *psyche* in Greek, which lived within each person and was accessible by the power of reason. He referred to this soul on occasion as a *daemon,* a power within like a voice which, if heeded, gave warnings and led in the direction of the Good, or the Supreme Being.

Tireless and always poor, Socrates spent little of his time maintaining himself or his family. He described himself as a gadfly biting the reluctant Athenian horse, stinging it into action and reflection. He taught purity of thought and action, honesty in all things, respect for the Good and the Beautiful. Plato was his student, as were many of the young aristocrats of Athens, but his thought confused most people. What many

Remains of the state prison where Socrates died—the Agora, Athens

thought was a disregard for the gods in Socrates was in fact a firm belief in divinity within himself and in any other who cared to seek it out.

By the end of the century Athens had lost the tolerance that had marked it as a great city. Reasons were sought for the defeat by Sparta. Many accused Socrates of corrupting the youth of Athens and teaching them to be critical of their elders and skeptical of the gods. At his trial Socrates spoke of his beliefs and his life. Again, little of what he said was understood. He said, "The simple truth, O Athenians, is that I have nothing to do with physical speculations"; and "Is there anyone who understands human and political virtue?" He told the Assembly what it did not want to hear, namely, that "I found that the men most in repute were all but the most foolish." He knew that "not by wisdom do poets write poetry, but by a kind of genius and inspiration; they are like diviners or soothsayers who also say many fine things, but do not understand the meaning of them."

These words, of course, belong to Plato, who reported what Socrates said at the time. We do not know how accurately they reflect Socrates' intent, but they clearly show that Socrates was both misunderstood and unwanted and that his values were not commonplace in the culture. When he died, an important spirit died out in Athens.

THE PELOPONNESIAN WAR

After the defeat of Persia, finally achieved in 449 BC, Athens and Sparta fell into a period of imperial competition. Both cities expanded their influence throughout the Aegean and on the mainland of Greece. The Athenians established the Delian League, with its financial center on the sacred island of Delos where the treasury of the league was guarded. The Spartans established the Peloponnesian League, which included the mainland cities of Thebes and Delphi. Although sporadic fighting broke out from 457 BC onward, a full-scale war did not begin until 430 BC.

The Peloponnesian War lasted for twenty-five years, an off-and-on sort of conflict, and was finally won by Sparta in 404 BC. There were many opportunities for this war to have been resolved peacefully, but as Thucydides tells us, vanity and arrogance combined with fear and ignorance kept the conflict alive—and eventually brought Athens to its knees. His account of the war is a powerful description of the changes that had taken place in the society from the period of the Persian Wars to the close of the fifth century. Our view of Classical Greece should not be clouded by fantasies of purity and heroic idealism. Rather, Greek culture at this time was convulsed with revolution, not only of cities and classes but also of values and ideas. Indeed, Classical Greece of the fifth century BC resembled our own time more than we might wish to admit. The signs of decadence, which we too often associate with Roman decline, were everywhere.

Although the Peloponnesian War ended in defeat for Athens, the terms were good and Athens soon recovered some of its influence, although not in terms of imperial power. A period of despotism set in, during which much of the glory that we think of as the height of the Classical Period diminished as those in power sought to assign blame and gain control. For example, Socrates was made the scapegoat for the failures of Athenian foreign policy and for the moral decline described by Thucydides. Many Athenians associated Socrates with the faction that favored Sparta, at least in terms of its aristocratic values, and the mob in Athens demanded and won the death penalty for him.

THE FOURTH CENTURY BC

The second half of the Classical Period was characterized by a movement away from the independence of the democratic *polis* in Greece and toward unification of the states under the power and leadership of King Philip II of Macedon, and then under his son Alexander the Great, who in a brief explosion of a lifetime created a temporary Greek empire. It was also a time of intellectual growth, as Plato and then Aristotle changed the culture by the power of their thought.

The years following the Peloponnesian War were, for Sparta in particular, years of frustration and disappointment. The city-states of Greece—first Sparta, then Thebes, then Athens once again, and so on—tried to gain supremacy over one another and to turn their attention once again to the east and Persia. The history of the first two decades after the defeat of Athens contains accounts of deceit, bribery, treachery, and intrigue as leaders scurried around seeking allegiances and developing plans for new conquest.

In 377 BC the Spartans attempted once again to assert their control and impose their rigid value system on the Greek world. The Battle of Leuctra ended that dream and Athens once again rose in influence, though only temporarily. The defeat of Sparta, however, meant that the Spartan way of life, so jealously guarded for a thousand years, had finally ended. That closed society of physical and mental discipline, of unquestioned obedience and high ideals, had finally broken down under its own weight and internal decay.

Philip of Macedon

For a time Thebes gained in prominence, only to decline again when Philip II of Macedon gradually gathered the cities of Greece under his control. The Macedonians, a people whose manner of life and temperament brought back memories of the Mycenaean kingdoms, began to gain ascendance in power and wealth. Their king began to look to the south as his first step in gathering the necessary force to attack Persia.

In 355 BC a struggle began over the control of Delphi, during which Philip seized his opportunity to play one city against another and impose control over the weaker states.

In 338 BC a battle between Philip and the federated Greek states, in which 75,000 men took part, saw a successful cavalry charge led against the Greek forces by Alexander, the eighteen-year-old son of Philip. This battle, in which the forces of Macedon prevailed over the remnants of the once-mighty Greek armies, marked the end of the age of the *polis,* and hence, the end of the Classical Age.

Philosophy in the Fourth Century
Before we leave the historical background of the fourth century BC we must recognize the impact of the work of Plato and Aristotle on the period. Plato was born in Athens in 428 BC, early enough to be exposed to the high points of the fifth century but too late to have seen its glory under Pericles. He was an aristocrat by birth and an intellectual by gift and inclination. Joining the group gathered around Socrates, he began to observe with care and devotion the words of the master. Most of his written work in later years would recapture the dialogues of Socrates in the *agora.*

From the historical point of view, Plato's Academy in Athens was really the world's first university, a place to withdraw temporarily from society to study. As such it was a new idea. Plato lived outside the walls of the city, near the *deme* of Colonus, not participating in the life of the *polis,* and there in his garden he taught and wrote. It was there also that he died in 348 BC at the age of eighty-one.

The short-term political impact of Plato's work is difficult to measure. He lived and wrote at a time when, although Athens was still independent and essentially democratic, the democratic impulse was waning and Greece was about to unite under the leadership of Philip of Macedon and his son Alexander. Plato was convinced that the ideal state would be ruled wisely by a philosopher-king, a man who understood

Romantic engraving of the philosopher's garden, with a view of the Acropolis

the relationship between divine Justice *(dike)* and the Good *(agathon)*. He had seen a democratic state condemn his teacher Socrates and had witnessed the greed and vanity of tyrants. His most important work is the *Republic,* which sets forth his concept of the just society.

Aristotle was born in Macedonia in 384 BC, the son of a court physician. He came to Athens at the age of eighteen and entered Plato's Academy. He remained there for twenty years and left upon the death of Plato to return to Macedonia, where in 342 BC he became the young Alexander's tutor. From what we know about Alexander's own philosophy, Aristotle's major impact on him was to instill a deep respect for the heroic values of Homer.

In 335 BC Aristotle returned to Athens and established the Lyceum, a rival school to the Academy. Aristotle's philosophy is much closer to Plato's philosophy than it appears on the surface. He took the concept of the Forms of Plato and applied it to the natural world. He also separated knowledge into its natural divisions and examined the nature and functioning of the human mind. His study of the relation of the world to the human mind signals the beginning of knowledge as a science. When Alexander died in 323 BC, Aristotle lost favor in Athens; he went into voluntary exile and died the following year.

THE HELLENISTIC PERIOD (338 BC - 146 BC)

Traditionally, the Hellenistic Period is said to have begun in 338 BC, when Alexander the Great undertook his campaign against Persia. The first aim of the young Macedonian king was to recapture for Greece the cities along the coast of Asia Minor. The king was only eighteen, but he possessed the scars of earlier battles and had qualities of leadership that made men willing to follow him throughout the world. Little did his armies know, however, just how far Alexander would ask them to go.

Alexander began the Persian campaign by hurling his spear ashore at Troy in honor of the heroes he so admired. In 334 BC he officially refounded Troy and captured the Ionian cities formally belonging to Greece. His style won him quick, thorough victories. He was a brilliant and ruthless general and an enlightened ruler. Rather than sacking cities and enslaving populations, he made it clear that he wished to institute democratic principles (with his own governance) in the conquered territories. As he moved south along the coast, Darius III, the Persian king, pursued him. In a masterful attack, Alexander surprised the Persian army near Issos. It was reported that 110,000 Persians died in this one battle, yet only 302 of Alexander's men were lost. Darius fled, leaving behind his queen and all the treasure of his kingdom.

ALEXANDER'S KINGDOM

Within the brief period of Alexander's life, the kingdom established by his military might and genius stretched south to include Egypt, east beyond the Indian Ocean to India itself, and north beyond the Caspian Sea to Armenia. At the end of the year 330 BC Alexander was far north in Afghanistan and planning a westward campaign to Italy when he became ill. Returning south to Babylon, he died in 323 BC at the age of thirty-two. Within his lifetime he had succeeded in creating a Greek empire that lasted, albeit in fragmented form, for several hundred years.

The chief influence throughout the Alexandrian empire was all things Greek: art, literature, philosophy, architecture, and scholarship. In Egypt, where Alexander was proclaimed a god, he founded his own city, Alexandria, which eventually replaced Athens as the center of Greek culture. Here the famous library was established that began to collect the world's literature. Scholars from around the empire gathered there to study.

HELLENISTIC CULTURE

After Alexander's death, the kingdom was divided into territories ruled by his former generals. The system was too loose and chaotic to last more than a generation, and soon local peoples began to revolt. Thus, the political structure dissolved quickly. The culture that Alexander had spread, on the other hand, lasted until the Roman invasions, and even then remained an influence for the next five hundred years, or until the Dark Ages of the Christian Era.

What seems most striking about these rapid developments is the sudden change in values brought about by imperial expansion. The splendors of the East, the sudden availability of large amounts of currency, and the appearance for the first time of large mercenary armies all contributed to the dramatic change of values in Greece. Private houses became opulent, art was created for homes rather than for temples, and expensive buildings were constructed for secular purposes.

Moreover, the *polis* disappeared as an independent political entity. The decisions affecting daily life and public policy were made somewhere else, by strangers. It was said that at this time the oracle at Delphi was asked who was the happiest man in the world. The answer was: a farmer tucked away in the hills of the Peloponnese, isolated from the world. There is in this story something of the loss of an earlier innocence, already long gone, of course, but only now understood. There is also an anticipation of the loss to come, when Roman armies would sweep into Greece to end this gloriously brief dynasty.

ROMAN CONQUEST

While Greek imperialism to the east held the spotlight of history, the Romans were gradually increasing their control of the western Mediterranean. By 200 BC Rome was in control of the city-states of the Italian peninsula and had defeated the powerful Carthaginians and their commander Hannibal's attempts to invade from the north. Toward the east, Rome concentrated its attention in the Adriatic and on the ambitions of local Achaean rulers. New federations of Greek states formed to counteract the influence of Macedonia, now led by Philip V. His feeble attempts at leadership were kept in check by Roman power.

During the next fifty years Rome increased its influence in Greece. Roman commissioners settled conflicts among the states and slowly but firmly established Roman-style rule. The instinctive desire for freedom, so typical of the Greeks, exerted itself finally in Corinth, where in 146 BC Greeks attacked Roman envoys. In response, a Roman army descended upon Corinth, completely destroying the city. Thereafter, Roman law and military control were imposed throughout the former Greek empire. Democracy was abolished, taxes imposed, land ownership controlled, and for the next thousand years events in Greece became a part of someone else's history.

Corinthian column from the Roman period with the Temple of Hephaistos in the background, the Agora, Athens

GREEK RELIGION

It is because we don't know who we are, because
we are unaware that the Kingdom of Heaven is
within us, that we behave in the generally silly, the
often insane, the sometimes criminal ways that are
so characteristically human. We are saved, we are
liberated and enlightened, by perceiving the hith-
erto unperceived good that is already within us, by
returning to our Eternal Ground and remaining
where, without knowing it, we have always been.
Plato speaks in the same sense when he says, in
the Republic, that "the virtue of wisdom more than
anything else contains a divine element which always remains."

— Aldous Huxley, *The Perennial Philosophy*

The story of Greek religion is a narrative of the human loss of
unity with the Eternal Ground and our efforts to reestablish
contact and relationship with the Divine. As we study the
ancient evidence, both in stone and words, in rituals and
myths, we are able to see how we have struggled with this
loss of intimacy, suffered in that loss, and molded our world
in an attempt to remember and regain a measure of intimacy
with the God within.

Regardless of our own culture and faith, we are indebted
to the ancient Greeks for the record they left of their struggles.
Their ancient temples and sanctuaries, their lyric poems, their
stirring dramas are, taken together, an expression of the
search for divine company and relationship. It is a characteristic of Greek religion that the divine presence had to be
invoked. Divine presence to the ancient peoples was cyclical
and temporary, like the seasons and the movements of the
sun and moon. Spirit was also related to the forces of impregnation, germination, and growth in nature.

The very existence of spirit at the level of human awareness depends upon aspiration and devotion. The birth of
Zeus, for example, embodies the belief that Zeus, as Bright
Consciousness, had to be protected from the brutality of his
father Kronos (Time) through human deception and devotion. Immortal spirit would survive only if it was not devoured
by time—quite literally swallowed, as the myth tells it. Human beings had to do their part to keep spirit alive, nurturing
it with invocation, sacrifice, and remembrance in the form of
festival, prayer, and ritual worship. To forget, to keep silent

was to destroy; or to reverse the old saying: out of mind, out of sight. In this way people "create" their gods, their myths of spirit.

The law is: if the gods are not remembered, they die. "To remember" means to embody or "to give members to" the idea of divinity. A god without members is a forgotten god. There are many examples of the dismembering of gods throughout Greek theology. When the Greeks molded their gods from clay and carved stone images in their own likeness, they were re-membering the gods of their ancestors, who as far back as Neolithic times lived with their gods in the natural rhythms of nature.

The Greeks were primarily a visual people, and they re-membered their gods not only in the suggestive landscape, but also on vases and in temples, sculpture, drama (a highly visual medium), and in vivid frescoes in their homes. More than other world religions, Greek religion is embodied and then reflected in the brilliant light that illuminates the sacred temples and passes over the sacred landscape in rays of sunlight.

Example of rounded hill as a symbol of the Earth Mother, Hagia Triada, Crete

THE EARTH SPIRIT

The prehistoric nomadic tribes, following the herds in season, were without permanent shelter or formal settlement. They moved or stayed according to weather and food supplies, completely dependent upon the geography. Such dependence instills worship, that is, exalted feelings based on revealed experiences. These nomads understood that the earth ruled them and that this rule was beneficial when the earth communicated its spirit. Later, in the times of settlement, a special communication was required, and there appeared especially sensitive people whose special knowledge and touch of the earth beneath their feet set them apart. They became shamans and, later still, priests and priestesses in the cults of particular gods.

But before the time of these selected intermediaries, all human beings took part in the life of the earth and felt no separation from it. The wind spoke, the leaves murmured, and the water bubbled up from the rocks, filling the night with meaning. This existence had a rhythm, which was instilled over thousands of generations, gradually developing patterns and formality. In cycles and patterns of the heavens, we saw our lives unfold. The natural patterns were related to human existence: sexual union, generation, birth, nourishment, vitality, decay, and death. Everything had its season (rhythm) and its proper shape (form).

The rhythms of life gradually became connected to nature's rhythms: day and night, summer and winter, calm and storm. The forms of divinity emerged in the landscape: mountains, rounded hills, horned peaks, gorges, caves, seas, lakes, streams, and springs. Of particular importance to the Earth Mother cults were those places where the fresh-water rivers and streams met the sea. Being points of interaction between creative forces, the earth in the form of these watersheds and marshes had special meaning. The famous site at Olympia is sacred to Hera because of the intersection of two rivers and their proximity to the sea.

At a certain point, probably before the Neolithic Period, this imagery gave to the earth a dominant feminine likeness. The earth itself acquired female characteristics in both rhythm and form. For example, it is generally believed that during the Stone Age the cave was regarded as the womb from where human beings emerged into the light and where they returned after death. The early cave paintings, so beautifully wrought in the darkest and most inaccessible parts of caves, might have been prayers of impregnation and hopes for eternal life.

The earth, then, became the Great Mother. A rounded hill was a breast in the mind's eye, suggesting the feeling of nourishment and dependent love. To keep the hill in view was to worship the earth as mother of mankind, and in Greece the breast of the mother was everywhere. There is also a literal sense, however, in which the earth was a mother—active, vibrant, productive, protective, nurturing. Thus, there was the reality and the metaphor of the reality.

THE EARTH MOTHER GODDESS

Before polytheism developed in Greece there was an era of monotheism, when a single goddess represented the idea of the divine. Those who consider human "progress" in terms of evolutionary change usually see religion developing in sophistication from a multiplicity of gods and animism toward monotheism to the One God of Western culture. Such a view ignores the evidence of tradition in most cultures and also suggests that polytheism is a primitive form of religious belief. The contrary is true.

In prehistoric times the productive powers of the earth and the facts of birth, death, and sexual generation created a divinity in which female characteristics predominated. The influence was primarily Eastern. In Mesopotamia, for example, this goddess was variously called Mah, Nintu, Aruru, or Ninmah. In the Aegean islands images of this goddess began appearing before the Bronze Age. Neolithic people made images of this goddess first from stone and then from clay. In Greece she may have had a shape before she had a name. The nourishing breasts, the ample hips, and clearly marked vagina dominate these images. Often, a male child appears as well, giving us an image of an early Madonna. Later, the child would become a man-child, a young god who is both consort and son and who dies each year to be brought to life by the generative power of the goddess.

It is evident that the Earth Mother Goddess, in whose mysterious power life itself resided, was the image of meaning for early human beings as well as the companion of their days and nights on earth. Other gods and spirits no doubt gradually made their way into the worldview, making their claims of power, expressed in the warmth of the sun, the waxing and waning of the moon, the raging storms and devastating fire; but the goddess nurtured and protected as the primary deity of worship.

As we will learn from Hesiod, contact with the gods eventually ceased to be a constant communion. There came a time when intimacy was lost. In order to recapture that unity, revelatory rituals of feasting, music, dance, and sacrifice developed, all with the intent of making people feel at one with the mother. Varying from place to place, these practices involved orgiastic celebration and blood sacrifice as a way to establish contact with the generative power, resulting in crop growth, human and animal fertility, and a safe journey for the dead. Blood is life, contains life, and was shed from humans and animals as sacrifice in recognition of this fact.

Today some might say that the images of the Earth Mother uncovered in the Cyclades and on the mainland during the Neolithic Period were merely primitive attempts at artistic expression and had no sacred intent or function. It is certainly true that the statues have a childlike quality, but perhaps this appearance describes the sacred relationship accurately. The goddess is the true mother as seen by the child.

The primacy of the Mother Goddess and her consort held sway during the Minoan and the early Mycenaean periods. The details of belief and practice left by these two Bronze Age cultures are unclear. The record has become clearer

*Venus of Willendorf,
30,000-25,000 BC,
Natural History
Museum, Vienna. Note
the exaggerated life-
giving features.*

through recent discoveries at Knossos and Mycenae, but generally, it is not until the Archaic Period that the mythology
and the meaning behind that mythology become understood.

HESIOD AND THE ARCHAIC MYTH

In the eighth century BC Hesiod composed the Genesis of the
Greek religion. In the language and imagery of the Archaic
Period he tells the stories of creation and of people separated from their gods. The fundamental idea expressed by
Hesiod is that the state of mankind has been in decline, that
contrary to the evolutionary view of progress, human beings
once lived in a state of grace but fell from it out of foolish-
ness and disobedience—not unlike the Biblical tradition of
Genesis.

In the epic poem we call *The Five Ages*, Hesiod describes
this decline, which cannot be located in time, although some
have tried. The age Hesiod describes as Golden is a spiritual
state and not a physical one. It describes an article of faith in
the human drama, although we can ascribe certain physical
conditions to it.

In Hesiod's account of the early, or prehistoric, human
state there is a description of union with spirit—not identity
exactly, but union, as in a relationship without the separation of selfish desire. All things were provided. The earth
yielded its abundance freely, without limits. That gods and
men sprang from one source is a critical ingredient in the
tradition. Human beings came after time (Kronos) came out
of chaos, and they were mortal. Their lives passed without

strife in their Eden.

Hesiod's description of the next stage, the Silver Age, speaks of a man playing childishly in his own home, isolated from the earth and the spirit he would encounter by moving through the landscape. He thus grows to be a simpleton, devoid of the wisdom of the earth, incapable of living fully or fruitfully in its bosom. This was the age of settlement. Settlement brought an end to unity with the gods. Dwelling in one place was not in itself evil, but it implied separation from the divine ground. Once settled, human beings had an obligation to serve the blessed gods in order to restore the former unity. Altars became a part of the process of settlement as places on the earth were selected as especially sacred, as sanctuaries. The sacred precinct was born. These special places were endowed with holiness, as places where the gods appeared and where human beings purified themselves for the encounter. Settlements, on the other hand, were regarded as not divine, as somehow separate, non-sacred.

Hesiod's "Brazen Age" marks the complete separation of humans from their gods. These people loved war and violence; they took no nourishment from the earth, and they depended solely upon the strength of their own arms and armor. The gods took no part in destroying them, but they destroyed themselves. Hesiod described this race as "hard of heart like adamant." The closed heart is incapable of seeing God. There is no room for the divine. The destiny of these people was the outer darkness from which there is no return. Separation meant oblivion.

In the fourth age of Hesiod's cosmogony, called the Heroic Age, we see the first glimpses of recorded history. The heroes spoken of here are the Mycenaean lords and warriors who, in the 1190s BC, sacked Troy. They are pictured as noble and "more righteous" than their warlike and hard-hearted predecessors. An important theme in Hesiod's work is that human beings must be noble as well as righteous. There is an aspiration to fulfill the possibilities inherent in being human, despite the loss of intimacy with the gods. The way back to the gods was to aspire to greatness, the reward for which was immortality in the blessed isles where sorrow had no place, although the human spirit now dwelled "far from the deathless gods."

By the Archaic Period, the time of Hesiod, the Greeks had little understanding of the Mycenaean way of life, although they may have grasped the true state of human beings' relationship to the gods. Bronze Age life was very different from Archaic life, as we will see in greater detail in the site discussion of Mycenae. But in religious terms, the *wanax* or priest-king of the hilltop fortresses replaced the gods as the semi-divine leader of his people and ruled absolutely: There was, as far as we know, a priest class who served the *wanax*, but its function was to carry out his instruction and his personal calendar of religious events.

Hesiod brings his story to his own era and the present

time, the Iron Age, when people live in isolation from one another as well as from the gods. Gone is the certainty of authority. And yet some good remains. The possibility of re-establishing contact with the gods exists. He does not speak of a divine spark within the human *psyche*—a concept that will emerge more clearly later on—but suggests that as long as a certain innocence remains, people can be saved from destruction. When Hesiod speaks of human beings reaching the stage when they have "grey hair on the temples at their birth," he refers to a loss of that innocent state when communion with the divine was commonplace.

THE MEANING OF THE THEOGONY

Hesiod is also the primary source for our information about the Olympian gods and goddesses who came to form the core of the Greek pantheon. The *Theogony* describes the attributes of generations of deities, from the god Chaos to the Earth Mother Gaea (Ge) to the powerful Uranus, who with Gaea fathered the race of Titans.

This cosmology also reflects the intrusion and imposition of northern and eastern influences. The masculine sky gods, we suppose, came from the north, perhaps as far away as Siberia. These sky gods come under a higher law, reflected in Zeus as Bright Consciousness, and are not supreme, immortal though they may be. In fact, the major feature of this northern tradition is the appearance of Zeus as the central spiritual force, the ruler of heaven and earth. He is not the ultimate creator described in the early myths, but he does establish himself as king of the gods and ruler of the spiritual realm. Indeed, Kronos is deposed by his son Zeus and confined in the western wilderness, where he lives with the blessed heroes, his powers usurped.

The *Theogony* describes the marriage of the Sky Father (Uranus) with the Earth Mother (Gaea), with lightning as the generative, possessive force. Seen by many scholars as a forced marriage representing the subversion of the religion of the Goddess, the actual "marriage" may have been a slower and more natural union as migrants from the north assimilated the traditions and customs of the indigenous peoples. The gradual domination by the Sky Father also reflects a maturing process in spiritual matters; for as human consciousness develops, the changing images of spirituality reflect the growth of awareness into maturity and full humanity. Thus, the Olympian gods are both male and female—six each, in fact—and they represent all aspects of the human condition, except, of course mortality. The Earth Mother was gradually subdivided into different female aspects and by the Classical Period was reflected in aspects of Demeter, Hera, Artemis, Aphrodite, Athena, and Hestia.

The story of the *Theogony* is long and violent. Out of Chaos came the gods, manifestations of consciousness in the cosmos, born through the power of Eros, the force through which all life begins and flourishes and all spiritual knowledge is transmitted. The *Theogony* is the account of the turbulence of the creative forces unleashed out of the primal mystery. Some of these are transmitted to humanity: the conflicts of power, the temptations of selfish desires, and the depravity of destructive instincts. In the birth of the minor gods also, such as Blame and Woe, powers are released, as when Blame grows untended by Reason into the Night and is enlarged by Dreams into injustice and ruthless vengeance.

Here is a myth of a people who have become aware of their own spiritual condition. The old security has been lost, and they are actively seeking new truths. If we see truth as spiritual, that is, as a reality other than what is perceived in the material world, then we can see these stories as attempts to work out the struggle by which human beings become, like the gods, spiritual beings.

Accordingly, the various Olympian gods were regarded as aspects of the human *psyche*, or soul. Zeus was the lawful spirit that is contained in all souls. Apollo was the force of harmony, moderating the desires and aligning the soul so that the spirit, or Zeus, could be lord of the human faculties. Athena represented intuitive inspiration, the voice of wisdom in the soul. Hades was repressed desire, the destructive tendency that ignores potential danger. Poseidon was the force that opposed the lawful spirit represented by Zeus. Poseidon is sensual pleasure and perversion as well. Hera, the wife of Zeus and one of the aspects of Earth Goddess, was the willing transformation of desire into spirit, the sublime union of human elements in their proper relation.

There is in nature a fundamental impulse to evolve to spirit, toward Zeus, and human beings possess the consciousness to undertake this struggle. To be successful, we must conquer or sublimate the destructive elements, the monsters of our unconscious nature, in favor of the intuitive wisdom of the spirit. We must also overcome the fundamental guilt that arises from the conflict between matter and spirit. To the Greeks this task was best accomplished by moderation and by recognition of the forces operating within us. As we examine the Olympian gods further, we will recognize many of these elements and see in the stories how the Greeks explained through myth the struggles of the spiritual way of life.

THE PANTHEON OF GODS

The twelve major gods of the Greek pantheon were finally established in Greece by the time of Homer. Although the rosters occasionally differed, depending on the city and the period, the twelve gods listed below were generally regarded as the chief gods in the pantheon:

Zeus
Hera
Poseidon
Demeter
Apollo
Artemis
Ares
Aphrodite
Hermes
Athena
Hephaistos
Hestia (sometimes
replaced by Dionysos)

Engraving of the twelve gods of Olympus gathered in the order of the zodiac

ZEUS

Zeus is king of the gods, lord of Olympus, ruler of the universe. The world is the city of Zeus. Thus, Zeus guards the *polis*, minds the home and the storehouse. In addition, as king of the gods, he is the special protector of those who approach kings in supplication, for those who ask a favor of someone in power put themselves in a vulnerable situation.

Zeus also protects the stranger who seeks hospitality. The traveler in ancient times was especially vulnerable to ill treatment on the road; yet a guest was also a special person, perhaps even a god, and so hosts were obligated to provide a warm welcome. Both the *Iliad* and the *Odyssey* emphasize the courtesies due to strangers and the swift retribution from the gods when hospitality is denied.

Zeus is also the protector of the sanctity of oaths. In ancient Greece, a man's word was the basis of the moral structure of the *polis*. A broken oath brought justice from Zeus in the form of public exposure and shame, the result of which might be banishment. It is Zeus, then, the god of mind and intellect, who sees into the intention behind the spoken word.

The myths surrounding Zeus portray him in images of power and generation. The lightning bolt is his special symbol. It is a weapon for punishment, a tool for generation, and a flash of enlightenment. Ideas, thought, and inspiration come from Zeus. They are a gift of spirit. If Zeus is invoked before a debate, for example, chances are that the thoughts and ideas that arise will be to the point and will represent the truth.

Along with generative lightning, Zeus also brings rain to impregnate Mother Earth to bring forth her fruits. As we trace the earliest appearance of the Olympians in the Bronze Age and earlier, it is this function of creative energy and generative power that first characterizes Zeus and suggests the

Zeus conquers the Titans; shown is the mastery of the four-horse chariot

sacred marriage of the Sky God to the Earth Goddess. In this sense he takes over the functions of his grandfather Uranus.

On the simplest, most popular level, Zeus was God the Father to the Greeks. He was the protector and creator in his role as father. He maintained order in the cosmic and domestic households by punishment. On a more sophisticated level, Zeus was the god of intellect and thought. The quality of mind over which he ruled is what maintains order in the intellectual life; we might think of it as the intuitive power from which springs enlightenment and revelation. At the spiritual level, Zeus was harmonizing spirit as well as the symbol of human consciousness and reason.

In mythology the birth of Zeus is given special treatment. He was born the youngest son of Rhea (also a goddess of the earth) and Kronos. Because Kronos had devoured all of his previous children (thus keeping them within his manifest nature), Rhea conspired to hide her new son from his father. She took the babe to a mountaintop cave in Crete, where he was nurtured by a goat, and gave a stone wrapped in swaddling clothes to Kronos to swallow. When he reached manhood, Zeus rebelled against his father and seized control of the heavens, there to rule the gods and human beings.

HERA

Hera is one of the earth goddesses, transformed by the Greek culture into an Olympian. Her special manifestation is as the single legal wife of Zeus. As such she represents the lawful marriage of matter to spirit. To the Greeks she was also the ruler of the social order as the patroness of marriage. She was the special goddess of the stages of a woman's life according to the Greeks: virgin maiden, loyal wife, and grieving widow.

Her marriage is celebrated in the springtime, in the month of Gamelion in the Attic calendar, corresponding to our January-February. It was said that the marriage of Zeus and Hera took place on Euboea, an island to the east of Attica that was a home of herders. Hera was protectress of cows and oxen, and she was called "ox-eyed" by Homer. She is a majestic goddess, honored by the other gods, and is spotless, indeed virginal, in her behavior. As such she symbolizes purity in marriage and, indeed, in all sexual matters.

In more psychological terms, what Paul Diel has to say about her is valuable:

> The wife of the spirit Zeus is Hera, symbol of the perfect sublimation of desire. Hera represents love, the highest form of sublime aspiration. She symbolizes objectified desire, which goes beyond subjective and physical satisfaction and aspires to the gift of the self and to the union of souls. Hera is desire which has surmounted its elemental ego-centricity; she becomes the ideal of sublime union between men. On the sexual level, she presides over the right choice of partner and over exclusive and lasting union.

POSEIDON

When the victory over Kronos put Zeus into power, the universe was divided into three parts, with Zeus in the heavens, Hades in the nether world, and Poseidon, the brother of Zeus, in the seas. Poseidon is also the god of horses, and his chariot is drawn with steeds hoofed in bronze and gleaming in gold. As he moves through his domain, the monsters of the deep, some given life out of the original chaos, swarm around him.

Poseidon bears the trident, which has the power to stir the oceans to destructive force and to strike rock and bring forth fountains and horses. He also keeps the sea calm for sailors who propitiate his fury with sacrifice. It was said that when a fisherman finally leaves the sea life, he places his net and trident in the temple of Poseidon and there prays for a peaceful old age, free from care.

Earthquakes are the work of Poseidon, and in the Aegean and the Mediterranean his work has left its mark. The palaces of Knossos were continually shaken to their foundations, and the island of Thera was left a shell of itself by an eruption that probably ended the Minoan culture. These manifestations of natural fury are gathered together in this god, who in spiritual terms was also the representative of insatiable desires. Positioned in opposition to the lawful spirit in Zeus, Poseidon is that force in human beings that is disobedient to the call of the harmonizing spirit.

DEMETER

Demeter is the daughter of Rhea and Kronos and the sister of Zeus. More than any of the other goddesses in the pantheon,

Demeter signifies Mother Earth and is a direct link to the Earth Mother of the prehistoric era. Her worship was particularly strong in the rural areas of Greece, and the Eleusinian Mysteries belonged to her. She is the goddess of agriculture, and her great gift to human beings is the art of cultivation and the annual wonder of fertility and harvest. As we shall see in much greater detail, Demeter brings the gift of spiritual insight through the sacred drink *kykeion* at the Mysteries of Eleusis.

APOLLO

Along with Zeus and Athena, Apollo is one of the three most influential gods in the pantheon. He is a latecomer to the Greeks, and scholarship has theories but no real trace of his origins. The current theories are that he came to Greece from either the eastern Hittite tradition, where he was known as Apulunas, god of the gates, or that he came from the north, perhaps even as far away as Siberia. Whatever his source, he quickly became a central god to the Greeks, who worshiped him throughout the Aegean and the mainland.

The spirit of art as expressive form is attributed to Apollo, as is the moral, social, and intellectual principle of moderation in all things. Along with form and moderation, Apollo represents law and order, particularly as a giver of law and a judge of murder and revenge. His most famous appearance in court was described by Aeschylus in the *Oresteia* and specifically in the *Eumenides,* where he comes to the aid of Orestes, who stands accused of matricide.

As a guide for human behavior, Apollo is credited with a series of precepts for the happy life. Some of those include such wise sayings as "Curb thy spirit," and "Observe the limit." He also advised against arrogance *(hubris)* before the

Apollo shown with his bow and Daphne transformed into a tree

gods. Also attributed to him is the statement "Keep women under rule." This last has prompted many to interpret his seizure of Delphi from the earlier goddess as the Dorian imposition of the male deity upon the Earth Mother cult. As we shall see, the seizure of Delphi had serious spiritual implications of another sort.

In matters of secular and religious law, Apollo was supreme. It was left to him to found temples, to establish sacrifices, and, in particular, to rule over the rituals of purification. He presided over the burial of the dead and whatever rituals were necessary to propitiate the spirits in the other world.

A child of Leto and Zeus, Apollo was born on the island of Delos. His twin sister Artemis is also one of the twelve Olympians. Their birth on Delos makes it fitting that Apollo is the god of light. Light is special to the Greeks. Any visitor to Greece and the Aegean knows about the remarkable quality of the light there—a luminous clarity that makes objects stand out from their contexts with sharpness of detail. Light is also spiritual knowledge, and Apollo has the special function of prophecy. It is Apollo who was designated to give out the word of Zeus through prophetic utterance at Delphi, where his dictum "Know thyself" is the foundation of spiritual knowledge.

More than in any other religion, the Greek expression of divinity is manifested in visual images. From the divine landscape itself with its forms of the Earth Mother to the temples containing cult statues, Greek gods are seen more than they are heard or experienced through ritual. The perfection of their form was most often expressed in the human guise, not out of human-centered arrogance but rather because divinity was an aspiration arising from the human condition and made possible through conscious expression of that condition. More than any other god, Apollo represented the perfection of that condition. His statues are more beautiful and more celebrated than any other in male form. Long-haired, clean-shaven, muscular, and always young, Apollo was the ideal of the ideal, perhaps most notably expressed by the marble Apollo from the Temple of Zeus at Olympia (which is in the museum at Olympia).

ARTEMIS

In the wild places of Greece, especially among the gorges and deep forests of Arcadia in the central Peloponnese, running with her favorite deer, is Artemis, the virgin goddess. The twin of Apollo and often worshiped in the same temples and cult sites, Artemis joins the other goddesses as an aspect of the original Earth Mother. She guards the wild places and the animals that are untamed. She is also the huntress, however, sometimes outwitting her prey. She retains the purity of the unspoiled earth with memories of life before settlement and agriculture.

Like her brother, Artemis is also associated with light, but in her case, it was the less brilliant light of the moon and stars. Thus she belongs to the night and is often seen pictured with a torch as well as with her traditional bow and quiver. By the Classical Period she was worshiped as goddess of the moon and had a full-moon festival in the month of Munychion (April-May).

As a virgin goddess she was the patroness of youth and especially of young girls growing up. Tall and graceful, idealized in full bloom, she was the most popular goddess because she kept guard over the youth. She was associated with ancient tree cults. She also had a darker, orgiastic nature. In Sparta, vestiges of this aspect were preserved in the yearly

Artemis pictured as the Earth Mother—the Artemis of Ephesus

flogging endured by young boys at her altar. The idea seemed to be that Artemis was a guide to proper conduct under the law, and the flailing impressed this conduct on young minds and bodies.

ARES

Reflecting the dark, bloodthirsty aspect of human nature is Ares, god of war. The Greeks understood that creative tension and conflict was a part of their character as a people. It is generally thought that Ares joined the pantheon of gods from Thrace in the north, where a more warlike culture evolved, and moved south to join the mix of peoples during the Bronze Age. Ares is joined in his bloody revels by his sister Eris (Strife) and his sons Demos and Phobos (Fear and Fright).

The violent nature of the war god is joined with sexual passion, and he is paired often with Aphrodite, who in later myths bore Eros from their union. As their child Eros is seen as the infantile creature of passion, playing at the feet of his father or cradled in his arm. In Hesiod's account, on the contrary, Eros is born of Chaos and is the power by which matter and spirit are joined in harmony. Thus, to see Eros as the child of Ares and Aphrodite is to see him diminished, made into a banal image of his more spiritual aspect.

It is not surprising that the worship of Ares was centered in warlike Sparta, where young dogs were often sacrificed at his altar. In Athens his sanctuary was the Areopagus, where the high court of justice met to judge crimes of murder. Thus, in Athens the spirit of war was sublimated to the exercise of law as the Council met to make judgments about acts of violence. But nothing is harder to quench than the thirst for war when a culture feels itself threatened and seeks the quick solution to its fears and feelings of injustice.

APHRODITE

Aphrodite is the foam-born goddess, rising from the sea without benefit of a normal birth, spawned in the violent dismemberment of Uranus by Kronos. In legend she rises from the sea near Cyprus, where she steps ashore to join the Phoenicians as one of the aspects of the Earth Mother Goddess, another symbol of fecundity and generative power.

In addition to her more familiar role as goddess of love, Aphrodite is also a nature goddess. Her realm includes the wind and the changing sky. She is the goddess of storm, both within human beings and in nature. To the Greeks, nature, or *physis,* included human nature as well as natural phenomena, and Aphrodite manifested the turbulent in all of nature. As such she was powerful and often destructive—a goddess to be respected.

Her powers were exercised in all the elements. In particular she was goddess of the sea and the seafarer. A calm sea fit for safe passage was as much her work as Poseidon's. She was also the goddess of plants and tender shoots, of fruitfulness in garden and grove. In human affairs she was recognized in the passion of love—the overwhelming power that drove men and gods alike to irrational behavior.

She is always pictured smiling and ideally beautiful. She carries magic charms with her to induce passion and subdue the will. In her company are her son Eros and the three Graces, Peitho (Persuasion), Pothos (Longing), and Himeros (Yearning). These personifications of the nature of passionate love demonstrate the subtlety and sophistication of the way in which the gods reflected human nature and show how myth served to explain and, to some extent, manage behavior among the Greeks.

In the most famous myth involving Aphrodite, the young mortal Paris is asked to choose which is the most beautiful among the great goddesses Aphrodite, Athena, and Hera. According to most versions of the myth, Paris chose Aphrodite over the other two when he was bribed with the prospect of acquiring Helen as his lover. In spiritual terms the myth represents a test for the mortal human being. Had Paris chosen Athena, he would have chosen spiritual wisdom of the highest order, a difficult but correct choice for the mortal in his quest for enlightenment. Had he chosen Hera, he would have taken the lawful path in which desire is sublimated properly to the rule of spirit. But Paris was tempted by the lowest level of human desire and was seduced by personal greed, and he chose Aphrodite in her aspect of sexual passion. His choice caused the Trojan War, which led to the death of Agamemnon, the agony of Orestes, and so on. In this way the myth of Aphrodite helps to delineate the struggle between matter and spirit in the human condition.

HERMES

The name "Hermes" means "he of the stone heap." For anyone who has followed wilderness trails and sought the correct path through forests and mountains, the sudden appearance of a cairn of three stones marking the way is a welcome sight. Hermes is the god of the sacred way, the guide on the path. In his more mundane aspect, he is the god of traffic, of roadways, but our interest is in his spiritual function.

Zeus, Hermes, and Aphrodite, in an engraving of the zodiac

Hermes is the son of Zeus and the nymph Maia, who was the daughter of Atlas, himself the son of a Titan and, according to Homer, a mischief maker. The myth of Hermes emphasizes his precocity and his inventiveness. Born in the morning, by noon he had already invented the lyre and stolen his brother Apollo's sacred cattle. Admitted to the pantheon of gods by nightfall, Hermes became the friend of Apollo and the messenger of Zeus. He possessed minor gifts of prophecy and was associated with flocks and shepherds, along with Apollo.

However, it is in his aspect as a guide that Hermes is important. His history has been traced back to Minoan roots in cults of mountains and caves. He was associated as well with tree cults, all of which suggest a strong connection in his function as an intermediary between man and god in the task of spiritual realization. Hermes may well be a link back to the Earth Spirit of prehistoric times. The nomadic peoples traced the Earth Spirit through the world, making contact with its powers along sacred paths and in sacred places, sensing the spirit in the landscape, and listening to its voice in nature.

Once ancient people settled, ringing themselves about with walls and citadels, they lost contact with that moving, informing spirit. Worship of Hermes was an attempt to honor and restore that contact. What Hermes became in the mundane functions of his worship is an indication of the loss of that impulse; but the connection remains anyway. He is the god of mining and digging for treasure. He is the god of roads, of the marketplace, of travelers. Heaps of stones, some marked with directions and inscriptions, were placed at intersections and doorways. In the fifth century BC, "herms," or busts of Hermes, were erected outside of homes to protect them from evil.

As a guide, Hermes is also the conductor of the dead to Hades—a connection to his original function as a spiritual guide. He is the god of sleep and dreams, which is another path of spiritual revelation and prophecy. Athletic ability, dexterity, physical beauty, and personal charm are his, as well as good memory and an agile mind. In sum, Hermes is closer to mankind than many of the other twelve gods, and more so than Apollo or Zeus, with whom he is most closely allied. It is in this perception of him as the friend of distant spirit yet the friend of lowly humanity that Hermes has his greatest appeal and importance.

ATHENA

Moreso than any other divinity, Athena represents a high order of spiritual development, a fitting symbol of Athens at the height of its glory. The rise of Athens in the order of Hellenic city-states either reflects the qualities of the deity who is patroness or is the result of the influence of her presence—perhaps a little of both. In any case, Athena is second only to Zeus in the spiritual purity of her being. She is wisdom incarnate, the perpetual maiden, or *kore,* of the human condition and symbol of the aspiration for wisdom in this life.

The legend of Athena is very old and the story unclear. She is at least as old as Mycenae and probably older. Although not Greek in origin, she quickly became one of the three most powerful gods in the pantheon, along with her father Zeus and her brother Apollo. She was not born but sprang full-grown from her father's head, which attests to her identity as Wisdom and Intellect. In spiritual terms Athena possesses a purity that can be attained only with great sacrifice and devotion, so precious is knowledge of her.

Her full name, Pallas Athena, means that she is of the

clan of the Pallantidae, a name synonymous with nobility in the history of Attica. She is also *parthenos,* the maiden or virgin, and her home, the Parthenon, is the maiden chamber where she resides. There, represented by the thirty-foot gold-and-ivory statue carved by the great Phidias, she stood as protectress of the *polis* and defender of the whole city of Athens. In her hand she bore the *aegis,* or shield, borne as well by her father as the symbol of power. On the shield glared the monster visage of the Gorgon, or Medusa, one glance at which turns men to stone.

Engraving of the statue of Athena by Phidias in the Parthenon

It is fitting that Athena bears the image of the Gorgon. Through her wisdom it is possible to overcome the death of the spirit at the sight of the Gorgon. To turn to stone is to die in spirit—to be nothing but matter, which is dead. In Athena resides the wisdom to give spirit its proper place, to turn away from the Gorgon. Athena's gifts include both intellectual and spiritual understanding. Her gift is the olive tree, the self-sown giver of oil and food. The arts of spinning and weaving are hers, as are health, safety, and security. Athena is always pictured as armed, the defender of Athens, goddess of victory and peace. She is a mighty warrior, but she fights with a wisdom that defeats Ares in his thirst for blood.

HEPHAISTOS

Hephaistos, "the lame god," the god of fire and of the arts requiring a firing process, is the son of Hera. Because he was lame and depended upon his genius and the skill of his hands to keep his place on Olympus, he was a favorite of the people and particularly of artisans. Because of his deformity, he was cast from the heavenly company and dwelt nine years in a cavern beneath the ocean. Eventually he was reinstated among the gods, but he remained associated with volcanoes and turbulence beneath the sea.

His affiliation with turbulence also connects him to Aphrodite, to whom he is married, although unhappily. The marriage is significant, however, in that both gods possess high levels of passion and unruly behavior, much to the displeasure of Zeus. But it is Hephaistos's connection with fire, symbol of consciousness and intellect, that makes him important. Along with Prometheus, who stole the fire of consciousness for mankind, Hephaistos was worshiped at the Academy in Athens, home of philosophy.

Hephaistos is responsible for the fine metalwork that appears in various legends of the gods. These include the great shields of Zeus and Athena and the famous arms of Achilles, celebrated by Homer. Armor is symbolic of the spiritual strength needed to meet the monstrous destructiveness unleashed in the world. These evils are well understood by Hephaistos, who in his limitations is closer to them than are other gods.

HESTIA

Hestia is goddess of the hearth, guardian of the home and by extension, of the *polis* as a social entity. She keeps watch over the family as the stabilizing force of the community. She never leaves Olympia, but remains there to guard it and preserve the foundation of divinity. Although she is the embodiment of the home, Hestia remains unmarried, refusing the advances of both Apollo and Poseidon. Symbolically, this signifies her moderating position between several spiritual forces.

Hestia is the daughter of Rhea, who represents the full joy of life on earth and simple desires. Hestia carries this quality to the center of the home. Her position in the pantheon accords her the privilege of being worshiped before and after ritual sacrifice at the temples of other gods. In fact, her name is mentioned before the name of any other gods in prayer and supplication. Indeed, the center of religious life in Greece may well have been the sacred hearth of Hestia at Delphi. Here the Greeks kept the stone known as the *omphalos,* or the world navel, the center of the world, from which all spiritual knowledge flowed.

DIONYSOS

After the time of Homer but sometime before the end of the sixth century BC, the god Dionysos joined the twelve Olympians, replacing Hestia, in most cases, in the hierarchy. His rise into the establishment of Greek gods was a long process,

Dionysos having been an itinerant god of mixed parentage for as long as history has recorded the myths of chaos, creation, and conflict.

The god known as Dionysos came to the Greeks from Thrace, a wild and mountainous country to the north, where his worshipers were known to be rude and boisterous. The cult of Dionysos was firmly resisted in many places and his followers were often expelled, but gradually acceptance of this powerful, magical god overwhelmed the Greek mainland and islands and moved south to Egypt and beyond.

Before we fix Thrace firmly as the original home of Dionysos, however, we need to give some attention to the other possibilities. The various myths and sources of information suggest that Thebes and Lydia in Asia might also have spawned the god. According to Hesiod, Dionysos was the son of Zeus and the mortal Semele, daughter of Kadmos of the House of Thebes. In the way of most mortals chosen to bear a god's child, Semele was killed by a lightning bolt and Dionysos was hidden, in his case in the thigh of Zeus, away from the wrath of Hera.

This myth affirms several important matters regarding Dionysos. Semele has her roots as an Earth Mother, even as the Earth herself, from whom Dionysos comes in the fire of spirit. He is of the earth and has connections in the underworld as well. He is also a son of Zeus, and as such possesses both power and spiritual nature. Thus he lives in several realms at once: heaven, earth, and underworld.

Euripides, in his play *The Bacchae,* places Dionysos's travels and the birth of his cult in Asia, suggesting exotic influences and an emphasis upon the mysteries. But Thrace remains the historical source of the Dionysiac religion, which gradually became part of the formal state religion of Athens and was famous beyond its rituals for the role it played in Greek drama.

Madness and Dionysos

In his fine work, *The Greeks and the Irrational,* E. R. Dodds helps us to understand the importance of Dionysos to the development and history of Greek religious experience. Dodds describes four types of madness having religious significance: prophetic madness (whose patron is Apollo), poetic madness (which is inspired by the Muses), erotic madness (inspired by Aphrodite and Eros), and telestic, or ritual, madness (whose patron is Dionysos). Ritual madness is always communal and highly infectious.

The purpose of ritual madness is essentially cathartic, purging the participants of those irrational impulses which when repressed produce sickness and hysteria. Heads of state and religious officials gradually recognized that to prohibit the expression of this impulse was to repress it dangerously. Transformation, on the other hand, imposed controls on the impulse and organized the madness in a religious form. Such control was deemed necessary, just as too much resistance

Fanciful engraving of prophetic madness, set in the Temple of Apollo, Delphi

was deemed disastrous.

Dodds also explains why ritual madness was so important. The rational mind resists the impulse to unite with spiritual forces because unity obliterates the personality or, in the Freudian tradition, the ego. The worship of Dionysos had the effect of eliminating the difference and simulating unity. In effect, Dionysos seemed to say, "Forget yourself in me and happiness will be yours now." Such immediacy was the basis of its popular appeal.

In the rituals of Dionysiac revels worshipers felt liberated from the restraints of society and self-consciousness. In the sixth century BC, this feeling coincided with the more democratic freedoms being instituted and probably accounted for the rapid acceptance of the new religion. In addition, the new freedoms left the individual without a sense of community, and any ritual that brought a communal experience with it was welcome. The music and dancing helped to erase the sense of isolation that resulted from the new awareness of individualism.

On the negative side of the equation, the figure and worship of Dionysos symbolize our Western view of hell. On one level Dionysos represents the subconscious triumph of earthly desire. He is an image of insatiability. Moreover, the divine madness produced in worship is nothing but a trap, in that the earthly sensation of oneness with the deity can lead to forgetfulness of true spirit. One who forgets one's spiritual nature forgets God and clings hopelessly to life.

Dionysos as a God

What then makes Dionysos so important? What makes him a god at all? For one thing, he is an antidote to stiff austerity, to the excessive rigidity of the state religion and the drastic separation of human beings from the Olympian gods. Dionysos also has the touch of humankind about him. He is of the earth and is nurtured by the fruit of the earth. Dionysus also died and was resurrected and re-membered. In the myth of his childhood, he was dismembered by Titans, those forces of destruction, and was born anew after three years in the underworld. This myth connects Dionysos with the nature gods of fertility and seasonal change. It also, of course, associates him with immortality and life after death.

However, the more immediate quality of his divinity is his love of life and his affirmation of the joys of the earth, the symbol of which is wine. Dionysos is celebrated as the god of the vine; wine is his special gift to humanity. The wines of Greece, less famous now than in ancient times, were treasured by anyone who could afford them. The great wines were produced in the volcanic soils of the islands, particularly of Naxos, Cyprus, and Lesbos.

The Greeks did not drink heavily. Their northern neighbors did, however, and were judged accordingly by the more moderate south. The Greeks understood the joys of intoxication and were able to use wine as a welcome ingredient in religious celebration. Festival drinking to the point of intoxication was acceptable. What was less acceptable, though, were the nighttime Dionysiac revels of the women in the hills, streaming through the woods with ivy-covered wands, occasionally dismembering an animal in the frenzy of their devotions.

It should be kept in mind, then, that against the austere purity of Apollo's temple on the slopes of rugged Delphi there lurked the irrational turbulence of Dionysiac revelry. Just beneath the surface of perfect form smoldered the fires of madness. The myths of the Olympian gods and goddesses, reflective of the spirit to which human beings aspire, also mirrored a nature capable of personal and collective destruction. Nor have we changed.

In the mystery religions, Dionysos is the mythical connection between mortality and immortality. He is of the earth and from the spirit, containing in his nature the source of human salvation.

STATE RELIGION AND FESTIVALS

The clan structure present among the earliest inhabitants of Hellas remained a source of continuity through three thousand years of turmoil and change in Greek history. By the late Archaic Period, ten noble families in Attica controlled most aspects of society. In religious matters the families controlled worship of the local cults, and they undertook to legislate the official state religion as well. In order to worship at all in any official way an individual had to have the sanction of family membership. To be outside the family was to be unable to worship in official sanctuaries. This changed in the Classical Period. When Cleisthenes imposed reforms in Athens, diminishing the power of the great families and creating the *deme* system, citizens who lived within a given *deme* could take part in any function of the *deme*, including religious worship. Thus, in Classical times every Athenian had a religious home, so to speak. Additional changes took place as further democratic reforms established the rule of law in Athens. Thus, by the time of Pericles, Athens had developed a complicated religious calendar administered by the state and carried out by the principal families.

The idea of a state religion does not mean there must be a codified form or a sacred book such as the Bible to serve as a standard. In Athens, for example, the state religion was a series of cults woven together along with practices and regulations governing the rituals of purification, sacrifice, and burial of the dead. On the Acropolis the cult of Athene Polias (the goddess of the *polis*), the cult of Athene Nike (defender of the *polis*), and the cult of Poseidon Erechtheus (a hero cult) all existed side by side and yet constituted a whole sacred entity.

If there was any uniformity in the so-called state religion, it might have been in the generally held beliefs about the human condition. A person's fate, or *moira*, existed separately from the gods, who ruled every aspect of life. The idea of *moira* goes back at least to the Dark Age and means not only fate but also portion and share. A person's *moira* might refer to family inheritance, the piece of meat served to that person at dinner, or it might mean overall destiny woven by the three Fates who ruled human life.

Homer's writings also reflected the Greek belief that the goal of excellence, expressed by the term *arete*, was the meaning of life. Proper respect for the gods throughout one's life might ensure happiness, but in general, suffering was human destiny, and it would have been better not to have been born at all. Once here, however, it was the task of the noble Greek to seek his *arete*, serving the *polis* as a citizen. A man's duties were to fight if called upon, to debate the issues of the day in the *agora,* to serve in the assembly or in whatever position the *polis* might assign him, and most of all, to support with his wealth the festivals and honors due to the gods. A woman kept the home, managed the household slaves, and stayed clear of politics.

FESTIVALS IN THE CLASSICAL PERIOD

In the very best sense, festivals were meant to shatter the limitations of time and place, to detach the individual from banal worldliness and from the bounds of body and personality in order to be reunited with the gods and heroes of the Golden Age. They were also meant to recapture the power of deified Nature and to promote uninterrupted continuation of the cycle of generation, growth, death, and resurrection,

*View to the north of
the Panathenaic Way,
Agora, Athens*

which formed the basis of the relationship with the divine.
At their worst, they were empty rituals, repetitive and spiri-
tually meaningless. Then mystery religions and minor cults
would often emerge to provide a more vital connection to
divinity.

The Attic religious calendar was originally lunar in structure, with the various festivals fixed on certain days of the
lunar month, particularly on the days of the full moon. Central to this arrangement was the understanding that the
waxing moon caused things to grow and increase and the
waning moon brought decrease and decline. Generally, the
twelfth day of the lunar month was the best for business as
well as for festivals. It is supposed that the calendar regulations emanated from Delphi and were the work of Apollo. In
fact, each *polis* had one or two chosen representatives of
Apollo who ruled on all matters pertaining to ritual and festival practices.

The names of Greek festivals, always given in the neuter
plural, expressed the feast as the central idea, not just the
god who was being venerated. For example, *Dionysia* really
means "the Dionysiac things present" rather than "a celebration of Dionysos the god." The *Lenaia* was a winter festival of
Dionysos in Attica and celebrated the winepress, the women
of the press, and the holy winepress house. The *Anthesteria*
was the feast of Dionysos celebrating the blossom-giving,
growth-promoting aspects of the god. In each case, then, the
idea behind the festival was a force usually associated with
life-giving energies.

The official state calendar of Athens began in the month

Hecatombaion at the height of summer with the Lesser Panathenaia festival—the Greater Panathenaia being every fifth year, or third year in the case of an Olympiad. As its name implies, this important festival honored Athena as the patron goddess of all Athens. In 446 BC Pericles added musical contests to those of chariot racing and athletics. Winners were given wreaths woven from the sacred olive branches and large vases filled with olive oil. The culmination of the festival occurred on the twenty-eighth of the month, the birthday of the goddess. A long, formal procession gathered at the Dipylon gate north of the city and wove through the *agora* up to the Acropolis. The procession included young girls and young men from the noble families, public officials, religious figures, brightly decorated animals destined for sacrifice, honored warriors, leading citizens—indeed most of the important people of the city.

The purpose of the procession was to adorn the cult statue of Athena with the *peplos*, a finely embroidered saffron robe. Then followed a sacrifice of a *hecatomb* of cattle. Normally a *hecatomb* meant one hundred, but it came in time to mean simply any very large number. In the case of the Greater Panathenaia, more than a thousand cattle may have been slaughtered. The meat was the basis of the feasting that followed. It was not, in fact, common for the Greeks to eat large quantities of meat, this being a northern habit. But on feast days the usual vegetarian and fish diet was set aside.

Behind the feast lay a sacred intent. Human being and god were present for one another, in the Greek sense of "knowing" one another. This idea of mutual presence is really the essential concept of the cult experience. The term "cult" for the Greeks meant local and private, as opposed to Panhellenic and public in nature. A cult was a sacred relationship between specific people and a particular god. Intimacy meant the feeling of presence.

To share a meal with a god meant that the meat was of

Engraving of a priest and a priestess pouring a libation at an altar

the god, and when it was eaten the god was taken in, absorbed, in the symbolic way of ritual experience. A feast of this kind was always associated with the sky gods and never with the gods or spirits of the underworld. For the latter, food and blood were offered to the chthonic (from Greek word *chthon*, the earth) powers but never shared by the living. No joining or "knowing" was desired in these cases because the soul being "nourished" existed in limbo in the underworld and the living were not meant to contact them.

This distinction reveals a principle of Greek festivals. The intent of the festival was to attract the god to be present in his or her sanctuary for the worshipers. The focus was on this world, the world of the living, not on another, invisible world. These were the gods of human existence, affecting life now and events in the living future.

The Greeks who regarded the festivals seriously, not merely as excuses for holidays, believed that the gods being celebrated might not appear again the next year if proper rituals were not performed. This fear made certain that human beings took part in this cycle and were not self-consciously disengaged from it in some existential way. The original idea was expressed by the legendary King Alcinous of the Phaeacians, with whom Odysseus found shelter in his wanderings. He said, "For the gods, at least until now, always appear clearly to us when we sacrifice glorious hecatombs, and they banquet with us, sitting where we sit."

THE MYSTERY RELIGIONS

Whereas the official religion of the Greeks now seems foreign and irrelevant, the so-called mystery religions may strike us as more immediate and vital. Here we are able to identify a set of beliefs and traditions both familiar and continuous. The essential idea of these mysteries was that the human condition included a divine element or potential which could, through knowledge, ceremony, and grace, be realized. Human existence was not, in this view, completely separate from the gods living in isolated splendor on Olympus.

There was not only a common divine source, as Hesiod claimed, but there was a common element of that source existent in every human being. Those involved in the mystery religions possessed secret knowledge transmitted through the special bond of membership from generation to generation. Indeed, we are able to trace the essentials of that knowledge coming down to our present time through this bond.

In the Aegean, the roots of the mystery religions were sunk in Cretan soil. The Minoans were the mystics of early Hellenic culture, celebrating the esoteric discipline of prophecy in the caves of Dikte and Ida and conducting initiations into the chthonic mysteries in their palace labyrinths. Since practices surrounding the cult figures of Orpheus and Pythagoras.

ORPHEUS

Orpheus was both a man and a legend. He was born in Thrace during the Bronze Age. Some place him in myth as a contemporary of Herakles. The legend fostered by the Orphics who claimed his name as founder identifies Kalliope, one of the Muses, as his mother. Orpheus was a poet and musician, and his lyric gifts soothed not only the gods but also human beings, animals, and trees. Part of the legend places him aboard the Argo as it sailed with the Argonauts and Jason to seize the golden fleece. His powers of music, god-given and spiritual in nature, kept the destructive voices of the Sirens at bay.

The central myth of Orpheus involved his beautiful wife Eurydice, who died of a serpent's bite and went to the underworld. Orpheus followed her there, charmed Persephone with his music, and won his wife's release on the understanding that on the way back to the light he would not look back at Eurydice, who was following him. However, he was unable to refrain from turning to look at her and as a result lost her forever. Some time later he was dismembered by Dionysiac Maenads, whose orgiastic celebrations he had offended. He was subsequently reborn by virtue of the cult which bears his name.

Orphism

Early in the sixth century BC the Orphic movement gained prominence throughout Greece, and particularly in Crete and in Athens. It came on the religious scene as a mystery cult, which meant that the knowledge of its rites was secret and that a ceremony of initiation was required of its members. There is evidence that the cult may have come to maturity in Crete many years before as part of the Mother Goddess worship and Dionysiac celebrations there, and that in fact its rites were not secret.

From the sixth century BC onward, Orphism refined its beliefs, taking the earlier myths of Orpheus and combining them with philosophical tenets emerging from the East. Orphism recognized the unity of God behind the many manifest gods; thus, the worship of many gods was possible. Knowledge of God came gradually, which meant that the divine mysteries had to be taught in stages.

The Cosmology of Orphism

Orphic cosmology was based on the principle that human beings contain an element or spark of divinity. The myth that worked out this truth was different from that of the Olympian tradition. It began with Zeus fathering a child with Persephone, queen of the underworld. The child, Dionysos-Zagreus, was a threat to the Titans, the immortal gods who always opposed Zeus for control of the cosmos.

Dionysos-Zagreus was deceived by the Titans, captured, and devoured. Zeus responded to this outrage by destroying the Titans with a lightning bolt, reducing them to ashes. Out of these ashes Zeus fashioned the first human being. In the nature of humanity, then, there is the ash of the immortal Titans and, most important, an element of Dionysos, son of Zeus the spirit. These two immortal elements, which might be called the *daemon* of Zeus and the *psyche* of Titanic immortality, form the basis of human immortality.

The initiation ritual of the Orphics remains a mystery in its detail, but must have involved purification with water and, according to several sources, being covered with mud and water, which symbolized the birth of humanity from ashes. Certainly the initiation would have imparted knowledge of the *daemon* existing within the individual and knowledge of the various practices within the tradition that helped one to realize this immortal nature.

Plato's philosophy was indebted to Orphic cosmology. He also mentions the Orphic ritual in an analogy: Lack of knowledge of man's true nature, he said, was like preparing for a rite of purification by carrying water to the bath in a sieve—the water running out before the moment of purification can occur.

The idea of purification by water is well expressed in one of the few extant tablets containing Orphic doctrine. Known as the Petelia tablet, it was discovered in Lower Italy near Sybaris. The poem was written on thin gold leaf, rolled up, and placed in a cylinder hanging from a gold chain. It was presumably hung around the neck of a dead person as an amulet.

The Orphic Petelia Tablet

Thou shalt find out to the left of the House of Hades
  a Wellspring
And by the side thereof standing a white cypress.
To this Wellspring approach not near.
But thou shalt find another by the Lake of Memory,
Cold water flowing forth, and there are Guardians
  before it.
Say: "I am a child of Earth and of Starry Heaven:
But my race is of Heaven alone. This ye know yourselves.
And lo, I am parched with thirst and I perish. Give me
  quickly the cold water flowing forth from the lake of
  memory."
And of themselves they will give thee to drink from the
  holy Well spring,
And thereafter among the other Heroes thou shalt have
  lordship.

The Lake of Memory symbolized to the Orphics, and later to Plato, the true path of spiritual knowledge. The idea is that through memory *(anamnesis)* we are able to re-member our divine nature, to assemble again what the Titans devoured when they killed Dionysos. In the Orphic tradition, Dionysos is the god who is re-membered by sacred practice and whose element is mingled in human nature if only we are able to remember it.

Transmigration of Souls
Through a process of purification, which included abstaining from eating flesh, an individual could be reunited with Zeus. However, the process required several human births. This suggestion of the transmigration of souls, or reincarnation, appears throughout Orphic fragments. In particular, an ode of Pindar dated 472 BC speaks of soul migration.

> In the presence of gods high in honor, whoso took delight in keeping oaths has his portion in a life free from tears; while the others endure pain that no eye can look upon, and all they that, for three lives in either world, have been steadfast to keep their soul from all wrong-doing, travel by the high-way of Zeus to the Tower of Kronos, where the Ocean airs breathe about the Islands of the Blest.

What we know of the Orphic tradition, then, speaks of specific practices that lead the individual to liberation and the attainment of divine status. Such a belief is very different from the orthodox beliefs of most Greeks, who suffered in what they perceived as complete separation from the gods. The received tradition saw humanity living in a degenerated age and condition in isolation from the gods, who if they existed at all, treated mankind with disdain and arbitrary cruelty. However, for those Greeks who followed the Orphic tradition, the Golden Age of Hesiod was possible now, in that an individual could, through knowledge and practice, be reunited with Zeus-nature.

THE PYTHAGOREAN MYSTERIES

The philosopher Pythagoras was born on the island of Samos in the town that now bears his name. As a young man he studied with the Ionian philosophers and traveled widely, particularly to Egypt, where he studied with the temple priests. He returned to Greece only to find an unfriendly climate for his work, so he traveled west and settled for a time in Crotona (Italy), where he taught and founded a community. In the late sixth century BC, in an atmosphere of mob rule, his community was attacked, and Pythagoras fled to Metapontum (Italy), where he died in 504 BC. As a result of the upheavals, his followers dispersed and founded other communities, thus spreading his beliefs to a wider area, including mainland Greece.

The Pythagorean cult developed a cosmology and spiritual practices based primarily on the study of number and devoid of traditional mythology. Because his mysteries were very close to the secret doctrines of the temple priests (see the section on sacred architecture), Pythagoras was in disfavor among the religious elite of his time. There are strong similarities between the Orphic beliefs and Pythagorean doctrines. Common to both schools of thought was recognition of the essential divine nature of human beings. Contemplation and devout practice produced the purity necessary for salvation. The doctrine of the transmigration of the soul was also important to Pythagoras. Love of wisdom, which is the purpose and meaning of philosophy, was also the very reason for existence, and all of human life could be properly understood in terms of such love. Pythagoras's community followed a strict daily regimen that involved spiritual exercises and a rigorous diet, which excluded meat. One exercise in particular that gives us a glimpse of his principles involved having students at day's end report exactly everything that had taken place during the day. This exercise helped the memory in its work of recalling deeper and more hidden facts of existence and excluding the mundane.

The Octave and Sacred Number

The most famous aspect of the work of Pythagoras was his discovery of the mathematical properties of the octave. This discovery was of great importance because it demonstrated the relationship between number and lived experience and thus demonstrated the relationship between divine principle and human life. Pythagoras discovered the mathematical relationship between the sound of a plucked string and its octave: the ratio of 1:2 and 2:1. When a string is halved, it vibrates exactly twice as fast and produces an exact octave. This demonstration proved to Pythagoras that the cosmos functioned on the level of number and thus according to principle.

THE ELEUSINIAN MYSTERIES

The section on the site of Eleusis examines this important cult in detail. However the essentials of these Mysteries need to be included here in the context of Greek religion, for they attracted a high level of participation and were prominent in the Athenian religious calendar.

The ancient Earth Mother cult maintained its power at Eleusis right in the face of Olympian dominion. The goddess of veneration at Eleusis was Demeter, and by extension her daughter, Persephone, was included. In religious terms the mysteries at Eleusis met the fundamental need of human beings concerning life after death. Part of the appeal in completing the six-month initiation process was the promise of an eternal existence, albeit unclear and cloudy in detail. It would seem that the inclusion of this cult in the state religion and the extensive fame of this celebration throughout the known world reflected a deeply held belief in cyclical patterns of life and death for all creatures and in the promise of immortality, which was central to the ritual. The climax of the nine-day celebration was the symbolic marriage of Zeus and Demeter, resulting in the birth of Dionysos, and included an overwhelming vision produced by ingestion of the sacred drink *kykeion*.

RELIGION AND PHILOSOPHY

The language used in seeking to understand the truth changed dramatically between the Archaic and the Late Classical Periods. Early expressions of the love of wisdom *(philia-sophia)* yielded to myth-narratives of human experience and aspiration told in highly figurative language. Still later, the Milesians in Asia Minor ventured into new territory by expressing their knowledge in words free of the petrified imagery of myth.

In the latter half of the fifth century BC in Athens, Socrates developed a new science of inquiry called the dialectic. His method was based on achieving self-knowledge through reminiscence *(anamnesis)*. The individual had to be carefully led to remember knowledge deeply imbedded in the soul. Guided by the *daemon* or spirit within, the seeker cleared away the impressions of the moment and the ideas and opinions *(doxa)* of others to arrive finally at the still center of being, where truth resided. Socrates himself taught nothing except this method. He asked questions that would expose falsehood and reveal truth, if the student was willing and adept.

The dialectic was Socrates' unique contribution to philosophical inquiry. In fact, more an approach than a scientific method, the dialectic was really philosophy itself, the love of wisdom working itself out in human understanding. The best way for human beings to express their love of wisdom was in intense conversation—the interaction of minds aspiring to the truth and willing to allow a higher law than ego to rule the process.

Some of these conversations have been passed down to us. In dialogue after dialogue, led mostly by Socrates and recorded by his faithful student Plato, the seeker is led to understanding and then to knowledge in the company of other seekers. We find in the dialogue entitled *Meno* an example both of the dialectic and of the purpose of philosophy. Socrates and Meno explore together the meaning of philosophical inquiry through question and answer:

> *Socrates:* I have heard from certain wise men and women who spoke of things divine that—
> *Meno:* What did they say?
> *Socrates:* They spoke of a glorious truth, as I conceive.
> *Meno:* What was that? And who were they?
> *Socrates:* Some of them were priests and priestesses, who

had studied how they might be able to give a reason of their profession; there have been poets also, such as the poet Pindar and other inspired men. And what they say is—mark now, and see whether their words are true— they say that the soul of man is immortal, and at one time has an end, which is deemed dying, and at another time is born again, but is never destroyed. And the moral is that a man ought to live always in perfect holiness . . . . The soul, then, as being immortal, and having been born again many times, and having seen all things that there are, whether in this world or in the world below, has knowledge of them all; and it is no wonder that she should be able to call to remembrance all that she ever knew about virtue, and about everything: for as all nature is akin, and the soul has learned all things, there is no difficulty in her eliciting, or as men say learning, all out of a single recollection, if a man is strenuous and does not faint; for all inquiry and all learning is but recollection.

Here, clearly stated, is the purpose and method of philosophical inquiry. Rather than merely filling the mind with information or acquiring a belief system passed on by the culture, Plato urges those who wish to know the truth to listen to the soul, the aspect of being that resides within and knows the truth from prior lifetimes. All of Plato is but the exercise of individual recollection. The participants in his dialogues remember through the discipline of rediscovery, peeling away the layers of acculturation to find the core of reality beneath.

AFTER SOCRATES AND PLATO

It is worthy of note that the influence of Plato and his Academy lasted formally in Athens until 529 AD, about a thousand years. Aristotle and his competing Lyceum extended the philosophical realm to natural science in one direction and to the true "essence" of things in the other. These two "schools" were the Oxford and Cambridge—or Harvard and Yale—of Hellas.

Under Aristotle, the Lyceum was mainly concerned with the "substance" of things, what lay behind sensual reality. Aristotle began with the tangible and went back to essence, whereas at the Academy, Plato and his followers began with essence as ideal form and regarded the tangible as an illusion. For example, Aristotle described the soul as having the form of the body. Beyond form is prime matter, which is expressed as potential. This approach to the mind and to philosophy does not lead so much to a standard of truth as it does to rational understanding and the birth of metaphysics, the process by which we begin to build systems of ideas about things. Aristotle gave human beings the freedom to become self-realized individuals, but there was a price to pay. Through his thought, human beings became isolated in a personal rather than a universal struggle for wisdom. Individuals found their own knowledge, struggled with their own self-realization. We were alone at last.

In the second and third centuries AD, the Neoplatonists focused on a single characteristic of Plato's philosophy: the concept of God as unity. The other gods were thought of as *daemons* in an intermediary stage of spiritual reality. The idea of the One, coming originally from Pythagoras and Heraclitus, was combined with the Orphic spiritual practices and evolved into the Neoplatonist vision. In particular, the works of Plotinus (AD 205-270) and his disciple Porphyry (AD 232-304) represent the culmination of the Platonic tradition in Neoplatonist schools.

It is Plotinus who framed many of the visionary ideas of Plato for modern seekers. He expressed the idea of the world soul, which anticipated the later concept of the *nous,* or universal mind, as a vision of how the unity of the One achieves multiplicity. Although held captive in a single body, a human being possesses universal mind, which allows liberation through contemplation upon the One. This line of reasoning later came to be known as the perennial philosophy and is the basis today of a growing unity between Eastern and Western traditions.

SACRED NUMBER
AND GEOMETRY

*And wise men tell us, Callicles, that heaven and
earth and gods and men are held together by communion and friendship, by orderliness, temperance,
and justice. . . . Now you, as it seems to me, do not
give proper attention to this, for all your cleverness,
but have failed to observe the great power of geo-
metrical equality amongst both gods and men: you
hold that self-advantage is what one ought to practice, because you neglect geometry.*

— Plato, *Gorgias*

We of modern times are Callicles, neglecting geometry in favor of self-advantage. We have forgotten the lawful relation
between heaven and earth, between spirit and matter. With
the help of the Greeks we might be able to remember this
connection through geometry—not the painful struggle to
prove the Pythagorean theorem, but rather the joyful relationship between the communion Plato speaks of and the
power of geometric equality that leads to the religious idea
of unity.

The important requirement for study at the Academy of
Plato was an understanding of the principles of geometry as
a basis for the study of philosophy. In the history and the
work of both Plato and his mentor, Pythagoras, the study of
geometry was a sacred devotion in which number and geometric form revealed the abiding laws of the universe. How
this came about takes us deep into the past, not only of Greece
but of Egypt and Northern Europe as well.

THE BIRTH OF GEOMETRY

Before the first stone structures were ever built, human beings scratched and painted signs and symbols onto cave walls
all over the world. Of all the shapes created by early human
hands, the most important was the circle, almost certainly
expressive of the sun and the moon. Since we also know that
these neighbors in space were worshiped as gods, we know
that the circle was a symbol of divinity. It had power to invoke divinity and was the first expression of our desire to
commune with the gods. It also expressed the sight of divin-

ity in the circle of another's eye.

The circle is whole, unending, complete, perfect. It is absolute and unchanging. It is the symbol of light, warmth, and life itself. It is also dual, in that it represents both the sun and the moon, each of which accumulated attributes and powers as the pantheon of gods grew in response to human need and understanding.

In many of these ancient drawings, a cross divides the circle into four segments, corresponding to the four directions and the four seasons. Indeed, the ancient lunar calendar may have developed with the discovery that dividing each of the four segments into seven smaller ones gave a circle with twenty-eight days—the lunar month. Thirteen months of twenty-eight days in turn gave a 364-day year with an extra day. This geometric calculation based on the circle placed the actual movements of the sun in its daily round and the moon in its monthly one into human hands and deified the symmetry of the circle.

The relation of the sun and moon to the circle and its natural divisions is one of the great discoveries of early cosmology. First, the simple circle, so expressive in its unity, represents the sun and moon, in themselves objects of power and awe. Then, divisions within the circle are discovered, which when drawn, express divisions within the year and events in the heavens such as the summer and winter solstices. Early Neolithic formations of stones following these patterns are evidence of early peoples' desire to understand and predict seasonal events.

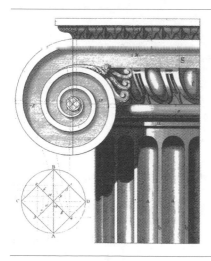

Engraving of an Ionic column with geometric patterns for the forming of a perfect spiral

GEOMETRY AND STRUCTURE

In the Neolithic Period, specific structures began to appear in which the geometry of the segmented circle was used to express human understanding of the movements of the sun and moon in relation to the earth. The most famous of these structures is Stonehenge, completed by early inhabitants of Great Britain before 1850 BC. As we now know, Stonehenge served as a solar and lunar calculator and most likely was also a temple. There were connections between these early geometric formations and Greek culture. Bladud, tenth king of the Druids, who lived long after the people who constructed Stonehenge, was a student of Pythagoras. He founded a Druidic center for the study of astronomy and geometry in Bath, England, and actually imported philosophers from Athens to teach there.

Similarly, in early Egypt, where the depository for all sacred knowledge was the temple, the priests possessed and controlled access to these same principles. The Egyptian priests understood the basic laws of the universe and embodied them in both temples and pyramids. Egypt became the source of esoteric knowledge and its schools transmitted that knowledge throughout the Mediterranean.

PYTHAGOREAN GEOMETRY

It was the secret knowledge of cosmic number and form that Pythagoras learned in the years he spent in Egypt. By then, two thousand years after the construction of the Great Pyramid but still during the active years of the great temples, the esoteric knowledge held in close secrecy by the priests was no doubt more generously shared than it had been earlier. By the sixth century BC, writing had opened the doors of hidden sanctuaries throughout the world.

During the years when Pythagoras lived (570-500 BC), Confucius, Lao-tzu, and the Buddha were also teaching esoteric knowledge, and their words being written down for a much larger following than could be reached by oral tradition. So it was with Pythagoras and sacred geometry. The secrets were emerging into the light, not without some danger to their integrity, however, and probably to their effective power as well.

Pythagoras is reported to have said that "All things are numbers." Taken in its full import, this means that the creation—all that may be perceived and understood—is number. That idea is usually understood in symbolic terms: that a number can be a symbol or a metaphor for an object or concept. Pythagoras, however, went beyond symbolism to absolute law. He said that a thing (object, state, thought) is as it is because it operates out of the Law of Two, or Five, or Nine. Thus, number is the same as law. These laws can be stated and are useful guides to an understanding of Greek form.

SACRED NUMBER

The Law of One
The One is the Eternal, the Absolute: indivisible, all-knowing, all-embracing. It is the All; the Greek *nous* in its broadest conception; the Monad; the Fire; the first cause; Universal Being; the Point which makes possible the circle. The idea of One does not consider the existence of zero, of negation or absence. The beginning is One, identity and unity.

The Law of Two
Self-awareness creates Two, polarity, the opposite. One becomes Two. In nature there is opposition: positive, negative; active, passive; male, female. Two is the duad, duality. Two points make a line. Two is the first feminine number; Eve; the Other; the tension of opposites.

The Law of Three
The synthesis of thesis (1) and antithesis (2); the resolving or holding of tension; the third point that forms the triangle; the first plane; surface. The Pythagoreans posited that the cosmic order manifested itself in Three; it is the first stability. Inspiration is the third force by which the artist (1) meets the medium (2). Three is the mysterious energy out of which comes the manifest world; the matrix. Inspiration, desire, eros in the third force. Balance is possible in the order of Three. The triangle establishes hierarchy. Like all odd numbers, three is male.

The Law of Four
The world is manifest in Four. The fourth point anticipates the solid. Principle articulated in sentences, expressions of law. Four is material; it is substance, the artifact created out of the One, Two, and Three. The Pythagoreans called Four the Eternal Principle of Creation. There are four directions, four seasons in nature, four regions in the sky. Four is Two and Two, showing the double aspect of duality itself. Four is Three and One, God in the individual, and thus soul. The first step in spiritual awareness and the first step in initiation into mysteries. Just as we begin to understand God by understanding the world, so we begin a spiritual journey with Four, the square, the solid, manifest world in which our senses play. We know God by knowing the presence of the soul within us.

The Law of Five
Five is the Law of Life, the union of Three (male) and Two (female). Five is Spirit arising from matter and is thus often connected to the resurrection of Christ. If Four is the manifest world, Five comprehends that world. It is understanding. Five is the measure of the pentagram, whose dimensions lead to the Golden Proportion, the geometric symbol of regeneration and rebirth. Because Five is a spiritual number, it also represents the potential of creation and the principle of eter-

nity, although not eternity itself. If Four begets the cube, Five forms the sphere. Five is the central number in the Tetractys, the Pythagorean diagram of number. In its position it relates to the One and is also half of the Divine Decad, or Ten.

The Law of Six

The Law of Six is a creative number, a partial resolution that proceeds to the divine Seven. Six is the feminine number of love and completion, Aphrodite's number. Six doubles to twelve and hence to the major time frames of creation, such as six days in the Bible. It relates to space in the same way, the hexagram emerging from the circle into multiple ideal forms. Six suggests a measure of completion and also anticipates the desire to unite with divine perfection. Thus, we often see temples with six columns on the narrow side. Here, the even number is both practical—allowing for the central door—and ideal, expressing the measure of earthly wholeness that aspires for eternal perfection in another order of experience.

The Law of Seven

The combinations of numbers making up Seven help us to understand its laws. Six, the number of earthly completion, plus One, the Divine Monad, equals a new stage in spiritual evolution. In Seven we experience a new understanding, a growth in divine knowledge. Creation took seven days—six of creativity, the seventh of rest. On the seventh day a new order arose. Seven is also the sum of Three, the sacred Triad, plus Four, the Principle of Creation. Thus in Seven there is a manifest union of spirit and matter.

The Pythagorean Greek word for Seven is *septas*, which also carries the meaning of holy, divine. Plato equated the Universal Soul with Seven, since the soul is generated from its law. In the Pythagorean system Seven is the most important number, presumably because its combinations and active principles are the core of spiritual work. In geometry we see the principle of Seven most often expressed in the relationship of a square (4) to a triangle (3). One expression of this sacred relationship is the pyramid, with its square base (the manifest world) and triangular sides rising to a point (divine principle and aspiration).

The Law of Eight

When we reach the numbers beyond Seven, we enter a world of complex principle and law because these numbers, like Seven, have their life in combinations of the lower integers. Eight, for example, is seen most often as twice Four—as the physical world regenerated at a higher level. Eight is the octave. It vibrates with the One and yet is a new note. Thus, Eight suggests beginnings that have divine sanction. In Christian numerology, Eight occurs in the octagonal shape of baptismal fonts and often in the number of steps descending to baptismal waters.

Eight is manifestation in its fullest development. Eight is associated with the Goddess as an expression of the perfection of the feminine. The eight columns fronting the Parthenon, consecrated to Athena, are an example of this relationship. The Earth Mother is Eight, breathing in and out in cycles, spiraling out and back in the figure-eight form (of later cultures), and embodied in the serpent that cures in the darkness of sleep.

The Law of Nine

When the human being has reached the culmination of life's journey, the point of fulfillment, the Law of Nine is said to be operating. The modern Armenian mystic Georgei Gurdjieff developed the best expression of this culmination in the enneagram, a universal symbol that represents all human knowledge. This expansive claim signifies the strength and breadth of the Nine as a law. Before we look at the enneagram, we might note some of the facets of Nine, which is the sum of 8 + 1, 7 + 2, 6 + 3, and 5 + 4. Included here are all the other number laws in relation to Nine, all in odd-plus-even combinations. Also, any integer multiplied by Nine yields a two-digit number that, when the two digits are added together, yields Nine again. Thus, 9 x 2 = 18, and 8 + 1 = 9. So too, 9 x 3 = 27, and 7 + 2 = 9. This means that as a law, Nine expresses a point of completion for the human cycle. From this point the only upward movement is to the Decad or Ten, the Divine Reality. Thus, Nine is the number of initiation.

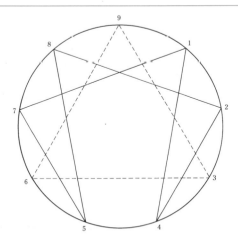

Fig. 1. The enneagram, showing the number configuration aligning geometry to number symbolism

The enneagram is a geometric expression worked out within the laws of a circle divided by Nine and expressing the Triad (see Fig. 1).

The Law of Ten

The Pythagorean system finds its completion in the Decad, the final number, which is really a beginning or a return to One. Ten completes the Tetractys and expresses the return to the source, which is the aim of all human aspiration correctly understood and pursued. And yet Ten is also more than One. It is One with steps taken. It expresses a completed cycle of action and manifestation. It is the perfected circle and the One whose sum is the One. The circle is the journey—the separation, the initiation, and the return. In the enneagram it is the circle that contains the Nine, that gives the Nine its form and meaning. Without the circle the other points would fall into chaos or align themselves in an arbitrary order. Without the circle, nothing. That is why the architects of sacred temples and sanctuaries always began with a point and a circle, out of which grew the manifestation in form: the line the triangle, the square, and so on.

THE SACRED TETRACTYS

The Pythagorean numerology is expressed in the Sacred Tetractys, which is a pyramidal arrangement of the numbers from one to ten (see Fig. 2). To understand the system of ten is to understand the relationships of the numbers as they appear in this simple configuration. One is at the apex of the form; it is the source, the aim, and the unity. A pair—Two, or the Duad—appears beneath it and forms a small pyramid with it which is Three. The form shows Three as One plus Two, but it also shows Two as two points, or a line. Three is also the next row. It extends to a larger pyramid made up of Six, which is also a point of resolution in the creation. The final row, Four, makes up the full perfection of the form and brings the total to Ten. The Tetractys, then, introduces us to the relation of the sacred numbers to one another and to the principles of geometry we now will explore.

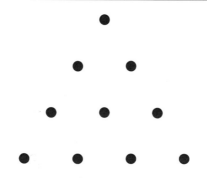

Fig. 2. *The sacred tetractys, a number pyramid from Pythagoras, key to his theory of number relationships*

SACRED GEOMETRY

Behind the outward appearance of the art created by the Greeks stood immutable laws of number and form. Expressed as geometric principles, these structural laws are based on relationships that were brought from Egypt, first by the Minoans and then by Pythagoras, and applied to the circumstances of a new culture.

Two of these principles in particular are embodied in the pottery, sculpture, and structures created by the Greeks. The first may be called the Circle and its Square; the second, the Golden Proportion. The Circle and Square is a simple enough principle and is based on the prehistoric relation of circle and cross described earlier.

First, a point is established and a circle inscribed. This is done on the ground if the resulting form is to be a structure, such as a tomb or temple. Then, working from the central point, a cross is drawn, from which a square external to the circle is constructed (see Fig. 3). In sacred terms, the point is the One, and the circle is an extension of that unity out into space as well as the basis of the square, which in turn is the basis of the resulting manifestation.

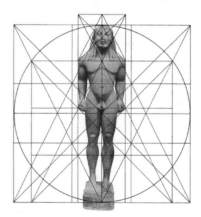

Fig. 3. Circle and square imposed on Archaic kouros, showing the geometric basis of design and universality of the human form

The second major principle of geometric form is the Golden Proportion, a form that was sacred to the Greeks and the Egyptians because it expresses a unique idea. The Golden Proportion is regenerative; that is, it describes a set of laws that return to the One or to unity from multiplicity. Thus, as a principle it expresses the idea of returning to the source or uniting again with divinity. The Golden Proportion also produces an aesthetically pleasing shape, one that has an immediate and compelling appeal to the eye because it articulates fundamental natural laws.

The Golden Proportion is created by establishing a rela-

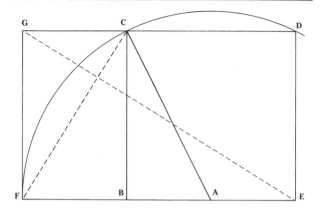

Fig. 4. *Constructing the Golden Proportion. From point A (bisected side of the square BCDE) inscribe an arc that passes through points C and D and falls on point F to form both the larger Golden Rectangle (DEFG) and the smaller one (CBFG).*

tionship between two unequal segments of a line. On any line only one point exists about which the following statement can be made: the ratio of the shorter segment to the longer is the same as the ratio of the longer to the whole. That point exists at a point approximately .618 units along a line one unit in length. The point, however, cannot be arrived at mathematically. Rather, the proportion is strictly geometric in nature and can be arrived at in several ways. One involves the construction of two squares within a circle, a diagonal (which corresponds to the square root of five), and an arc that corresponds to the original circle, which in turn creates the so-called Golden Rectangle.

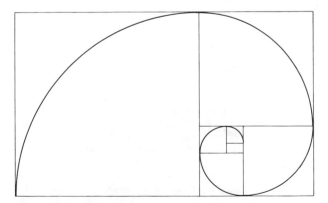

Fig. 5. *The Golden Proportion, with spiral that follows and forms a series of Golden Rectangles*

The importance of this rectangle is that it creates an image or illustration of a return to unity. It does so because the geometric relationships always create the same proportion, one which embodies itself in every smaller or larger form. The principle can be shown in the spiral form created by the evolving pattern (see Fig. 5). In nature, the pattern repeats itself in numerous forms of animal and plant life and is one of the crucial laws of growth and form. Those interested in further study of the Golden, or Divine, Proportion should refer to the works by Lawlor and Doczi in the section "Further Reading."

The Greek philosopher Protagoras said: "Man is the measure of all things." This statement expresses two related principles. First, the role of human beings is to express the laws of the universe as they are perceived through the human instrument. Second, the laws that make up the universe are expressed in microcosm within the human being, in both body and mind. To understand and articulate those laws is to know the creator of the universe.

In this way sacred geometry, particularly as expressed in the Circle and Square and in the Golden Proportion, makes manifest the laws by which matter appears from spirit and returns to spirit. In the Greek culture, these proportions were expressed clearly in pottery. Minoan and Mycenaean pottery reveal the Golden Proportion as the ruling form in the work. The shapes of the *amphora* in Archaic and Classical times show the same laws in use. The measure here is based on the principle that working from this form and perceiving it in the finished product is a sacred act. It is a prayer as well as a sacrifice to the gods, who revealed the form in the first place. The Greek artist did not sign his work, did not claim it as his creation as the modern artist does. The work came from a higher source and was an exercise in revelation expressed in form. The artist was merely a willing instrument of immutable principle.

Engraving of Temple of Hephaistos, Athens

GREEK TEMPLES

Similarly, in the temples built in Greece and surrounding areas during the Archaic and Classical Periods, the laws of sacred geometry ruled every line, angle, and shape. Whether laid out by the principle of Circle and Square or the regenerative laws of the Golden Proportion, they expressed within the landscape the power to transform matter to spirit. We say that these temples demonstrated the characteristics of the gods they represented. Indeed they did, but in geometric terms they also reminded the Greeks that the gods were lawful aspects of themselves which, when properly aligned, could bring benefit as well as knowledge through the geometric structure within which the law was being celebrated.

SACRED ARCHITECTURE

Architecture is harmony, rhythm, melody, and form in space. In the case of the ancient Greeks, a unique harmony emerged from the desire to recover lost communion with the gods and to invoke the power those gods possessed. Elements in the composition were the female forms of the landscape, the forms of nature, and the ideal form of the human being. The Greek architectural creation was always harmonious and always intimately connected to the landscape. Context was crucial to the sacred intent.

As we saw in the overviews of history and religion, the ancient Greeks developed their culture from their relationship to the landscape as goddess. The Earth Mother lay across the land in the hills, valleys, gorges, and caves. Her shape and nature nurtured and protected early inhabitants as they followed the herds along sacred pathways worn in the body of the earth. Over time, the sacred places in this landscape emerged as sanctuaries where altars were erected, usually oriented to a particularly dominant feature of the goddess-landscape.

THE SACRED LANDSCAPE

Early in the period of settlement, the Minoans selected building sites according to these same principles. Valuable work on sacred architecture and landscape has been done by Vincent Scully, formerly of Yale University, who studied the relationship of the Earth Goddess to palaces and temples throughout the Mediterranean. In his 1962 book, *The Earth, the Temple, and the Gods,* Scully sets the stage:

> From roughly 2000 BC onward, a clearly defined pattern of landscape use can be recognized at every palace site. More than this, each palace makes use, so far as possible, of the same landscape elements. These are as follows: first, an enclosed valley of varying size in which the palace is set; I should like to call this the "Natural Megaron"; second, a gently mounded or conical hill on axis with the palace to north or south; and lastly a higher, double peaked or cleft mountain some distance beyond the hill but on the same axis. The mountain may have other characteristics of great sculptural force, such as rounded slopes, deep gullies, or a conical or pyramidal

The Palace at Knossos in Crete, resting in its sacred landscape

massing itself, but the double peak or notched cleft seem essential to it. These features create a profile which is basically that of a pair of horns, but it may sometimes also suggest raised arms or wings, the female cleft, or even, at some sites, a pair of breasts. It forms in all cases a climactic shape which has the quality of causing the observer's eye to come to rest in its cup. Though there are many overlaps in shape and probably many unguessed complexities in their meanings, still the cone would appear to have been the earth's motherly form, the horns as the symbol of its active power.

Scully's text describes these features of the landscape as they appear throughout Greece and as they relate to the later functions of temple siting as well. Consequently, we cannot look at these sites isolated from their natural context. The architecture and the landscape are a unity. The "natural megaron" in which a palace or temple sits is as the name suggests: a sacred enclosure in which religious ritual takes place.

Without including the function and power of the landscape, the ritual invocations at the palace altars or temple sanctuaries would have become isolated, too personal in nature. To know that the whole community was held, quite literally, in the protection of the goddess naturally engendered the belief that the activities and devotions taking place at her sites were controlled by her rhythms and a structure greater than human desires or thoughts. The goddess was a context within which the entire life of the community was motivated and carried out.

The landscape also had aesthetic value, and temple design was influenced by setting. Scully is adept at sensing the aesthetic considerations involved in design and placement. For example, he speaks of the Temple of Hera at Paestum (Italy), "which was intended to sit in deeply shadowed heaviness upon the plain." In contrast, the Parthenon was designed to lift upward in order to suggest the spiritual nature of Athena as opposed to Hera's more physical influences, even though these two goddesses shared characteristics of the earlier Earth Mother Goddess.

CELESTIAL ALIGNMENTS

In addition to features of the landscape, temple and sanctuary placement corresponded to celestial elements: the movement of the sun, the rising and setting of stars in relation to landscape features, and the orientation of the sun and stars at the summer and winter solstices. Close attention was paid to the exact moments on a certain date when the rising sun's rays would enter the temple and strike the face of the god or goddess. The birthdays of gods were determined by the rising of stars in the notches of the mountains to which temple were aligned.

Another factor in the placement of a sanctuary was the alignment of sites to one another across great distances in relation to constellations in the zodiac. For example, sanctuaries devoted to Hera at Olympia, Argos, and Samos share an alignment of latitude and align themselves in Taurus at important times when the planet Venus is in transit through that constellation. Other key sanctuaries, such as Delos, Athens, Delphi, and ancient Sardis in modern Turkey, also share similar alignments.

ARCHITECTURE AND NATURE

The earliest extant examples of architecture in the Greek context are Minoan and Mycenaean. The palace remains at

The Hall of the Colonnades at Knossos, showing early use of the column, originally an inverted tree

Fig. 6. *Minoan coin and matching Hopi Indian spiral showing the image of the labyrinth*

Knossos and the Lion Gate at Mycenae both reveal early use of the column. Evidence shows that the column was initially simply a tree trunk, cut and trimmed to serve as a support for roof, porch, or second story. Though often considered merely phallic, the function and symbolism of the column is more properly related to the goddess because it suggests the growth, fertility, protection, and fruitfulness of the tree more than it does generative sexual power. Later, the column was fashioned in stone and later still in marble. At Knossos the stone column retained the tree shape of the wooden columns used earlier. Trunks were cut and then reversed so that the narrow portion of the trunk served as the column base. The idea seemed to be that reversing the trunk prevented the tree from sprouting again and allowed water to run off the column without gathering at the base, thus preventing rot. The natural imagery of the tree later evolved into the voluted and leafy capitals of the Ionian and Corinthian orders, emphasizing the symbolism of fertility and fruitfulness.

The labyrinth was another important feature in early architecture. A fundamental symbol of life, death, and fertility, the labyrinth (not to be confused with the maze) is a pattern of twisting and turning paths leading always to the center. It was designed to balance and still the mind. Its purpose was to shake the mind from its illusions of exterior place and certainty to prepare it for a sacred experience. The labyrinth has been expressed as a spiral motif in nearly every culture. For example, the spiral labyrinth is an Earth Mother symbol to the Hopi Indians of the American Southwest (see Fig. 6).

The Minoan palaces were built on the principle of the labyrinth, with the Earth Goddess herself in the form of the palace within which the people lived and worshiped. Coming and going through passages, passing from darkness into light and back to darkness, shifting from level to level, turning and suddenly emerging within sight of the sacred symbols of the goddess, the architecture was the substance of life and meaning worked out in ritual movement and form. Later approaches to temples retained this sense of the labyrinth as ritual preparation.

THE ARCHITECT IN ANCIENT GREECE

The architect in Greece was the *arche techne*, or the primary leader in the craft of design, the one responsible for coordinating the construction of the temple. The architect worked with simple tools: the line (rope), the divider, and the straight edge. The secrets of the profession and its symbols formed the basis of the Masonic order in Western culture. Without knowing exactly how the secret process of temple design worked, we can speculate about it from tradition and myths. As it was a sacred process, the chosen site must have originated with an altar, the location of which had been established many hundreds or even thousands of years before.

The architect selected the exact spot from which the temple would be generated. At the point of the altar, a stake was driven into the ground, thus fixing the spirit of the god to the site. A large circle was inscribed, symbolizing the god and the abundance of spirit to be celebrated. From that circle, either additional circles were constructed to form the Golden Proportion, or a square was constructed from which large triangles formed the final dimensions, both vertical and horizontal, of the temple. The triangles established the matrix and stability of the design. The squares or Golden Rectangles set out the exact physical distances and maintained the sacred intent.

It is perfectly possible, then, to accomplish all the geometric requirements of temple design using only the basic tools mentioned above. Refinements of design, the shape and separation of columns, the height of entablature, the extent of foundation platforms were all generated from the initial laying out of the geometry on the ground. In the detailed design of the Parthenon, for instance, factors such as sight lines, aesthetic considerations, sculpture requirements, and the demands of working with marble all entered into the final design.

THE FEATURES OF TEMPLE DESIGN

The temple, as an expression of human form and natural law, symbolized imperishable spirit emerging from matter. It was not meant for human habitation and was used only in a limited way for worship. Its purpose was to express the divine nature inhabiting it. When human beings entered the space, either as priests or worshipers, the architecture carried them away from the ordinary into a higher realm. For example, the effect of walking through the Parthenon (alas no longer permitted) is to lift our awareness to our relationship to the divine. It is an elevation of the spirit into the space where divinity dwells.

The entrance to the temple was always articulated in terms of an equilateral triangle formed from the roof peak to some point on the floor, or stylobate. The triangle always represented spiritual aspiration, a rising of matter (expressed as the base line) to the point of spiritual unity at the peak. The very structure of the temple entrance, then, symbolized the approaching worshiper's hope for unity with the presiding god.

The temple first appeared in Greece in the twelfth century BC. Temples were Olympian in nature, celebrating the new gods in their marriage to the earlier earth deities. In many ways the temple represented control over the sometimes chaotic forces of nature and the underworld. In some of the Bronze Age sanctuaries the forces unleashed were unpredictable and frightening. The temple served to fix the deity to the laws of form as expressed in the actual temple design. At the same time there was the impulse to unity, to establish human communion with the gods on a regular, predictable basis.

As indicated earlier, the temple was not only linked to the landscape but was also connected to movements in the heavens. Usually oriented to the east, the temple faced the sunrise and might also have been designed to fix the movements of the morning star as a guide to the festival days for the enshrined god.

There are eight general principles of temple design and function:

Most temples are oriented to the east, with exceptions made for special landscape features or site requirements.

The function of the temple was to bring the human being to the divine point of view, or as we have said, communion.

The temple expressed in formal design the natural enclosure of the entire site.

Each temple created a complex inner landscape for the purpose of worship.

The temple was a sculptural entity reflective of the god enshrined there.

The temple was a complete expression of art in its own right, reflecting the vision of the *polis* and the *arche techne*.

The later temples were forced to reassert the principles of enclosure rather than depend on their relationship to the landscape.

The character of the temple's design was determined by two factors: the landscape and the deity enshrined.

TEMPLE NOMENCLATURE

Before describing some further principles of temple design and construction, it will be useful to define a few constituent parts. We begin with the various ground plans for temples, including the names, some in Latin and some in Greek, that are traditionally used to describe various features. Then, we will examine the three basic orders of Greek temple design.

Temples are generally classified according to the arrangement of columns in relation to the walls. In Figures 7 through 11, solid walls are shown in thick black. In general, doors were placed in all openings. The platform or temple base is represented as a thin-lined rectangle.

Fig. 7. *The simple temple in antis*

The term *in antis* refers to the projections of the temple walls beyond the enclosing walls. *Antae* are the extended walls that reach beyond the basic rectangle of the inner section. The sacred enclosure or inner room of a temple is known as the *naos* in Greek, or the *cella* in Latin. The *pronaos* is the porch or entranceway to the *naos*. There was sometimes an additional room inside called an *adyton*, an inner sanctum where only the priests or priestesses were permitted.

In the Prostyle temple design, there are no *antae* and the *naos* is fully enclosed with a simple *pronaos* formed by a row of columns. Figure 9 illustrates the Amphiprostyle design, with columns at the rear, but no rear entrance. The Peripteros design, the most common for Greek temples, describes a temple in which the *naos* is designed *in antis* and is surrounded by a single row of columns supporting the roof elements. In the Dipteros design the *naos* and *pronaos* are surrounded by at least two rows of columns, creating the illusion of a forest.

These basic designs also vary in the number of columns across the width of the temple front. The number is always even, to provide for a central door, and varies from four to twelve. The usual six-column front is known as hexastyle.

In the nomenclature, the column is the vertical shaft with all its features. The entablature refers to everything above

Fig. 8. *The Prostyle temple design, typical of simple treasuries*

Fig. 9. *The Amphiprostyle temple design*

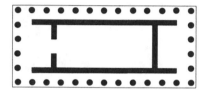

Fig. 10. *The Peripteros temple design*

Fig. 11. *The Dipteros temple design*

the column, including the roof elements. So, when we speak of the vertical elements we are speaking of the column and its features, and when we speak of the horizontal elements we are speaking of the entablature and its features.

As the concept of the temple evolved, there developed principles of construction based on the relationship of key elements, namely, the vertical and the horizontal forces involved. The vertical columns rose organically to a point of union with the heavy horizontal forces pressing down. This point of union became the focus of construction.

The Doric Order

The first order of column and entablature design was the Doric, named for the people who migrated south into Greece in the twelfth century BC, bringing the elements of this temple design with them. In the Doric order the column has no base.

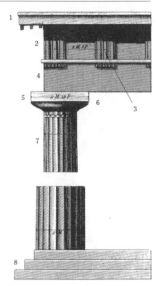

The Doric Order
1. Cornice
2. Frieze
3. Triglyphs
4. Architrave
5. Abacus
6. Echinus
7. Shaft
8. Stylobate

The Ionic Order

The Ionic order appeared after the Doric and is attributed to the Ionian people, later settlers in Greece. This order has greater elegance and a more organic quality than the Doric,

The Ionic Order
1. Cornice
2. Frieze
3. Architrave
4. Capital

and was used either alone or in conjunction with the other orders. The major differences from the Doric are the spiraled volute of the capital and the elaborate column base with torus.

The Corinthian Order

The late addition of the Corinthian order, seen sparingly until Roman times, introduced a new capital design featuring small volutes at each corner and elaborate leaf designs taken from the acanthus plant, common to Greece. The illustration shows the major contrast to the other orders.

The Corinthian Order
1. Cornice
2. Frieze
3. Architrave
4. Capital

THE DYNAMICS OF TEMPLE BUILDING

The Doric order reached its ultimate expression in the Parthenon. The architectural expression of the vertical and horizontal union results in a column which has a slight bulge or *entasis* as it descends from the point of union above. The capital has a slightly flattened look, as if the top of the column had been spread by the weight. The effect is one of balance and stability and yet a certain springy sense, as if the entablature might rise rhythmically only to fall back into place. The effect is one of dynamic balance.

The Ionic order presents a slightly different, more organic sense of union. Here, the weight of the entablature seems to curl the top of the column down to a point of stability. Because of this impression of curling—suggesting either vegetation or water—the Ionic column itself is not affected the same way as the Doric. It is generally thinner, shifting the impact of union to the capital.

In the Corinthian order, a fine example of which can be seen in the museum at Epidauros, the effect of the union is more mystical, in that the leaves do not appear to carry any weight at all. The sense of weight disappears in the upward thrust of vegetation, with only a slight curl in the volutes. In this order the union of vertical and horizontal is hidden or ornamented away, more suggestive of miracle than of tangible interaction.

As we proceed now to discuss the various sites in Greece, we will encounter specific examples of these orders. The variety of articulation within each order speaks to the exuberance of the Greek imagination and its sensitivity to each context. We can say that the Greek experience expresses itself through the lawful application of principle to individual context with sacred intent.

2
THE PALACE CULTURES

CRETE AND THE MINOANS

When we speak of the palace cultures in ancient Greek history, we refer to those archaeological sites called Minoan or Mycenaean where the remains are predominantly from what we call the Protopalatial and Neopalatial periods, the years from 2000 to 1200 BC. In the two most important of these sites, Knossos and Mycenae, the palaces were relatively undisturbed by later construction. In both cases, indeed, only minor traces of later Archaic or Classical temples remain, and in neither case do these traces obliterate major evidence of the earlier architecture.

A few other sites in Greece (such as Tiryns and Phaestos) offer some evidence of Minoan or Mycenaean remains, but most ancient sites—the Acropolis in Athens, for example—offer nothing of the earlier settlement for us to examine. We have evidence of prior occupation only in the form of isolated walls or pottery shards or fragments of frescos uncovered as the archaeological teams penetrated the layers of history down to bedrock.

However, even though they are limited, the palace remains we do have reveal a remarkable record of human culture and achievement. Here were cultures in which a priest-king ruled a tightly organized communal hierarchy. All the elements that made up the culture were present in one complex—a palace made up of royal apartments, connecting living quarters for the ranking members of society and their retainers, shrines and altars, storage areas, courtyards, public meeting halls, even grave sites in the case of the Mycenaeans. There were, of course, separate dwellings outside the palace complex, but the culture was defined by and centered on the palace.

Living as we do now in separate and private dwellings, isolated from those who govern and those who conduct our religious rituals, we can have no clear idea what communal existence was truly like. In the palace culture, secular and religious life were integrated in the person of the priest-king. Service to this monarch and to the gods and goddesses of the culture defined daily life. We might even speculate that private thought was of a different order. So integrated were these cultures that even individual consciousness as we know it might have been different in some way—more collective, perhaps.

The only experience we can have of this life is to visit the palaces and attempt to move through their spaces in a sacred manner with our attention focused on the elements before us: the landscape that frames the palace and the overall shape and design of the rooms and courts. The understanding this brings might in some small way allow us to pass over the stones and through the doors as the original inhabitants might have done.

The author in front of the Horns of Consecration at Knossos, Crete

KNOSSOS

Knossos is one of the great treasures of the world, and what remains today for the modern pilgrim to experience offers enough to make certain that a visit to the island of Crete and a full day on the site form an important part of any itinerary. Overnight cruise ships leave from Piraeus for Iraklion, the major city of Crete and site of the ancient port of Knossos. The cost of passage with room and bath for this voyage is about the same as a night in a Class A hotel, thus providing a saving for those counting their drachmas. But for those who prefer the convenience of air travel, Olympic Airways flies into Iraklion on a regular basis from Athens, and the flight is both short and reasonably priced.

Although the cruise ships throb with the rhythm of powerful engines, the traveler still rides on the waves under the clear Mediterranean sky to land on Crete as the Minoan sailors did in the third millennium BC. It is exhilarating to experience those things that never change, such as the movement of the sea and the feeling of solid ground under the feet after a voyage.

THE PORT OF IRAKLION

Iraklion is an unusual city. It is still ringed by ramparts built by the Venetians, who ruled Crete from AD 1204 to 1669. The city is named for Herakles, the mythical hero whose twelve great labors included (as the seventh) capturing the mad bull of Crete and transporting it alive to Mycenae. Herakles is usually pictured in late mythology wrapped in skins and carrying a huge club with which he subdued most of his enemies, and to this day the youths of Iraklion roam the streets of the city on New Year's Eve bopping each other over the head with air-filled plastic clubs. It is a rather poor honor for the great hero.

The city offers a full range of hotels and easy transportation to the ancient sites. Finding a good restaurant in Iraklion isn't easy, but the sidewalk cafes offer fresh local produce and the winding streets hide numerous shops. Crete is one of the agricultural centers of the Mediterranean, and the countryside boasts miles and miles of olive and orange groves, as well as fertile valleys that furnish fresh vegetables for the mainland.

THE PALACE SETTING

The palace of Knossos sits on a small hill called Kephala, just over 3 miles (5 km) south, or inland, from Iraklion. The site can be reached by city bus or taxi. Kephala Hill is surrounded on three sides by ridges and is dominated to the south by Mount Jouctas, a notched mountain sacred to the Minoans. To the north the valley forms a gentle bowl that opens out and down to the sea, visible in the distance from the upper floors of the palace. The location of the palace is ideal from the point of view of living conditions. The site is protected from winds, the Kairatos River flows nearby on its way to the sea, and the fertile valley provides ample grazing and rich soil for cultivation.

More than any of the later Archaic or Classical sites, the Minoan palaces on Crete seem ideal expressions of harmony with nature. These structures appear to have grown organically into the hillsides on which they spread over many generations. There is no such thing as a final palace, a culminating structure. That is why an artist's rendering of a palace should not really be attempted, although some efforts have been admirable. We can have no sense how the palace complex looked at any given period, but we can appreciate the concept behind the changing details.

Knossos is a microcosm of the landscape in which it sits. The Central Court mimics the valley of the Kairatos River. The surrounding two- and three-story chamber complexes echo the ridge lines to the east and west of the palace. The great Horns of Consecration and the Propylon to the south are the images of Mount Jouctas and the Lower Gypsades hill, which rises gently in the foreground. The original wide, sloping ramp to the north (now much narrower) mimicked

Mount Jouctas, sacred mountain of the Minoans, south of Knossos, Crete

the gradual incline to the sea. The palace, then, is the Minoans' construct of the sacred land where they founded their culture and took their place in the cosmic scheme.

To what extent this analogy was a conscious articulation on the part of the priest-builders of the past is a modern question without an ancient answer. Our sense of what constituted "conscious" in 2000 BC cannot be measured in the framework of the twenty-first century AD. It might best be said that the planning of the palace was "natural," meaning in harmony with nature and the gods, whose power was sought and heard and felt in every undertaking.

HISTORY

NEOLITHIC TIMES

The story of Knossos begins in the seventh millennium BC, in the Neolithic Period. The earliest evidence of a settlement on Crete is found on Kephala Hill. Presumably these early people came to Crete from the south and east, and there is enough similarity to early Egyptian culture to support that conclusion. Beneath the floor of the Central Court excavators discovered at a depth of 20 feet (6m) various tools and pottery detailing the history of a Neolithic settlement and suggesting the worship of an Earth Mother goddess.

Part of that worship was related to the presence of Mount Jouctas, the peak visible to the south of Knossos on which Neolithic cult remains and Minoan sanctuary buildings were discovered. There is precious little evidence anywhere concerning Neolithic religious belief or practice in relation to either landscape features or cult figures, so conclusions must be based on a few finds at various sites and on the general theories about the importance of the Mother Goddess in the pre-Bronze Age Mediterranean.

What the archaeological record does show clearly is that prior to the Bronze Age, the Neolithic settlement at Knossos was one of the largest and most prominent settlements in Europe and that the palace culture we see today followed with little apparent upheaval. Thus, the palace culture that developed later on the site was not wholly new, but was probably a continuation of existing religious beliefs and practices.

MINOAN MIGRATION

Some time in the third millennium BC the people we now call Minoan came to Crete. There is no evidence that these migrations took the form of conquering invasions. The new population intermingled with the earlier inhabitants, and as they began to build palaces, the same locations valued by the previous culture seemed to serve the new arrivals. The difference was that this new population exhibited extraordinary artistic knowledge and skill.

As outlined in the historical overview, the beginning of the early Minoan Period (roughly 3000-2400 BC) coincided with the beginning of the Bronze Age in 3000 BC. Evidence has been found from that period of two- and three-story rectangular dwellings made of sun-dried mud brick and plaster. All of these dwellings were leveled when palace construction began in the Middle Minoan Period. There are a few of these early remains well to the south of the present remains and at the bottom of the walled pits in the West Court.

PALACE CONSTRUCTION

Current dating procedures place the first palace construction near 2000 BC, in the period known either as Middle Minoan II or by the more current term, Protopalatial (which is sometimes assigned the dates 1900-1700 BC). The construction of the Central Court, the West Court, and the Theatral Area are dated to this period, as also some scattered buildings no longer in evidence. Wall and foundation remains from this period, found throughout the site, suggest that the broad outlines of a design for the palace as a whole were already in place. Late in the period called Middle Minoan II, the palace assumed its monumental proportions. From 1900 to 1700 BC the fundamental forms of what now remains were erected. To this period we can assign the development of the palace as a connected series of elements. Any later additions and repairs, including the modern reconstructions that greet visitors today, were imposed upon the forms erected during these two centuries of development.

The main features of this design included the enclosure of the Central Court by multistoried structures, the develop-

The West Porch of Knossos, showing multistoried construction

ment of the Grand Staircases on the western and eastern sides of the Central Court, the elaborate storage magazine to the west, and the royal living quarters to the east. Also included were the cult areas to the north and south, including the Lustral Basins, the Shrine Rooms, and the general processional passages that were used to approach the Central Court, where the sacred life of the palace reached its culmination.

PALACE DESTRUCTION

Between 1800 and 1700 BC a disaster, probably an earthquake, destroyed the early palace. This marked the beginning of the period known as Middle Minoan III, or Neopalatial. From this time until 1450 BC, when all the palaces on Crete were destroyed, Knossos saw constant remodeling of its major features. Much of what we see today are products of these two or three centuries of construction. The history of the palace in these times is complicated by the arrival of the Mycenaean overlords, who assumed control of the palaces and made changes according to their own vision of culture—changes that probably included modest fortifications. The important construction of the Throne Room and attached rooms to the west are attributed to this period.

The date 1450 BC is generally agreed upon in the history of the Mediterranean for the great volcanic eruption of Thera, the modern island of Santorini. There are Minoan remains on Santorini at the ancient town of Akrotiri that give silent witness to the disaster. Beneath the volcanic dust of Akrotiri archaeologists have uncovered priceless frescoes (now in the Archaeological Museum at Athens) depicting details of Minoan culture. The theory that the Cretan palaces were destroyed by this volcanic eruption would be more generally accepted if the Cretan sites contained definitive evidence of layers of volcanic ash or similar direct connection to the eruption. However, earthquakes and massive tidal waves that very likely accompanied the eruption could also have destroyed the palaces. When the palace at Knossos was first excavated, there was evidence of sudden destruction rather than the more gradual deterioration of a declining culture. Someday we may know the full story.

Historically, the end of the Minoan culture on Crete in 1450 BC marked the close of Eastern influences in ancient Greek history. Although Eastern influences may be dimly perceived until modern times, from this point on the influences on Greek culture were mostly northern and "European," and the dominant themes of culture were hereafter Western. Thus, the preservation of Knossos until the present affords a rare opportunity to explore the connections to the mysteries of ancient Egypt and the sacred worlds of the East.

MYTHOLOGY

... Knossos, the great city where Minos, who spoke with the great Zeus, was nine years king.

— Homer

A myth is both the narrative of a culture and a universal drama of the human condition. Myths explain the histories of peoples, tribes, and individuals in their struggles to know and understand destiny and the meaning of life. The myths surrounding Knossos are some of the most intriguing ever told. They tell the stories of Minos, the legendary priest-king; his wife Pasiphae, the moon goddess; the Minotaur; the artist Daedalus and his unfortunate son Icarus; and finally, Theseus and the lovely Ariadne.

EUROPA AND ZEUS

The story of Minos, the founder of Knossos and of the culture that bears his name, begins in Asia Minor, in what is now Israel, where the fair Europa lived with her father, King Aganor. As often happens in sacred myths, this story begins with a dream. Europa is visited by two goddesses in the form of two continents, rival earth goddesses, who inform Europa that Zeus, Bright Consciousness, will visit her and plant his seed in her. The girl is frightened and seeks peace and forgetfulness with her friends in the nearby hills sacred to the goddess.

Engraving of Europa being carried off by Zeus as a bull

Zeus descends from Olympus in the form of a splendid bull with delicately curved horns and majestic head, and he grazes near where the girls are picking roses on a gentle green mound. Europa is induced by the beauty and gentleness of the bull to climb upon its back, whereupon the bull moves swiftly down to the sea and swims over the sea to Crete. Europa is deposited, frightened and alone, on the shore. Soon, however, Zeus appears again, this time as a handsome stranger, and takes Europa to wife. The union of Zeus and the princess Europa produces three offspring, one of whom is Minos, future king of Crete.

MINOS AND THE MINOTAUR

Minos lives in Greek memory in several vivid myths and in an utterance from the Delphic Apollo. Found in the works of the third-century AD philosopher Porphyry, the oracle of Apollo cites the greatness of the philosopher Plotinus and says that his soul had returned to the heaven of Plato and Minos and all the choir of love.

That Minos should be included in the company of Plato in heaven and that Apollo should single out his soul as having attained such heights are an indication of Minos's reputation as a sacred figure. In legend, Minos was a son of Zeus and himself possessed oracular powers. When he claimed the throne of Knossos, he prayed to Poseidon to send a sign that he had a just claim to the throne. Poseidon immediately sent a sacred white bull from the sea as a fitting sign and as a suitable sacrifice to himself.

Minos was so struck with the beauty of the bull that he kept it rather than sacrificing it to Poseidon. This affront to the god was an act of spiritual greed, keeping for oneself what was due to the gods. Later, when Minos married the beautiful Pasiphae, worshiped in her own right as a moon goddess, Poseidon caused Pasiphae to fall in love with the white bull, which still roamed freely with the king's herds. Pasiphae confessed her lust to Daedalus, the Athenian artist living in exile in Knossos, who agreed to fashion for Pasiphae a likeness of a cow in which she would be able to receive the bull. From this union came the monster Minotaur, half man, half bull, which Minos confined to the darkest recesses of the labyrinth.

MYTH AND SPIRIT

In this myth are framed all the elements of humanity's relationship to divinity. Knossos itself, the palace and its environs, is the stage upon which human beings act out their role in the cosmos. Poseidon, god of the sea, is the dark mystery of divinity, responding to the prayer of a noble son of Zeus, Bright Consciousness, to assume his proper place in the hierarchy. The prayer is answered with the sacred white bull, symbol of prophetic power.

When Minos refuses to sacrifice the bull, to relinquish power to the gods where it belongs, he is guilty of greed and arrogance (hubris). Pasiphae, who represents the powers of the subconscious symbolized in myth by the moon, seeks union with the bull, acting out an inappropriate desire made possible by the greed and neglect of Minos. The result is the birth of a monster, symbol of the deep flaw in the sacred hierarchy of the kingdom.

The labyrinth, representing the harmonizing power of nature and the subconscious of the culture, is crucial to the drama. The Minotaur is improperly confined in this structure, in the darkness where greed and desire flourish unattended and are repressed and hence nurtured. In these circumstances the proper development of consciousness is inhibited. Minos does not establish his relationship to the gods while the Minotaur—his repressed nature—remains in the darkness.

All the elements of this myth are evident in the landscape at Knossos. Poseidon's mysterious sea is visible to the north, at the end of the long valley. Mount Jouctas, a mountain expressive of the horns of power and the authority of the gods, lies to the south, exactly in line with the important passages of the sacred procession and the Central Court where the bull-leaping myth is acted out. The palace sits on a raised mound, the body of the goddess where human life acts out its role in the cosmic drama. The dark passages of the labyrinth—the subterranean Shrine of the Double Axes—are where the destructive powers of the underworld must be met, propitiated, and transformed.

That Minos should eventually succeed in transforming this destructive power and attaining the status of a wise man is a measure of his struggle as a human being and is the story of the evolution of a soul. The light and sun of the Central Court mark the place in the open where the struggle of the soul is made manifest. The rituals of the Minoan religion most likely culminated in the Central Court, where bull leaping and other symbolic rites acted out the human aspiration for unity with and propitiation of the gods.

In a fragment of a play by Euripides called *The Cretans* we learn that when the Minotaur is born and confined in the depths of the labyrinth, King Minos sends for the Idaean Daktyls, who were priests living in a sanctuary on Mount Ida, the mountain sacred to Zeus on Crete. The Daktyls are called upon to purify the palace and bring peace and moral order back to the culture. It is interesting that a special priesthood is sought out to bring their particular powers and understanding to this crisis. Because we have only a fragment of the play, we do not know the outcome of the purification, but doubtless many of the sacred processions and rituals of Knossos relate to these acts of purification.

THESEUS AND ARIADNE

The hero Theseus was in legend the founder of Athens. When he became king, he united the families and tribes of Attica under the leadership of Athens and became its wisest ruler. When his father Aegeus was still king, Theseus sailed to Crete with thirteen other Athenian youths in payment of a tribute to Minos. (Some say the tribute was seven boys and seven girls, others say just seven youths.) Athenian youths were sacrificed to the Minotaur every nine years for crimes committed against the Cretans by Athenians. Theseus had pledged that he would destroy the monster and end the tribute.

Before leaving for Crete, Theseus sought the council of the Delphic oracle, who pronounced that Theseus should perform sacrifices to Aphrodite before he embarked. After doing so, Theseus and the other Athenian youths set out in a ship rigged with black sails, symbolic of the mourning associated with payment of the tribute. King Aegeus, however, also put a white sail aboard the ship and urged Theseus to hoist it upon return if he met with success.

In Crete Theseus appeared at Minos's court and took part in the games that formed a part of the rituals of sacrifice. So noble in form and manner was Theseus that he captured the love of the beautiful princess Ariadne, who in her desire to save him gave him a magic sword and a skein of sacred thread to find his way out of the depths of the labyrinth. With these gifts Theseus killed the Minotaur, found his way out, and with Ariadne escaped from Crete and sailed for home. On the island of Dia, according to Homer, Ariadne was claimed by Dionysos as his bride, and Theseus returned to Athens in mourning, thus forgetting to hoist the white sail of victory. King Aegeus, seeing the black sail, assumed the worst and threw himself into the sea, named for him in memory of his tragic error.

Engraving of Dionysos and Ariadne riding off in triumph. Centaurs are typical participants in myths of Dionysos.

According to a later myth, Theseus abandoned Ariadne on the island of Naxos and set sail for Athens. The grieving princess was then saved from despair by Dionysos. As king in Athens, Theseus was thereafter obliged to honor the memory of Ariadne and to proclaim special festivals in Athens to Dionysos to expiate his guilt.

THE JOURNEY OF THE HERO

In Theseus's long and illustrious history he undergoes all the trials necessary for spiritual development. In Crete, he meets the terrors of the underworld in the form of the Minotaur in the labyrinth, the subconscious where we may become lost in our journey. Theseus is given the simple tool of a skein of linen thread with which to find his way out of the maze. Giving his love and promise of escape to Ariadne brings him this tool—the gift from her that ensures success.

By abandoning Ariadne Theseus shows that he has not understood the nature of his victory. Thus he sails back to Athens under the black sail of darkness, which results both in the death of his father and the animosity of the god Dionysos. It is only in dedication to proper duty and sacrifice to the god that Theseus learns from his suffering to be obedient to powers greater than those of his personal mastery of the circumstances of his world.

In these myths of Minos and Crete we learn much of why Knossos has lived so long in the Greek imagination as a place of mystery and power. Knossos is synonymous with the human attempt to build a palace of human dreams and aspiration and to risk the wrath of the gods by exceeding the powers proper to human life. We are in awe of the attempt and of the gods whose powers brought destruction to the dream.

MINOAN RELIGION

Very little is known of Minoan rituals and the names of the Minoan gods. We can only speculate from a wide variety of sources what may have constituted the patterns of Minoan belief and practice. The main elements of the religion were apparently the sacred pillar (column), the tree cults, and the bull. Various images from frescoes, rings, seals, pottery, and the famous sarcophagus from Hagia Triada in southern Crete suggest that the religion had to do with the shedding of bull blood (the essence of life) at or on the pillar, which represented the power of the goddess to renew life and the growing cycle each year.

The bull was always netted or else snared by the foot, to make certain that no blood would spill prior to the sacred ceremony. During the ritual, bound and still alive, the bull's throat was cut, permitting the blood to drain into sacred vessels. This sacrifice celebrated the life force of the bull and the divine connection of that force to growth in nature. As we visit the site, we shall see the images of the bull and the pillar in relationship to one another in the architecture of the palace.

THE SITE

Those looking for the famed labyrinth at Knossos need look no farther than the palace itself. The pre-Hellenic word *labrys* means "double ax," which no doubt gave rise to the association of the word *labyrinth* with Knossos. But myths have a way of speaking more truth than simple etymologies can explain. The palace itself is a labyrinth, a mass of connecting rooms and passages that penetrate the darkness, emerge into light, and articulate the story of the Minoans and their culture. The ancient visitor entered the labyrinth at the West Porch entrance to the palace. However, our visit of necessity begins at the modern entrance to the site.

THE ARCHAEOLOGICAL RECORD

At the entrance to the site is a bronze bust of Sir Arthur Evans, the famed British archaeologist who in 1900 began excavations here. Evans was present in 1935 at the unveiling of the bust, having just completed work on a four-volume account of his work at the site. Although minor excavations in 1877 had uncovered storerooms and various walls, it was Evans who first began extensive digs. He had been keeper at the Ashmolean Museum at Oxford and there developed an interest in the ancient scripts found by Heinrich Schliemann at Mycenae. The theory at the time was that the site at Knossos was most probably the source of the Mycenaean culture. Few realized just how important would be the discoveries on Crete as they revealed an entirely new culture.

Having purchased the land around Knossos and signed an agreement with the Greek government, Evans hired diggers and began work. Within two years he had uncovered most of what we see today. At the time, little remained intact. The sheer volume of rubble was awesome, all the various floors having fallen into a single mass. Evans and his colleagues determined that in order to understand the proper relationship of levels and supporting columns, some form of reconstruction would have to be attempted. Moreover, many frescoes were found in the rubble, and their location in the palace had to be determined. Most of the restoration of these frescoes was finally accomplished by the Frenchman Jules Gillieron, under Evans's watchful eye.

What we see today is a compromise of archaeological principles. Without any reconstruction we would see little but outlines of walls and column bases at the lowest levels of the palace. Only models, similar to the ambitious wooden reconstruction at the museum in Iraklion, would show us the complexity and beauty of the original. What Evans attempted was a partial rebuilding of the palace according to his understanding of the evidence uncovered. For example, only a few of the wooden columns remained and these had been charred by fire, but some remaining pigment showed that the columns were painted white, red, or black.

It became clear that the Minoans had mastered the technique of multistory construction, using stone walls and columns for vertical support, and logs and plaster for ceilings. Hewn logs were used as door frames and lintels, giving the entranceways a graceful, even modern, look. Evans made every attempt to reproduce Minoan masonry and decoration, even using the same materials, except for the decision to use concrete rather than wood for columns and ceilings.

Purists may decry the results of Evans attempts, pointing out justifiably that important early remains were obliterated by the modern reconstruction, but the result for the contemporary visitor is a rare opportunity to step back in time—albeit a time chosen for us by Evans—to share the beauty of a very special place. Careful observation will permit the visitor to distinguish original construction from Evans's reconstruction. A visit to the palace at Phaestos will reveal a more disciplined example of archaeological research still in progress.

The West Court

The modern entrance to the site is from the west across a bridge, beneath which we can see the ancient ramp leading up to the West Court. Elements of an early retaining wall are still visible, as are foundations of houses that would have been outside the original Middle Minoan palace (before 2000 BC). Several striking architectural features are immediately evident. (See Fig. 12.)

The Minoans built raised walkways through their courtyards. From their placement and proximity to altars, it is clear that these were designed for processions. Since religious and secular life were fused in one ceremonial vision of life, we have come to call these walkways Sacred Ways or Processional Ways. Their narrowness suggests that the processions were single file and moved along a route that permitted large crowds to view the participants.

Two altar sites in the West Court and the Processional Way slicing through the open area seem to indicate that this western court was always an important sacred area for the Minoans. And its remains are some of the earliest at the site, further suggesting a long and continuous ritual history.

The Walled Pits

Also from the Middle Minoan II period (2000 BC) are three walled pits used by the Minoans as places to deposit refuse from ceremonies and sacrifices. As we have seen from later Greek depositories, arrangements were always made for the used ceremonial items to be disposed of properly. Sacred items could not be left around or simply thrown down an embankment. A careful examination of the walled pits, particularly the two nearest the Processional Way, reveals the foundations of houses from the Prepalatial Period. Still evident are the red plaster floors and walls, demonstrating the fine workmanship of this early period. Evidence of such early remains is rare at the site.

Royal Road and Theatral Area

Rather than enter right into the palace at this point, visitors might approach the complex from the north by the ancient Royal Road, which is found by turning left from the West Court and walking to the stepped platform or stage known as the Theatral Area. This stepped court seems to have been used in a later period (Late Minoan I) as a place of reception, perhaps a kind of reviewing stand from which processions might be observed. Earlier the whole area was organized as a large courtyard similar to the West Court. The present raised position would have provided a dramatic stage from which the king might have held court outside the palace—among the people, and yet still very much in command.

The ancient road, or Royal Road as it is sometimes called, has the reputation of being the oldest road in Europe. Certainly most of the paving stones are original and date from the third millennium BC. The height of the modern side walls

The Sacred Way leading to the Theatral Area at Knossos

indicates the extent of the digging needed to reveal the original stones. The occasional breaks in the wall expose some of the old houses and shrines that lined the road in ancient times. This road may have provided a short connection to the Little Palace, the remains of which (not open to the public) have been excavated on the other side of the modern road, or it may have turned north and gone all the way to the sea. To date, no remains of the road have been discovered beyond its present state of exposure.

The North Lustral Basin

Just beyond the Theatral Area, to the north and at the end of the palace complex, sits the reconstruction of the North

Lustral Basin. Its location here suggests that the area served as a point of purification for those about to enter the palace. The lustral basins were probably not used for bathing but rather for purification, which must have involved ritual pouring of water over the body combined with prayers and other ritual devotions. We can experience the purification ritual by descending the sixteen steps to the basin, which is approximately seven feet square and was fed by the natural level of water in the palace system.

The Processional Way

Once purified, the visitor entered the Processional Way at the Theatral Area and moved south along the western side of the palace. Altars to the right and then to the left may have been stops along the way as the single line approached the West Porch. Traces of blackened gypsum—evidence of the fire, either set or accidental, that destroyed the palace for the last time—can still be seen along the way.

Several elements of the West Porch are significant. First, a single column is placed right in the middle of the doorway. Its position commands attention and causes the procession to move around it. The column was a symbol of the goddess— of her strength, her support of the world, and her fecundity. This column in particular lines up precisely with Mount Jouctas to the south, reminding us of our dependence upon divine support as we move into the palace.

The West Porch also featured wall frescoes relating to the bull leaping that was such an important part of the sacred life of the Minoans. The images of bull leaping, the presence of the column, and the sight of the mountain served

The North Lustral Basin, Knossos, where visitors may have purified themselves before entering the palace

to draw attention to the sources of power that give this palace its reason for being.

The Corridor of the Procession

The way narrows as we continue south. This long corridor was decorated with frescoes of the procession itself: life-sized figures of men and women, elaborately dressed, carrying gifts and ceremonial vessels for libations. Similar frescoes have been reproduced on the walls of the Great South Propylon. Our own artistic traditions tell us that these frescoes served to elevate the procession to an art, to remind the worshiper of the heritage as well as the beauty of this act. Since they mirrored the procession, they may also have served as a manual of how to move and look.

The way then turns left, and our attention is drawn to the floor of the corridor. The procession moved along carefully laid gypsum slabs, raised slightly to control and direct the movement. On either side of the raised walk was inlaid a greenish schist, a crystalline rock having a closely foliated structure.

The route of the ancient procession from this point is speculative. From the evidence provided by fragments of frescoes, one route took the celebrants into the South Propylon, up the Grand Staircase and into what Evans called the Piano Nobile, or the main story, where Evans located the state apartments and the ceremonial halls. Another, more direct route to the Central Court makes its way past the South Propylon and then left directly to the court. Since there were no doubt many kinds of processions, they may have used various routes.

The Great South Propylon

Certainly the most impressive entry into the palace is through the Great South Propylon. The Minoan, Mycenaean, and Greek cultures all emphasized the importance of the entrance. Most of the sites in this book feature monumental entrances—places where attention is focused, energies are gathered, prayers offered, and greetings extended.

The sacred importance of this area is emphasized by the presence of the large sculptured Horns of Consecration, which have been restored and placed where the original fragments were discovered. The horns represent those of the sacred bull, symbol of the power beyond human control. They are placed so as to frame and echo the peaks of Mount Jouctas. At the time of writing this book, a cypress tree presumes to interrupt the direct line of sight.

The procession into the Great South Propylon passes through a gateway, past a great column and the frescoes on the wall to the left, up two steps, past two square columns and then two round columns to the Staircase to the Piano Nobile. There are twelve steps in this staircase as there are in all of the major staircases in the palace. This uniformity was certainly intentional, although the reason for it is not

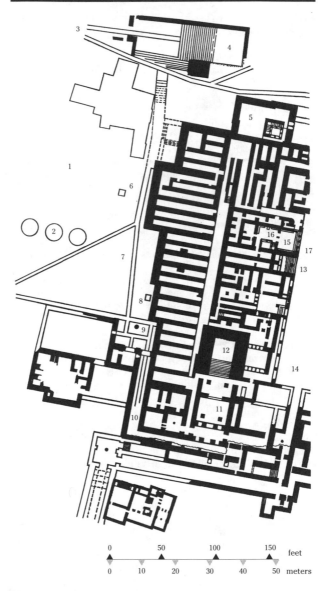

Fig. 12. *Knossos, Crete*
1. *West Court*
2. *Walled Pits*
3. *Royal Road*
4. *Theatral Area*
5. *North Lustral Basin*
6. *Altar*
7. *Processional Way*
8. *Altar*
9. *West Porch and Column*
10. *Corridor of the Procession*
11. *Great South Propylon*
12. *Staircase to Piano Nobile*
13. *Staircase to Central Court*
14. *South Procession Corridor*
15. *Outer Throne Room*
16. *Throne Room*
17. *Lustral Basin*

N ▲

18. *Grand Staircase*
19. *Hall of Colonnades*
20. *King's Megaron*
21. *Queen's Megaron*
22. *Queen's Bath*
23. *Shrine of the Double Axes*
24. *North Entrance*
25. *West Bastion*
26. *Giant Pithoi*
27. *Workshops*

clear. It could be that twelve steps is the proper height for a story. It could be that twelve marks a calendar division, or is meaningful as the multiple of the threes and fours that seem to dominate other architectural features of the palace.

Twelve represents a certain spiritual fulfillment, such as the twelve labors of Herakles. Twelve are the signs of the zodiac, the tribes of Israel, the loaves of bread in the tabernacle, the disciples of Christ. In many traditions twelve represents achievement and resolution, as well as initiation and spiritual transformation. We shall see the number twelve reappear elsewhere in the palace.

The Piano Nobile

Once we reach this level in the palace, our procession moves past a single column to a vestibule, through double doors (note the marks in the floor for the doors) into a central lobby, and then through double doors once again into the Tricolumnar Hall. This impressive room, with its sets of three circular and square columns and various doors to adjoining rooms, must have been ceremonial in nature. It suggests a point of arrival at a place where ceremonies can be held. Evans's discovery of many ritual vessels of superb quality, such as those pictured in the processional frescoes in an adjoining room called the Treasury supports this view.

As Figure 13 indicates, the Piano Nobile contains a multitude of rooms and corridors, which are connected to the major line of procession. To the left is the Great Hall, which covered the lower level of magazines used for storage. This hall overlooked the West Court. The presence there of an altar, along with the connecting sanctuary hall (so named from

The Great South Propylon at Knossos, with frescoes of the sacred procession

the sacred subjects of its wall frescoes) suggests it was an area devoted to religious ceremony.

The goal of the procession is the Central Court, reached by the staircase that takes us to the right and down to the court. The staircase, again with twelve steps, was covered, the roof supported by the single columns whose gypsum bases are evident on the way down the steps.

The Central Court

The Central Court was the focus of life at the palace. Its broad expanse, 180 feet, 6 inches (55 m) by 92 feet (28 m), insured generous light and air to most areas of the palace and strongly asserted the palace's public and participatory qualities. Such an open area at the center of a complex of connected rooms and passages suggests that the Minoans treasured and maintained an open society within a contained, sacred environment.

There is no evidence to suggest that the famous bull-leaping ritual occurred at any place other than the Central Court. Most likely the ritual was a culmination of religious festival and procession. As we learn from frescoes, the ritual involved both young men and women who, with great skill and courage, seized the horns of a lunging bull and swung themselves up, landing in a flip on its back, and then leaped to the ground. No doubt some were killed or maimed in the attempt.

It is interesting that the frescoes show young men and women with both light and dark skin. The explanation has been offered that the mixture of the original Minoan stock (dark) with the Mycenaean (light) is reflected in the artist's choice of colors.

The function of the bull-leaping ritual was most likely related to the symbolism of the Horns of Consecration and the Shrine of the Double Axes. The bull represented divine power, both a gift and a danger if it was ignored or treated with arrogance. In the ritual the youths seized the horns, symbolic of this power, and with great athletic skill used the natural power of the bull's charge and goring reflex to fly through the air and land safely. Accomplished as part of a broader religious ceremony that included ritual sacrifice of the bull with the double ax, bull leaping united the participants with divine power and renewed the strength of the society for another year.

The Throne Room

To the left of the stairs that lead down to the Central Court level are the Throne Room of the palace and its anteroom. Since the actual royal quarters and reception areas appear to be in the eastern half of the palace, this western Throne Room may well have been the ceremonial province of the priest or priestess of the labyrinth. Here, however, is where the speculations become fanciful. This Throne Room did contain a number of sacred vessels and other signs of religious

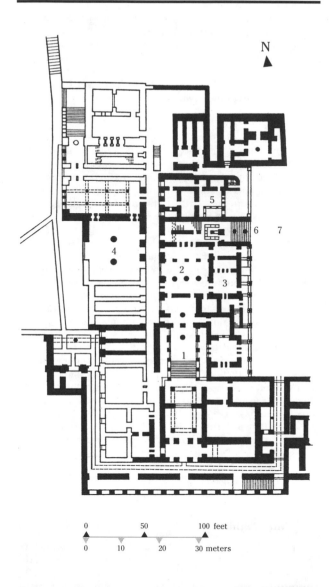

N

Fig. 13. Piano Nobile, Knossos, Crete
1. Staircase
2. Tricolumnar Hall
3. Treasury
4. Great Hall
5. Terrace Rooms
6. Staircase
7. Central Court

function when Evans uncovered it. Since the Minoans unified the functions of priest and king, priestess and queen, this room may have been used by the monarch in the role of religious leader. But, again, what was left from an abandoned palace may not represent normal use.

At present, the room is closed to the public in order to preserve the original gypsum throne—the oldest throne in Europe—from further wear. Gypsum is a very soft stone, as is evident from the water erosion affecting other exposed gypsum throughout the palace. From our side of the barrier, however, we are still able to see how the room was laid out and guess at how it functioned.

Set against a wall decorated in frescoes, the throne faces a supporting column, symbol of the goddess as upholder of order. Thus the occupant of the throne acknowledged the power that sustained the throne. The fresco is balanced—in red and white, in horizontal line and vertical waving plants, in red-and-white waves that remind us of the natural patterns of the sea close to the shore when the tidal sand is stirred. The throne is flanked by mythological griffins, the eagle-lions symbolic of insight and power. The room is ringed with benches upon which lesser authorities perhaps sat during ceremonies. The throne itself is a graceful seat, delicate yet solid, flowing and yet firm. Behind the column, down six steps, is a private lustral basin, perhaps open to the sky, where ceremonies of purification may have taken place. In the western wall of the Throne Room there is a door leading into another small room called by Evans the inner sanctuary. Here the evidence suggests that preparations for ceremonies took place. This entire section of the palace is a late addition, perhaps constructed in the Late Minoan II period. During that time the palace was ruled by the Mycenaean overlords, and

Exterior of the Throne Room, Knossos

The Throne Room, with the oldest throne in Europe, Knossos

the images of the griffins and the single column echo the famous Lion Gate at Mycenae.

The Frescoes

Above the Throne Room, up a spiral staircase to the left, Evans reconstructed a terrace and a room to house several reproductions of frescoes found in the palace. The so-called Miniature Frescoes are significant because they show ceremonial scenes in which crowds of celebrants fill the court or the Theatral Area. These illustrations give us the best information we have of the actual form of the ritual celebration. The arms flung skyward suggest an ecstatic moment in the ritual. Another fresco portrays dance as part of the rites, while a third illustrates the bull-leaping ritual.

Before crossing the Central Court to the eastern complex, the visitor might walk south toward the South Procession Corridor. This entrance to the Central Court may have been used by participants in the bull-leaping ritual. The reproduction of the priest-king fresco on this wall indicates just where the original was found at the time of excavation. The original sections are now in the museum at Iraklion. The king holds a rope in his left hand, on the other end of which may have been a bull, a griffin, or possibly even a sphinx.

The Royal Labyrinth

Across the Central Court, in the eastern part of the palace, we find the depth and complexity of construction associated in legend with the labyrinth. We have no physical evidence of official procession in these rooms and corridors, but since we do find ceremonial rooms and evidence of shrines, initia-

The priest-king fresco of Knossos. Much of what is known of Minoan royalty has been gleaned from this fresco.

tory rituals involving mock burial or the journey to the underworld may have taken place here. Part of the purpose of such rites was to expose the initiates to the forces of death in order for them to be reborn as members of the community. No better place exists to celebrate such a rebirth than in this complex of rooms and halls.

Diodorus, the first-century AD Greek historian, said:

> The rite of initiation at Eleusis, which is perhaps the most celebrated of all, and the rite of Samothrace, among the Cicones, whence came Orpheus, its inventor, are all imparted as mysteries; whereas in Crete at Knossos, from ancient days it was the custom that these rites should be imparted openly to all . . . who wished to know such matters.

Linking Minoan ritual to the Mysteries at Eleusis and the rites of Orpheus means that initiatory ritual was part of the Minoan culture, and the association of that ritual with the palace and its labyrinthian structure leads to the myths of the labyrinth. Did the rituals grow out of the structure, or did the structure manifest the rituals and beliefs of the inhabitants? The latter seems more likely in a culture where the presence and power of the gods were a part of every action and filled each moment with meaning. The palace is a construct of myth. Ritual created it. What we see here is a ritual in constructed form, and that is why we can descend into this labyrinth in a sacred manner.

The Grand Staircase

The Grand Staircase of the east wing is a monumental accomplishment. The gypsum staircase has four sets of twelve steps, connected by landings and sets of three steps, making it two full stories down from the Central Court. Here again we find the patterns of threes, fours, and twelves that greet us throughout the palace. Such a pattern may have been practical (for instance, for counting steps as one descended in the dark) and/or symbolic. One can imagine hymns or chants linked to movement up and down these steps.

In daylight the stairs were lit by an adjacent light-well supported by columns all the way to the bottom. At the first level is the upper hall, which features frescoes of the great figure-eight shields. These shields were made of a bull hide with the backbone of the bull hide down the center, appearing as a brown band, and the rest of the hide scraped clean for lightness. Recalling the similar shapes of early Cycladic goddess figures we can see that these shields were images of the Mother Goddess in her protective aspect.

At the bottom of the staircase is the Hall of Colonnades. From here we can proceed along the corridor adjacent to the stair landing to the Hall of the Double Axes, or to the King's Megaron.

The King's Megaron

Mason marks on the wall to the right indicate that this is the king's chamber. The glass panel on the north wall protects what is left of the spot where a wooden throne sat. Eroded gypsum fell to this spot from above. One of the special features of this room is its system of doors and partitions, which controlled air flow in summer and winter and also provided privacy when needed. Note the holes in the floor where doors supported on pegs swung open or closed. The doorjambs are constructed in such a way that the doors folded away to make flush pillars and open up the two halves of the Megaron.

Decorating the King's Megaron is the spiral motif seen throughout the palace but particularly evident in the eastern quarters. This spiral, which also appears on Minoan coins, symbolizes the sacred snake as well as the intricate design of initiatory ritual. At the center of the spiral is the rosette design, also featured everywhere at Knossos. The rosettes usually have twelve outer petals and twelve inner rays or petals radiating from a central point. In most cases in these rooms, the rosettes form patterns of twelve around doors, with six across the top. The designs are closely connected to the heights and widths of doors, which suggests that the decoration was planned with the architecture and not simply added later.

The Queen's Megaron

Opposite the door from the north corridor is another door, which leads by several turns into the queen's quarters. The main hall, decorated with dolphins and rosettes (see illustration, page 8), opens out to two light wells, one of which is decorated with frescoes of dancing women. The ceiling features spiral designs, giving the entire room a wonderful feeling of movement and lightness.

A system of connecting corridors and small rooms fill out the queen's quarters. The first room contains a plaster reproduction of the queen's bathtub. The next little room is the toilet, with plaster piping arranged to provide running water from a cistern above. The water system was quite elaborate, running constantly through the eastern portion of the palace to a drain outside on the eastern slope and hence to the river below.

The corridors connecting the queen's quarters to the rest of the living area are constructed so as to allow the curious wanderer to explore a multitude of routes through the complex of rooms. Indeed, if several of the corridors and stairways were not now blocked off, even more possibilities would exist. The visitor can now return to the Hall of Colonnades or leave at the lower level to explore the southeastern extension of the palace.

Beyond the queen's quarters, farther south at the same level, is the Shrine of the Double Axes. The present remains are from a very late period in the history of the palace, but the area may always have been the location of a shrine. Found here were several small sets of horns that have holes for placing the image of the double ax, plus a clay figurine of the goddess and several smaller figures. This shrine seems to have been connected to the royal quarters and may have been a private area of worship.

The North Entrance

We can now return to the Central Court and examine the North Entrance to the palace, passing out to the Lustral Basin and the Theatral Area once again. The outstanding feature of this entrance was the ramp that approached the Central Court from the large pillar hall, or custom house, as Evans called it. The hall must have served a ceremonial purpose for this entrance to the court. In the Protopalatial Period the ramp was wide and open, leading up to the Central Court. It may have been an access to the court for the bulls and all the attendants involved in the bull-leaping ritual. At a later time, the ramp was widened and contained on both sides by bastions.

The West Bastion supports the bull fresco relief, which pictures a bull charging from the north. Combined with the image of the priest-king fresco at the South Procession Corridor, we may have here a complete history of the ceremony beginning in the west corridor of the Processional Way. The bull is pictured charging in an olive grove. This representation may portray the capture of the bull outside the palace, or it may symbolize the vitality and fecundity of the bull as celebrated by the ritual.

The West Bastion, with bull fresco, showing an exterior scene outside of the Central Court

The Domestic and Craft Center Remains

Visitors who have the time to look at the hundreds of rooms that remain might wish to explore the area to the northeast of the court. Here were pottery stores, magazines with Giant Pithoi, and the east bastion with its elaborate ramps and drainage pipes, which by their clever design help to control the flow of water down the slope. In this section as well we find evidence of the artistic life of the palace, the rooms where artisans worked to fill the constant demands for pottery and ritual items.

THE HILLS BEYOND

When the site closes at the end of the day, the visitor can take a picnic and, turning down the narrow paved road to the little village of Makrytichos to the north, cross the Kairatos stream (which is very shallow), and hike up the dirt road into the olive groves above the palace. Here the remains of the Royal Villa, a beautiful Minoan structure that seems to have been a guest facility or a private dwelling for the royal family, becomes visible across the valley. The villa is not open to the public.

Above Knossos on the hillside, the grass is soft and the view magnificent. One is able to see just how well this palace is located in the landscape, protected on all sides and yet open as well. Continuing excavation has revealed the extent of the Minoan city that existed beyond the palace. Ruins have been uncovered along the river to the south and on the opposite hill to the west.

In these relaxing moments it is possible to assemble the impressions one has gathered into some sense of the whole. The total effect of Knossos is one of complex coherence, massive ease, and random order—in effect, a paradox of architectural vision and construction. The frescoes add to the effect by relieving the right angles and sense of bulk with graceful lines, colors of sea and sky, images of plant life, and figures of human and animal beauty. One senses that the occupants of this palace lived in peace. They lived consciously in the presence of the goddess and conducted their lives under her nurturing influence.

Henry Miller best expresses the mood at this moment. At Knossos, he said, "I do not pretend to know, but I felt, as I have seldom felt before, the ruins of the past, that here throughout long centuries there reigned an era of peace."

PHAESTOS

At Phaestos it is possible to touch the sky. So claimed many ancient visitors to this magnificent site in southern Crete. It is not that Phaestos sits so high on its acropolis, only two hundred feet off the Mesara Plain. Rather, the site seems to float at the end of one of the largest and most beautiful valleys in Crete, surrounded completely by distant mountains, snow-capped in winter. To the east, down the long stretch of the Mesara Plain lies Mount Dikte, sacred as the birthplace of Zeus and a center of oracular power. To the north, behind the surrounding ridge line, is the Ida Range, with the twin-peaked Mount Ida, also sacred to Zeus and famous for the great Kamares Cave, where the beautiful pottery bearing that name was first discovered. The mouth of the cave is visible from Phaestos.

The journey to Phaestos from the north rivals the visit to the site. The trip from Iraklion is not a long one, although it may be delayed by stops at several points to admire the dramatic landscape. Along the way the visitor will want to pause at Gortyna, the ancient Greek site famous for the Classical remains of the Code of Law. These original stones were under water for two thousand years. They were revealed in 1884 when the marsh was drained and are now displayed at the site, which also features Roman remains and a charming sixth-century AD Christian basilica.

The approach to Phaestos takes the visitor over a mountain ridge and down a winding road into the Mesara Plain and then up once again to the site. The first settlers back in Neolithic times must have comprehended the power and sacred harmony of this modest hill above the plain.

SACRED LANDSCAPE

Vincent Scully was the first to articulate fully the details of the relationship of sacred landscape to palace and temple siting in Greece. His analysis of the features of landscape as symbols of the Earth Goddess and the corresponding orientation and structure of Minoan palace sites is most vividly seen here at Phaestos. The fertile Mesara Plain forms a natural enclosure within which the palace hill is held. The twin peaks of Mount Ida to the north, representing the sacred horns of power, rise behind the intervening rounded hill. The cave sanctuary on the mountain is the sacred cave of the goddess in her capacity as the deity of birth, fertility, and death. The shape of the mountain is echoed by the twin-pillared north-

The palace remains of Phaestos from upper court, including the Grand Staircase

ern entrance to Phaestos's Central Court, leading to the royal apartments overlooking the mountain.

All of the Minoan palaces on Crete (Knossos, Phaestos, Mallia, Gournia, and Kato Zakros) display similar relationships to their physical contexts. Like Knossos, Phaestos is a microcosm of its setting. The reason the palace looks as it does can be read in the landscape surrounding it: the Central Court as the plain, the structures to its north and west echoing the adjacent hills. Our understanding of this site is enhanced by the widest possible attention to its context. As we pass over the remnants of a civilization, its importance emerges according to our sensitivity to its elusive genius.

HISTORY

Like Knossos, the hillside and surroundings of Phaestos yield evidence of extensive Neolithic settlement. Between 2000 and 1900 BC the Minoans began building their palace here. The same disaster that destroyed Knossos some time after 1700 BC also leveled Phaestos. Th construction of a new palace marked the beginning of the Protopalatial Period. The destruction in 1450 BC brought an end to Minoan/Mycenaean culture here, although the site continued to be inhabited.

The historical record shows that Phaestos took part in the Trojan War and that it continued to be a *polis* into Greek times. The record also shows that in 180 BC Phaestos was conquered by Gortyna and came under its domination. Such a continuous history suggests that study of the site might be complicated by the overlays of many cultures. However, what we see today, with few exceptions, are the remains of the Minoan site.

In terms of its sacred history, Phaestos was a center of oracular law and revelation for the entire Minoan culture. Indeed, as the myths of the site reflect, kings of Phaestos were often credited with attributes similar to those associated with Moses and other lawgivers to the tribes of Israel.

MYTHOLOGY

The ancient sources link Phaestos with Rhadamanthys, who was brother to Minos and second child of the union of Zeus and Europa. Other myths connect Rhadamanthys with Herakles, in connection with the great hero's journey to Crete to remove the sacred bull from Cretan shores. In another account Rhadamanthys is the son of Hephaistos, who as the god of fire and craft—and by extension of volcanoes and earthquakes—was confined in a cave for nine years to fashion works of art for the gods. The number nine suggests the Sacred Tetractys (see p.72) and communication with the gods through revelation. Thus, part of the myth of Rhadamanthys is that, similar to his father, he retired to the cave of Mount Dikte for nine days every nine years and returned with a body of sacred law. In this way Phaestos is associated with revelation in the myths surrounding the Minoans.

THE SITE

In 1900, at the same time that Evans began his dig at Knossos, the Italians began an extensive dig at Phaestos, following earlier work by the Americans. Work continued on and off for thirty years and included some restoration work as well. In 1949 the Italians resumed excavations, which have been continuous to the present.

When Henry Miller arrived at what was the visitor's pavilion at Phaestos just before World War II, he found there waiting for him Kyrios Alexandros, guide, caretaker, and lover of Phaestos and all it stands for. Alexandros wiped the dust off Miller's shoes and offered him a meal, including a bottle of sweet dessert wine from Samos called *mavrodaphne*. Miller was overwhelmed by the surroundings and commented:

> At the very gates of Paradise the descendants of Zeus halted here on their way to eternity to cast a last look earthward and saw with the eyes of innocents that the earth is indeed what they had always dreamed it to be: a place of beauty and joy and peace. In his heart man is

angelic; in his heart man is united with the whole world.

And so it is. The first task of the contemporary visitor is to grasp the orientation of the site with the surrounding landscape. To the north, Mount Ida presents her twin-peaked summit as the dominant feature of the Ida range and marks the center of the island of Crete. Down the valley to the east Mount Dikte, the dominant mountain of Eastern Crete, rises in the distance. The mountain range to the south is the Asterousian, the coastal range, with the Libyan Sea beyond.

The Upper and West Courts

At the first level, or Upper Court, the ancient road, no longer evident, came down from the north and into the West Court. Most of the stone foundations remaining in this upper area date from Hellenistic and early Christian times, but there are vague traces near the long staircase of a Minoan Protopalatial processional way. The stairs bring us to the West Court, where early remains form most of what we see.

The Theatral Area reminds us of the ancient road at Knossos where the narrow paving divides and the steps provide a place for ceremonial viewing or religious ritual. The nine steps of the Theatral Area may have sacred numerical significance. We have already heard that nine years and nine days appear in the mythology of Phaestos and in the patterns of revelation involving Rhadamanthys. Nine in Pythagorean symbolism—which the Minoans might well have absorbed much earlier from Egyptian sources—denotes the human struggle to unite with the divine, to return to the source.

The ancient road leading to the Palace and Theatral Area, Phaestos

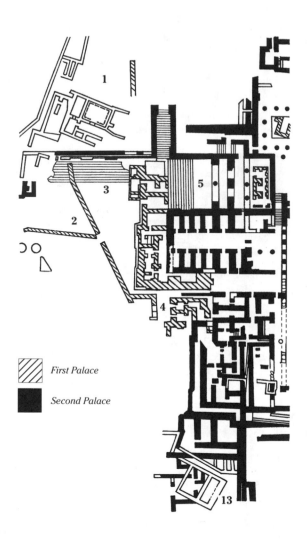

Fig. 14. Phaestos
1. Upper Court
2. West Court
3. Theatral Area
4. Early Propylon
5. Grand Staircase and Propylon
6. Central Court

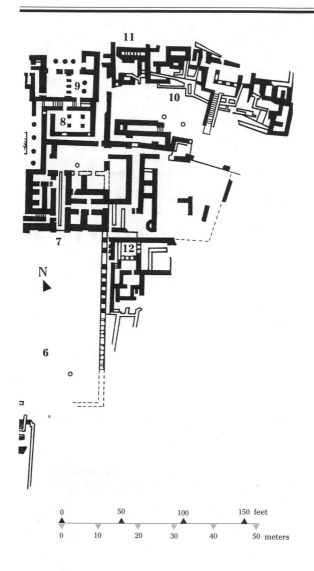

7. North Corridor
8. Queen's Apartments
9. King's Apartments
10. Northeast Complex
11. Archives (Phaestos Disk)
12. Sacred Area
13. Archaic Temple of Rhea

Early Propylon

Although the natural progression from the Theatral Area would be to approach the Grand Staircase, we can also follow the ancient road as it moves southeast from the Theatral Area toward the Protopalatial entrance to the palace and the Central Court. As the plan shows, this entrance turns left (east) and enters the palace approximately at the middle of the court. A long corridor leads straight ahead at this point. Nothing remains now of this entrance, but we can speculate from the design at Knossos that a proper entrance and walls lined with frescoes led the procession on its way to the court.

Grand Staircase and Propylon

Returning to the northern entrance via the Grand Staircase, we now enter the Neopalatial portion of the palace, which replaced the earlier structures after the disaster of 1700 BC. These grand steps, 40 feet wide (12 m), are twelve in number, again reminding us of the sets of twelve steps throughout the palace at Knossos. As the procession made its way up these steps, the participants approached, directly ahead, a single column whose base suggests an oval shape, the symbol of the goddess and an echo of the rounded hill due west of the site. The extended Propylon continues into three more chambers before turning right (south) to descend another flight of steps to the Central Court, which is oriented on a north-south axis aligned with Mount Ida.

The magnificent Grand Staircase of Phaestos

Royal Apartments

The northern gate to the royal apartments presents a massive entryway leading to the North Corridor. The entrance reminds us of the North Entrance ramp at Knossos leading to the Central Court, but in this case the corridor leads to the

Queen's and King's Apartments. No chambers in the palace appear to have provided a separate throne room complex. This absence has led archaeologists to conclude that Knossos may have been the seat of a centralized government where the kings of the other palaces gathered under the Knossos ruler.

The area now covered to protect recent excavations reveals details of the royal wing of the palace. This series of rooms, corridors, and courts provided a spacious and dignified living area, one well suited to ceremonial functions. The North Corridor from the Central Court leads into a wide court framed by a foundation wall that once belonged to the Protopalatial palace. Another corridor to the right leads north to the royal apartments off to its left. First we encounter a double-columned room with a terrace, which may well have been the queen's quarters. Farther along, a complex of rooms leads to the main entrance to the royal or King's Apartments. Still apparent are the early floor paving and walls, which contain window frames and door supports. To the north we see the remains of a porch or portico, which leads to the left to a lustral basin.

This entire complex of rooms was used for ritual and purification, in keeping with the dual-role life of a priest-king. The chambers are connected and fluid in their arrangement. They face north toward the sacred mountain, which signifies power and protection. The rest of the palace spreads out to the south and includes its ceremonial entrances, its magazines for storage of the riches of the culture, and the Central Court, where much of the life of the community took place.

Northern gate to Royal Apartments, Phaestos. Mount Ida lies due north from this entrance.

The Northeast Complex

To the east of the royal apartments are Protopalatial buildings that must have served both a religious and an artistic
function. As we have seen, in Minoan times the religious life
and artistic life of a palace were integrated into a single purpose. The goddess was served by both priest and potter. The
Northeast Complex shows this unity of function. It was in the
first series of small rooms that the mysterious Phaestos Disk
was discovered. This clay disk, eight inches (20 cm) in diameter and half an inch thick, has successfully defied decoding

Phaestos Disk, eight inches in diameter, found in Northeast Complex

for years. We still do not know what it says, let alone what it
means. It may be a great sacred key or a toy or a guide to
economic development. A sacred key to something is more
likely, but so far, efforts to explain its spiral form and forty-five
different symbols have been inconclusive. The disk may be
examined at the Archaeological Museum in Iraklion. The world
awaits its translation.

Eastern and Southern Sections

To the east, off the Central Court, we find a sequence of interesting rooms that were probably dedicated to religious ritual.
From the northeast corner of the court, we can explore the
rooms that connect and lead to a lustral basin at the southern end of the complex. These rooms seem to have
accommodated a ritual of purification that took place in various stages. The only information we have of these rituals lies
here in the layout and artifacts of these ruined shrines.

At the southern end of the Central Court we see that the
hillside has fallen away, perhaps in the disaster of 1450 BC,
but more likely at a later date in a more local tremor. Over
the fence to the south are the remains of the houses that sur-

rounded the palace hill and formed the outlying community. At the very southern tip of the site, beyond the remains of the southwest apartments, lie the foundations of an Archaic Temple to Rhea, daughter of Uranus and Gaea and usually called the mother of the gods. Her worship here in Archaic times signals recognition by the Greek settlers of the importance of this site to the Earth Mother. It was here on Crete, in a cave on either Mount Dikte or Mount Ida, as various legends have it, that Rhea gave birth to Zeus.

HAGIA TRIADA

Only a few minutes by road to the west of Phaestos, toward the Libyan Sea, lie the remains of a small Minoan palace called Hagia Triada, named for the fourteenth-century Church of the Holy Trinity that overlooks the site. Very little is known about this palace. Various scholars have speculated that it might have been a summer villa for the kings of Phaestos. Its proximity to Phaestos argues that it is unlikely to have been separate, either politically or economically, but it may have had a unique ritual function. In any case, the little palace is an archaeological gem and possesses some fine examples of Minoan architectural design and construction.

What we do know about this small palace has emerged from steady excavation by the Italians throughout the twentieth century. Notable finds at the site have included the 1911 unearthing of a large number of inscribed Linear A tablets, the 1938 discovery of a seascape painted on a floor and dated to the Late Minoan Period, and the 1962 discovery of Minoan figurines and votive remains nearby. The site was built in the Middle Minoan III Period, was important in Late Minoan times, and later became a cult site and was occupied through Hellenistic and Roman times.

The assumption that it was important as a cult site is not surprising given its location and relationship to the sacred landscape. Mount Ida appears clearly in the distance to the north, directly in line with the major staircase that must have served as part of the processional way. In the middle distance appears a perfectly conical hill, which is echoed in the stonework and column construction of the main palace.

Worked carefully into the hillside to orient it to both Mount Ida and the sea, the palace first took shape in its western section, culminating in the main hall at its western extreme. In later times, under Mycenaean influence, the northern addition filled out the present design. The Mycenaeans also built a *megaron* over existing Minoan structures in the western section. An interesting feature of the northern addition is the presence of an *agora,* or marketplace, characteristic of the Mycenaean period. The *agora* suggests that this site was used year round in later times and served as village as well as palace.

There are two views on the function of this site. The first is based on the absence of two of the major ceremonial features of the Minoan palace sites—the central court and the theatral area—suggesting that this "villa" was devoted to pleasure and relief from the summer heat at the central palace at Phaestos. The other view is that this small palace was ceremonial in some unique way that did not include the functions of a central court and theatral area. Enough ritual items have been uncovered here to suggest use of the site as a cult center of some sort.

At the museum at Iraklion the visitor can see a major find from Hagia Triada that has added significantly to our understanding of Minoan customs. This is a painted stone sarcophagus, showing on one side a procession (or processions) related perhaps to burial or perhaps to the worship of Dionysos. Pictured in the procession are seven figures. Three figures with libations and musical instruments approach a shrine decorated with columns, double axes, and sacred doves. Four figures are pictured in a sacrificial ritual within the palace. More will be said about this interesting piece in the section devoted to the Iraklion Museum.

THE LESSER SITES OF MALLIA, GOURNIA, AND ZAKROS

For those with the time and interest to explore the other Minoan sites in Crete, a trip to the eastern half of the island will provide the opportunity to visit Mallia, Gournia, and the latest gem in the Minoan crown, Zakros. These sites contain the familiar landscape elements so important to palace siting and reveal unique features that add to our appreciation of the richness of Minoan culture.

MALLIA

The palace at Mallia is a short drive east from Iraklion, too long perhaps for a taxi drive but accessible by bus. The site was first excavated in 1915 by the French, who continued until the 1930s and picked up the work again after World War II. In addition to the palace site, archaeologists have uncovered two large houses, an underground crypt west of the palace, and an extensive burial enclosure north of the palace.

The palace itself is oriented on a north-south axis, with the sea to the north and the sacred Mount Dikte to the south. On Mount Dikte is the sacred cave dedicated to the goddess and connected in later myth to the birth of Zeus. Although Mallia does not possess all the landscape elements other Minoan sites have because of its proximity to the sea, the palace itself was constructed so as to contain within it the necessary ritual elements.

From the Sacred Way in the West Court visitors enter the Central Court from either the north or the south. The south entrance is the more direct and ends at a Theatral Area in the southwest corner of the court. The North Entrance features an ancient flagstone walkway, a main entrance hall, and a north courtyard. A long corridor leads to the Central Court, at the north end of which is a ceremonial Pillared Hall. This interesting hall is entered through a narrow door "guarded" by a single pillar. A right turn reveals the six-pillared hall.

Two items in the Central Court are of particular interest. First, a Sacrificial Pit was uncovered at the southern end of the court, near the Theatral Area. This pit is the only such ritual element discovered at a Minoan palace. It may have been located at this place because the Theatral Area was constructed within the enclosure rather than outside, which again may relate to the unique placement of the palace in the landscape. Here the Central Court and Theatral Area were combined in their sacred functions.

The other item of interest is the Kernos, or offering table, near the ceremonial stairs. This round stone is placed in the direction of Mount Dikte on an axis to the stairs. The stone is unique in its design and mysterious in its function. A central cup, ringed with a shallow depression, is surrounded by thirty-three smaller cups or depressions plus one larger cup extending from the circle. This stone could have held offerings of grain and produce from the area or blood from animal sacrifices. The central hole may also have held a post or column with the double-ax symbol, as pictured on the Hagia Triada sarcophagus.

Also of special interest at the site are the two giant pithoi, or storage jars, which tower above the visitor. The detailed rope designs in the terra-cotta are obviously decorative, but

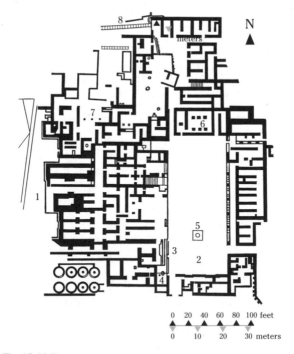

Fig. 15. *Mallia*

1. Sacred Way—West Court
2. Central Court
3. Theatral Area
4. Kernos

5. Sacrificial Pit
6. Pillared Hall
7. Royal Apartments
8. North Entrance

may also have been functional. They show the pattern by which these huge containers were roped so that they could be moved or tipped.

GOURNIA

Further along the eastern coastline from Mallia, at the Gulf of Merabello, is the Minoan site called Gournia. Although this site is clearly Minoan, it is less clearly a palace. It is valuable to archaeologists as an example of an early (1600 BC) town. The site covers a ridge and shows evidence of royal quarters—a small palace perhaps—on the top of the ridge, with the rest of the town spreading out below. To the south of the "palace," linked to it by what may have been a ceremonial staircase, is the *agora* and a courtyard.

Gournia is valued for the picture it suggests of a secure, integrated culture. The central shrine located on the northern slope, the palace on the ridge, and the *agora* below all fit into the landscape to form an enclosed whole, where the population was held in the embrace of the goddess. One has the impression of a secure world where foreign powers were kept at bay. Finds at the site have included large numbers of both ritual artifacts (figurines of the goddess, tripods, and double axes) and craft elements (carpenter's tools, weaving tools, mortars and pestles, knives, saws, and tools for producing olive oil). At Gournia one feels the close relation of work and worship—the two were woven into one activity.

ZAKROS

Farthest to the east is the newly uncovered site of Zakros. The name of the site comes from the nearby town of Zakros, which is at the end of the main road from Sitia and Palaikastro to the north. High mountains separate this palace from the rest of Crete, and in ancient times this city must have been isolated and accessible only by sea. Zakros was certainly an important trading port throughout its history.

When the city was destroyed in the great conflagration of 1450 BC, the site was abandoned abruptly and completely, never to be reoccupied. Therefore, the thorough excavation of the site that began in 1961 has revealed valuable treasures of the Minoan culture. Discovered were Linear A tablets, frescoes, and sacred vessels, plus household materials and tools left behind as the inhabitants fled.

There was also evidence of volcanic ash, suggesting that the general destruction of the Cretan palaces may have been related to the great Thera eruption. But intriguing questions remain. Why weren't the sites ever reoccupied? Could the destruction have been so very complete? Was a tidal wave involved? Could it have struck Phaestos to the south and Zakros, too, hidden behind mountains to the east?

IRAKLION:
THE MUSEUM

The purpose of this section is not to provide a comprehensive guide to the Archaeological Museum in Iraklion. Guides are available for that purpose. Included here are highlights from the twenty galleries, along with a few interpretive observations. Comments will not cover those items in the collection that date from the period after 1100 BC, generally accepted as the end of the palace cultures.

GALLERY I

The first gallery in the museum contains representative items from Neolithic sites in Crete dating from 5000 BC to 2000 BC, the beginning of the palace cultures. In Cases #1 and #2 are examples of the figurines we suppose to be Earth Mother Goddesses from this period. The earlier the figures, the less distinct the female features, leading to the caution that they may not be sacred figures at all, but the later examples leave little doubt as to their religious symbolism.

An interesting figure in Case #12 (#4676) is the clay sculpture of a bull with male and female figures clasping the horns. The image expresses the complexity of the sacred role of the bull in the myths and rituals associated with it. Case #13 contains Mother Goddess figures and human figures in gestures of worship. The folded arms indicate the formal position seen in many Minoan illustrations of ritual activity. The stone seated figure from Tekes is particularly striking. He sits with back straight, head held high, arms folded across his chest. The position is relaxed but formal and suggests a king on his throne, full of authority and yet not threatening.

GALLERY II

In Case #19 we see the Goddess Vase from Mallia, most likely used in votive ceremonies. The liquid poured from her breasts. In Case #23 we see some fine examples of Kamares-style pottery. These delicate pieces were so named because they were first discovered in the Kamares Cave on Mount Ida. We know from their location that they served a sacred purpose.

In Case #25 are the so-called Town Mosaics, which were no doubt inlays for wooden boxes or decorative panels. The glazed earthenware figures show various architectural features of Minoan houses or sections of palaces. We are able to

The bull-leaping fresco, restored from scant fragments, Knossos

see two- and three-story construction, flat roofs, door and window beams, and floor construction consisting of rows of small logs bound together and plastered over. Also in Case #25 is a pictograph of a standing man, spear in his right hand and his left hand touching his heart. This must be a position of either worship or salute to a leader.

In Case #24 is the model of the Tricolumnar Shrine, a typical Minoan configuration of three columns supporting a roof element and three doves. The presence of birds in such models or frescoes suggests an epiphany of the goddess.

GALLERY III

This gallery features finds from Phaestos in the Middle Minoan Period, from 2000 BC to 1700 BC. The effect of seeing these pieces arranged together is an appreciation of the very special quality of work from this palace. The people of Phaestos seem to have enjoyed a unique relationship to nature and to their gods—one of openness, playfulness, and imagination.

The major treasure in this gallery is the mysterious Phaestos Disk (Case #41). This round clay disk, about 8 inches in diameter, was found in the palace ruins of Phaestos and has baffled scholars ever since. The majority opinion now is that the disk had a sacred intent, perhaps holding a hymn or a guide to ceremony. What we do know is that it was made by pressing damp clay with seals marked with some symbolic or linguistic meaning. There are 45 different seals used a total of 241 times on both sides. Each side is generally in a spiral form, though the figuration is not quite a spiral in that the outer ring of twelve sections is broken by the spiral as it turns to reach the outer edge.

The presence of twelve segments in the outer ring suggests a calendar, perhaps related to festivals. On both sides there are 49 figures in the outer ring. Other interesting features include the eight-leaf rosette design, which was sacred to the Minoans as well as the later Greeks, and the circle with seven dots arranged in a circle of six with one in the center. Because the shape is round, the disk may represent the heavens and the symbols various heavenly bodies, including the zodiac. Oriented to the sky, the observer might be able to determine important ritual dates by the position of the stars. We use similar star charts today.

This gallery also contains fine examples of Kamares pottery, beautifully inscribed with geometric designs fluidly intertwined with images of nature. The unique vase in Case #43 with its attached rosettes suggests the fecundity of nature and the exuberance of growth as these flowers seem to grow out of the vase as if out of crevices in rocks. In Case #33A a unique column design features a sea scene sculpted around a post. Dolphins sport among the seashells and seaweed in a balanced image of great beauty.

GALLERY IV

The Bull's Head Rhyton in Case #51 is one of the treasures of the museum. Made of black steatite (soapstone), with eyes of rock crystal and jasper, this libation vessel was used in sacred rituals at Knossos. The vase was filled through a hole in the neck and emptied through the nostrils. The horns were probably gilded wood, although the present horns are a restoration made to give the appearance of gold.

Bull's Head Rhyton, a libation vessel found at Knossos, Case #51, Iraklion

Also important in this gallery, in Case #50, are the two glazed earthenware goddesses. The snake goddess in particular gives us a vivid sense of the chthonic aspect of the Earth Mother Goddess in Minoan religion. The snake cult combined images of the renewal of life, of curative powers, and of prophecy. The statues also tell us a great deal about the dress of Minoan women—the constricted waist, breasts left bare, and the heavily embroidered flounced skirt.

Among the interesting sacred vessels in this gallery are the alabaster lioness head in Case #59 and the collection in Case #58. In particular, note the shell vessel on the top shelf as an example of the superb craftsmanship of the period. Case #56 contains the ivory bull-leaper. The famous fresco upstairs will show the daring routine of these leapers as they transformed the charging power of the bull into feats of daring and agility.

GALLERY V

Featured in this room are items from the so-called Palace Style of the Late Minoan Period, just after 1450 BC. A variety of items from are Knossos. In Case #62 are examples of Egyptian and Near Eastern art, demonstrating the wide-ranging trade of the Minoans and their Mycenaean overlords. In Case #66 is a stone vase found by Evans in the throne room at Knossos. In Case #70 is a miniature showing the capture of a bull with a net, a method that prevented injury to the bull and the premature spilling of its sacred blood.

The model of a house in Case #70A shows us a good deal about Minoan architecture, including the use of wooden columns, the cross beams, and the use of small logs tied together to form the roof. In Case #69 are displayed some of the many examples of Linear B script found at Knossos. The numerical system of lines and circles permitted the tabulation of items into the tens of thousands. The phonetic signs were both ideograms (signifying specific objects like figs, men, wheat, and wheels) and numerals.

One interesting example of the symbolism of phonetic signs is the figure for *ka*, the circle with a cross. The crossed circle is one of the earliest forms inscribed by human beings to express the cosmos. Linear B may well have an extensive internal symbolism similar to its Egyptian counterpart.

GALLERY VI

These Late Minoan artifacts from Knossos, Phaestos, and Archanes feature attractive ritual dancing motifs, such as the

Large amphora showing the famous double ax. Noteworthy is the fusion of the ax into the natural imagery of plants

clay figures in Case #71. Four men in a round room *(tholos)* perform a sacred dance, as evidenced by the inclusion of horns of consecration. Dance was an important feature of Minoan religion, part of the rites of fertility associated with seasonal festivals.

In Case #87 are several rings, including the famous Isopata Ring, which has intrigued scholars for decades. Engraved on the gold are four female figures engaged in an ecstatic dance. They are without heads and from their necks appear to come beads or drops. One might assume that this portrays some brutality, but more likely it suggests a state of frenzied ecstasy in which all interfering thought (the upper brain) is gone and a state of freedom and unity has been reached. The ring also contains symbols that appear to float in the space around the women, one of whom also appears to float above the ground. The symbols include two organic images suggestive of growth and fertility, and an eye, which may indicate spiritual vision achieved in the dance.

GALLERY VII

This room contains several fine examples of steatite carving, three of which are particularly striking. In Case #94 the Harvester's Vase illustrates a sacred procession from the grain fields. A priest leads the file of celebrants as they joyfully return laden with the harvest. The successful harvest is, of course, the culmination of the ritual year. A rich harvest provides security for the winter months and affirmation of the nurturing protection of the goddess.

The vase in Case #95 shows two male figures, one clearly a king or leader and the other making a presentation. Called the Cup of the Report, this vase gives us a more accurate picture of palace life than do the more formal frescoes. The images are impressive and quite handsome. Case #96 contains a vase with scenes from the games, including the bull-leaping ritual. The bull is shown charging at the leapers, a reminder of the danger and difficulty of this ritual act.

Two other displays in this room deserve attention. Case #100 contains two potter's wheels. Note the double-ax carvings on one of the wheels. In Case #101 are examples of gold jewelry. The gold bee pendant is particularly significant. It has a delicacy and a balance that remind us that, for the early Greeks and perhaps the Minoans as well, the bee was an image of spirit, a buzzing presence producing nectar, which the Minoans considered a sacred medium.

GALLERY VIII

The finds in this gallery are mainly from Zakros, the most recently excavated site in Crete. The stone vessels stand out as superbly crafted pieces. The rock crystal vase with gilt ring and a delicate handle of beads in Case #109 was carefully assembled by the museum staff from hundreds of fragments. In Case #118 a stone *amphora* illustrates the high quality of attention and workmanship of the Zakros artists.

GALLERY IX

The collection in this room dates from the Late Minoan Period in Eastern Crete. In Case #123 several items of sacred importance stand out. The two figurines, one male, the other female, show postures we have come to associate with religious ritual. The female stands erect, right hand resting on her left shoulder, left hand resting on her right hip. Similar poses are typical of women in attitudes of worship.

In Case #122 is an ox-shaped rhyton, very naturalistic in rendering. Careful examination reveals a faded decoration that looks like a net. As mentioned earlier, the bull was captured with a net so as not to spill its sacred blood until the sacrificial moment. The net was considered sacred as well, being a critical part of the ceremony. The net on the sculptured bull would mark the rhyton as worthy of devotional care.

GALLERY X

The Late Minoan III collection in this gallery features several interesting goddess figurines with hands held aloft, eyes closed. In Case #133 is figure #9305, the Poppy Goddess. She is crowned with opium poppies in her function as provider of sleep, dreams, revelation, and death. Her posture evokes images of her sublime state, her stillness and serenity. A contrasting state is depicted in Case #132 where we see the ecstatic dancers with a lyre player.

One of the most popular figures is the female swinger in Case #143. Discovered at Hagia Triada, this lovely piece is also sacred, as we know from the rituals of swinging that formed a part of festivals welcoming the arrival of spring. The posts supporting the swing relate to the tree cult and are crowned by the representation of the goddess in her form as a bird.

GALLERY XII

Before going upstairs, pause to admire the wooden model of the palace at Knossos, constructed by Z. Kanakis in 1967. The care lavished on this model reflects a personal interpretation of the latest information on the appearance of the palace. Since the palace remains do not permit us to know exactly what the structure looked like at any given moment in its history, what we have here is a composite picture.

GALLERY XIV

The second floor of the museum holds the display of frescoes and larger pieces that deserve greater viewing space. Close attention to the mounting of the fragments recovered from the palace sites reveals the sometimes daring interpretations by scholars and artists as they extrapolate original works from the fragments.

In Gallery XIV one of the major pieces is the bull-leaping fresco from Knossos. Roughly one-third of the original was recovered and then pieced together. The reconstruction was aided by the presence of fragments at crucial points in the action of the scene. What we see is a representation of the sequence of a leap. The leapers, both male and female, are in the key positions of the acrobatic leap. The first grasps the horns of the lunging bull and is tossed back over the bull's head; the second leaper is pictured springing from the bull's back, having flipped over the head; the third lands with arms raised, completing the leap with perfect control.

Some have speculated that the bull-leaping ritual was initiatory, meaning that every youth attempted the feat at some point as part of the rite of passage to adulthood. This conclusion ignores the extraordinary difficulty of this feat and its probable function as part of a seasonal ritual relating to the renewal of Nature's power each year. The feat was probably undertaken by a few select athletes, both male and female, as a vivid and nearly magical expression of human mastery of powerful life forces as embodied in the sacred bull.

The other major piece in this gallery is the Hagia Triada sarcophagus. The scenes painted on the stone of this piece have intrigued scholars for half a century. On its four painted sides are scenes of procession and sacrifice. What we can say about this extraordinary piece is that all of the decoration taken together gives us more information about Minoan religious practices than any other single source.

The scenes are framed by the typical sacred border decorations of spiral and rosette. The flux and cycle of natural life are represented by the spiral motif, which is held at the center by the rosette, expressing the unity and symmetry of universal law. On the sarcophagus these decorations are framed by straight lines in red, white, blue, and gold. Here are the columns, the upholders of the culture, and the beams, protecting and supporting human life.

Some scholars conclude that the scenes depicted on the sarcophagus relate exclusively to the burial ceremony, befitting the piece's function. However, they may well represent worship of the gods related to death and resurrection. On the long side devoted to processional themes we see a figure without arms or legs "standing" with a symbolic tree and receiving sacrifices. In this case the god must be Dionysos, the dismembered god of death and resurrection, receiving his tribute in a moon-shaped boat and in the form of two young, vibrant bullocks.

On the other long side a bull is trussed and sacrificed, but very much alive, on a sacrificial table. Surrounding it are priestesses in various poses of worship and sacrifice, reaching out to touch and to receive the power from this bloodletting ceremony. The blood of life and divine power will be symbolically and literally joined to the sacred tree-column as an affirmation and a prayer for renewal of the growing cycle and the journey of the soul after death.

GALLERY XV

Our knowledge of various Minoan ceremonies is enhanced by the presence of several miniature frescoes discovered at Knossos. In the first, #25, we see a ritual dance performed in a sacred grove, perhaps in the West Court of the palace. We can see Egyptian influence in the forms and gestures. These scenes depict the public nature of religious ceremony and the ecstatic nature of the experience.

Note the decorative relief from a Knossos ceiling. The spirals and rosettes form an orderly sky as yellow rosette stars float in blue wavy clouds and swirls of air. Such symmetry and color remind us of the notion of the palace as the context where human beings play out their earthly drama, where architecture transforms sky, earth, and underworld into a vision of human understanding and belief.

THE MAINLAND AND
THE MYCENAEANS

The identity of the people who by 1550 BC would establish the culture we call Mycenaean is uncertain. The migrations that began in 2000 BC introduced a new culture with a new language (a form of archaic Greek) to the mainland. Homer referred to them as Achaeans, Danaans, and Argives. The accepted theory now is that these people were Indo-European and entered Greece from the Balkans or from southern Russia.

Engraving of a cross-section of a Mycenaean tholos tomb, Mycenae

We can follow their tracks down from the north around the Black Sea. They rode horses, made gray pottery (called Minyan), wore armor, and conquered their enemies with bronze weapons. Their men were bearded and were fearsome warriors. Excavations at Troy at level VI show that these people occupied Troy beginning in 1900 BC. The extent to which these peoples had contact with the already stable Minoan culture in Crete and beyond is documented by changes in pottery design. There are artistic and architectural connections that indicate strong Minoan influence, resulting in a gradual fusion of "Minyan" and Minoan culture on the mainland.

The major ruins associated with the Mycenaean culture are centered in the Argive Plain at Mycenae, Argos, and Tiryns. More recently, the remains of the famous Mycenaean palace of Nestor at Pylos in the western Peloponnese have been extensively excavated.

MYCENAE

Soil of my fathers, Argive earth I tread upon,
In daylight of the tenth year I have come back to
*   you.*
All my hopes broke but one, and this I have at last.
I never could have dared to dream that I might die
In Argos, and be buried in this beloved soil.
Hail to the Argive land and to its sunlight, hail
To its high sovereign, Zeus, and to the Pythian King.

—Aeschylus, *Agamemnon*

From the acropolis of Mycenae, north on the Argive Plain,
the fertile valley opens out to the west and the mountains,
and to the south and the sea. On a recent mid-January afternoon, on the day in myth and history when Agamemnon
landed in Nauplia and returned from Troy to his palace, a
cold wind blew across the hill, and through the black clouds
to the west the sun streamed in piercing rays. As the clouds
scudded to the south, the sun swept across the god-shaped
mountains like a searchlight. The goddess lay revealed.

Mycenae broods. Henry Miller said, "I feel the approach
of the cold breath from the shaggy gray mountain towering
over us." Behind the citadel the chasm of Chavos drops away

The Argive Plain from the citadel of Mycenae

to dizzying depths. This is no Knossos, redolent with the buzzing, fragrant life of its surroundings. Instead, Mycenae is cyclopean walls and overhanging mountains and deep gorges and the remains of conspicuous wealth, all speaking of a glorious and violent past.

HISTORY

The story of Mycenaean culture has been pieced together from excavation, epic poetry, written history, pottery, and from the deciphering of Linear B script. The accounts of the economy on tablets found at Mycenaean sites give us a glimpse of the culture. In many ways, it is as if the history of our own culture were to be assembled in AD 5000 from a scattering of sales records, inventory lists, and news magazines that survived a fire and were buried for three thousand years. The difference, of course, is that in the case of Mycenae we are working with a small palace that had a limited population and far fewer cultural elements to catalog and analyze.

By the time writers such as Homer and Plutarch sought to describe the Late Bronze Age, a Dark Age had intervened. Most of the traditions and values of the earlier time had dissolved into dim memory and were now filtered through an entirely new social and political system. Thus our study of Mycenae begins from a perspective described as the Heroic tradition. We carry with us from our school days Homeric images of heroes and kings courting the gods and gaining fame for themselves in monumental battles fought over questions of personal honor. Shifting attention slightly to the daily lives of these superhuman figures reveals a unique and historically significant time in the sacred and secular history of the Mediterranean world.

THE DIVINE STATE OF KINGS

The Linear B script tells us that the king, the sole holder of power in the culture, was called *wa-na-ka* or *wanax*. He was the chief priest, commander in chief, regulator of events, and supreme judge. The *wanax* was surrounded by a hierarchy of officials and minor lords whose duties overlapped and who also lived in the palace. As a result the culture was highly centralized. Wealth in the form of gold, silver, bronze, grain, and herds was carefully controlled and allocated according to the wishes of the king.

The power of the *wanax* was supported by a warrior class whose task was to control access to the territory ruled by the palace, and by a class of scribes whose task was to record taxes and master the details of the complex economy. In addition, there was a priestly class who carried out the rituals of worship and gave prophecies when asked—and presumably, sometimes when they weren't.

By 1500 BC, when the Mycenaean culture dominated Greece, there were at least 320 citadels under the general leadership of the *wanax* of Mycenae. Domination of the rest of the mainland and the Aegean was complete. The great northern sky gods now ruled, with Zeus supreme among them. For over three hundred years all was Mycenaean.

DECLINE AND DESTRUCTION

By 1100 BC, when the era was over, only forty citadels remained. By that time Mycenae itself was reduced to a minor town as Greece slipped into the Dark Age from which it was to emerge three hundred years later. No record remains of the social changes and political revolutions of this period. By the beginning of the Classical Period, the story of Mycenae surfaced once again in a minor way as a result of the Persian invasions. A small band of Mycenaeans (probably soldiers from the district) stood with Leonidas of Sparta at Thermopylae in 480 BC and again at Plataea in 479 BC. By the time of the Roman Era in AD 200, when the Greek traveler and geographer Pausanias passed through, Mycenae was an abandoned ruin. Only the Lion Gate, some outer walls, the chamber of Atreus, and the suggestion of a grave circle were in evidence.

Although it is not possible to know what caused the decline and eventual disappearance of the Mycenaean culture, we can speculate about it from the later so-called Geometric Period, when conditions in Greece were heading toward the establishment of the city-state. Increased population, increased trade and contact with the east and south, far-flung military campaigns such as the conquest of Troy—all these must have contributed to lessening the centralized power of the *wanax*. It must have been impossible after 1100 BC for the king to command absolute obedience and to maintain the same degree of religious authority. Those citadels such as Argos and Athens that were able to overcome their physical limitations and shift their vision of political and religious rule survived the changes and evolved successfully into a new age.

The culture that had so completely controlled the mainland of Greece and had ventured to the islands, including Crete, could not withstand the pressures of the migrations that swept into its lands like an avalanche. Not only Dorians but many others, most of them speaking dialects of Greek, invaded or simply migrated to the south, no doubt responding to pressures from the north as huge population shifts took place. The Mycenaeans who survived fled mostly to the east and to Asia Minor, where they became immigrants or else seized temporary control of palace cultures similar to their own. Eventually, what was distinctly Mycenaean blended into the changing cultural patterns, and for thousands of years all that remained of ancient Mycenae was the haunting monument of the great Lion Gate protruding like a tombstone from what became only a minor village in Archaic, Classical, and Hellenistic times. But the storied past would not be forgotten.

MYTHOLOGY

The myths of Mycenae are the stories of Perseus, who was the legendary founder of Mycenae, and of Tantalus and Pelops, who were the ancestors of Agamemnon, Orestes, and Electra. Other legendary figures are connected by marriage and alliance: Clytemnestra, Menelaus, Helen, Odysseus, and the other heroes of Troy.

These myths took form early in hymns and dance and later in the epic poems of Homer and the great tragic poets. They acquired religious sanction in the decorations of pottery and the friezes of Archaic and Classical temples. They became the education of all Greece and the foundation of moral philosophy and law. Only the myths of Oedipus rival the stories connected to Mycenae. Even today, shepherds speak of encountering the spirit of Agamemnon on the slopes of Mount Euboea, where he is said to wander seeking rest from foul murder at the hand of his wife and her lover.

PERSEUS AND THE MEDUSA

The sacred founding of Mycenae is attributed to the hero Perseus, son of Zeus and Danae. Like many heroes, Perseus began life under the cloud of a prophecy linking him to the death of a progenitor, in this case his grandfather Acrisius. These myths all portray the ancient cycle of fathers who hold power and sons who seize power in the natural course of events. Informed of the prophecy, Acrisius confined his daughter Danae and her baby son Perseus in a wooden ark and put it to sea, hoping they would die. Like the child Moses and the Egyptians Isis and Horus, Danae and Perseus were saved, and Perseus set out on his heroic journey of separation, initiation, and return.

As a young hero, Perseus had to accept his spiritual heritage as a son of Zeus and overcome the temptations of destructive earthly desires—in his case represented by the terrible Medusa, whose face turned all who looked upon it to stone. Stone was a symbol of spiritual death or the permanent sleep of the soul. Guided by Hermes and inspired by the wisdom of Athena, Perseus overcame the Medusa by seeing only her reflection in his sacred shield. Seeing earthly desire only as a reflection of a greater reality permits the hero to awaken the soul to its proper destiny. Such is the nature of the sight of the soul. So Perseus was able to conquer the Medusa, acquire the love of the beautiful Andromeda, and become a noble leader of his people. After many adventures,

Perseus became the king of Tiryns. He then founded Mycenae with the help of the Cyclops, who built the huge walls of the citadel.

TANTALUS AND PELOPS

The other memorable myth attached to Mycenae involves the figure of Tantalus, whose destiny it was to live in human memory as the most brutal and frustrated of men. Tantalus was so close to Zeus (spiritual reality) that he was invited to dine with the gods on Olympus. In return, seeking to please the gods—or, in other versions of the myth, to show his superiority over them—he sacrificed his son Pelops by cutting him up as a meal for the gods. Only Demeter, the Earth Mother, took a bite before the other gods discovered the sacrilege. As a punishment, Tantalus was eternally "tantalized." He is described standing in water he cannot drink, while overhead dangles fruit that the winds blow from his outstretched hand whenever he reaches for some.

The myth of Tantalus and Pelops has been variously interpreted as the fall from divine grace and as the ritual dismemberment of the year-god in the cycle of seasons. Pelops was saved by the gods and restored to life with their divine protection. This resurrection story echoes the myths surrounding Dionysos, also dismembered and restored to life. Pelops became a companion to Zeus and eventually returned to earth as king of the Lydians and Phrygians near the Black Sea. His role in the myths of Mycenae was as father of Atreus and Thyestes, two brothers who fought for the right to rule the kingdom.

ATREUS AND THYESTES

The great House of Perseus came to an end when his descendant Eurystheus went off from Mycenae to fight a war and was killed. The nobles of Mycenae chose Atreus as the new king, thus ushering in a new dynasty. Atreus and his combative brother, Thyestes, had sought sanctuary in Mycenae from Elis (Olympia), where their father Pelops was busy with myth-making of his own. The myths surrounding Atreus involve his efforts to solidify his claim to the throne at Mycenae against the efforts of Thyestes to dislodge him.

One such myth, coming to us from Apollodorus, reminds us of Minos and the white bull of Poseidon. Atreus had sworn he would sacrifice to Artemis the finest sheep in his flock. Knowing of this oath, Hermes planted a horned lamb with a golden fleece among the herds, knowing that Atreus would be tempted to keep the lamb for himself. Once again we see a hero tempted to claim what rightly belongs to the spiritual realm. Atreus compromised by sacrificing the meat of the lamb but keeping the fleece for his own pleasure.

Thyestes stole the fleece and claimed kingship on the basis of it, since the fleece was a necessary element in the important rainmaking rituals conducted by the king. Whoever controlled the rain controlled the kingdom. Atreus countered this deception by demonstrating control over even more elemental forces than rain. He reversed the movement of the sun so that it set in the east. Such awesome power was considered proof of his right to rule the kingdom because control was everything. Thyestes was banished.

Myths involving the shift of the sun's path occur in many traditions. In the Hebrew Old Testament, in 2 Kings 20:111, Yahweh reverses the movement of the sun as a sign of His love of King Hezekiah and His intention to extend the king's reign for fifteen years. Such myths are associated with portrayals of the reign of kings in terms of the natural cycles of growth and decay. It is natural for kings to serve for a time (often in multiples of nine) and then to give way to their sons or other younger men. In this case Atreus righted a wrong by demonstrating his astronomical knowledge and power, and thereby regained control of the kingdom.

THE HOUSE OF ATREUS

The myths of the House of Atreus take us through the darkest labyrinths of the human *psyche* and finally into the light of a new order of justice and divine mercy. They tell a tale that haunts the stones of Mycenae and finds its resolution on the sunlit acropolis of Athens, where Orestes is cleansed of the blood of his ancestors, thus ending the curse.

The essential story begins with the birth of Agamemnon, son of Atreus and Aerope, who also bore Menelaus, future king of Sparta and husband of the beautiful Helen. Also in this story is Aegisthus, the incestuous son of Thyestes. It is Aegisthus who will seduce Clytemnestra, war bride of Agamemnon and mother of his four children: a son, Orestes, and three daughters, Electra, Iphigenia, and Chrysothemis.

The myths of Atreus and his descendants are linked as well to the famous judgment of Paris, the divine beauty contest won by Aphrodite that resulted in the abduction of Helen to Troy and the disastrous Trojan War. This campaign to regain Helen forms the basis of Homer's epic poems and much of the subject matter of Classical tragedy. It is to Aeschylus and his famous trilogy, the *Oresteia*, that we owe most of our knowledge of these myths.

The Death of Agamemnon

There never was love between Agamemnon and Clytemnestra. Theirs was a marriage of power politics and war, made in violence and ending in betrayal and death. As king of the most powerful citadel in Greece, Agamemnon was chosen to lead the expedition against Troy. In order to gain favorable winds for the journey across the sea to Troy, Agamemnon sacrificed his daughter Iphigenia on the altar of his own ambitions. It was this outrage that Clytemnestra cited to the people of Mycenae as justification for the assassination of her husband when he returned after ten years to sit once more on the throne.

But deeper than Clytemnestra's claim of revenge lay her lust for Aegisthus and his vengeful intrigues to seize power in Mycenae. After the fall of Troy, Agamemnon sailed home, preceded by signal fires set on a string of sacred mountains to announce his arrival. He landed at Nauplia and took the ancient road to Mycenae, where he was greeted by his wife. Led to a warm bath and fresh garments, he was snared by a net and killed with the sacred double ax. The myth clearly draws a parallel between the death of the king and the sacrifice of the sacred bull in Minoan ritual.

After the death of Agamemnon, Clytemnestra and Aegisthus ruled in Mycenae under the cloud of murder and the realization that the young Orestes had escaped and might someday return to avenge his father's death. His sister Electra had remained behind, crying out to the gods for *dike* (dee-kay), the justice that must be done. Eventually, in the gods' good time, Orestes did return, disguised and guided by Apollo, whose clear command was to kill his mother by stealth and deception.

Orestes and Electra lured their mother with false news of the death of Orestes. Unaware, Clytemnestra welcomed the disguised Orestes who, after revealing himself to her, struck her down. The same fate awaited Aegisthus.

The Trial of Orestes

Rather than assuming the throne of Mycenae in his turn, Orestes was driven out by the avenging Furies, whose wrath descended upon him for the murder of his mother. Orestes sought shelter in the Temple of Apollo at Delphi, where the god sheltered him, but the Furies continued to sting him with guilt and retribution. Driven to Athens, Orestes was brought to trial for matricide, and Athena resolved the impossible quandary of crime and retribution by voting to absolve Orestes of his guilt. The cycle of death and vengeance was at last broken.

It is fitting that the myth of the House of Atreus ended outside the walls of Mycenae and that the citadel was left with the memory of the carnage that characterized its history. Soon after the death of Agamemnon, the Mycenaean citadels were burned and abandoned as centers of power. Certainly, at their best these outposts produced a heroic age that glorified the human capacity for monumental achievements. That the age also produced monumental crimes of the spirit speaks to the loneliness of humanity once severed from its gods.

THE SITE

THE ARCHAEOLOGICAL RECORD

The story of excavation at Mycenae begins with Heinrich Schliemann and his vision of the Bronze Age as described by Homer in the *Iliad*. Schliemann was a German industrialist whose financial success permitted him to spend his later years searching for the sites made famous by Homer. His successes at Troy and Mycenae make him the father of Aegean archaeology. After his world-famous discoveries at Troy in 1871, he turned his attention to Mycenae in 1874, and within two years he had excavated most of Grave Circle A, again with world-shaking results. His finds included the famous gold masks now on display at the National Museum in Athens.

It was not difficult for Schliemann to discover Mycenae because the site had always been known. Even in Classical times the Lion Gate was visible, exposed enough to reveal the monumental construction so typical of Mycenaean architecture and engineering. So awed were the later Greeks by these visible remains that they credited the construction of the gate and walls to the mythical Cyclops. We still refer to this type of construction as cyclopean.

In 1886, after Schliemann's discoveries, B. C. Tsountas began his long-term work on the site, clearing most of the citadel and discovering over seventy chamber tombs. Further work was begun by the British in 1920. In 1950, after the interruption of World War II, the British resumed work and discovered many more grave sites dated in the Late Helladic and Geometric periods. The Greek Archaeological Society began work at the same time, resulting in the discovery of Grave Circle B in 1951. Major discoveries were made under the supervision of George Mylonas beginning in 1958. Of particular interest was the discovery along the southern walls of rooms whose function was certainly religious. Thus, it was not really until the 1960s that we began to understand more about the religious life of the Mycenaean culture.

The Landscape and Citadel Hill

The site of the ancient citadel of Mycenae is approached either from the north, through the mountain pass from Corinth, or from the south from the modern city of Nauplia. Mycenae sits proudly at the northern end of the Argive Plain, facing the citadel of Argos across the Inachos River, with the Gulf of Argolis within sight to the south.

At its back, rising 2,600 feet (800 m) on either side, are the mountains Marta and Zara. As Scully has argued so forcefully, this site embodies the ancient vision of the Earth Mother and affirms the devotion of the founders of Mycenae to her power. Terra-cotta figurines of the Mycenaean goddess commonly have upraised arms. That figure is represented in this landscape by the two mountains within whose protective shadow the fortress sits. The image of being protected be-

Approach to the Lion Gate, Mycenae, showing remains of cyclopean wall

tween conical mountain shapes is seen everywhere in Mycenaean sites, as well in the *tholos* tombs, whose architecture embodies the form of the goddess in her function as underworld guide to the dead.

As the visitor approaches the Lion Gate, the conical Mount Zara is perfectly framed behind it. The triangle above the massive lintel appears as an image of the mountain. As in the culture of the Minoans, whose influence is felt here, the column that appears in the sculpture is always associated with the goddess and is her symbol.

The Outer Court and Lion Gate

We know when we approach the citadel of Mycenae that we are in the presence of an impressive fortress. We know much about the structure of this bastion, but very little about its success in withstanding assaults. We assume it was never breached from without. The destruction that occurred in the twelfth century BC might well have been the result of betrayal from within. Certainly there was no breach in the outer walls that history or archaeology has recorded. The famous walls of Troy were of similar construction and extent, and Homer recorded the ten-year attempt of the Achaeans to breach them. Finally, it was the ruse of the Trojan Horse that won entrance to the city. The walls held firm.

The fortification walls of Mycenae are extremely thick and were once much higher than they are today. In thickness the circuit walls averaged 20 feet (6 m). In height the walls probably averaged 40 feet (12 m), but nowhere is that height preserved in the present remains. Prior to the thirteenth cen-

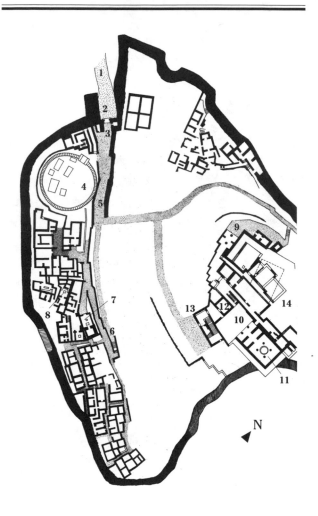

Fig. 16. Mycenae
  1. *Outer Court*
  2. *Lion Gate*
  3. *Inner Court*
  4. *Grave Circle A*
  5. *The Great Ramp*
  6. *Entrance to Cult Area*
  7. *Shrine*
  8. *Temple*
  9. *Palace Propylon*
  10. *Great Court*

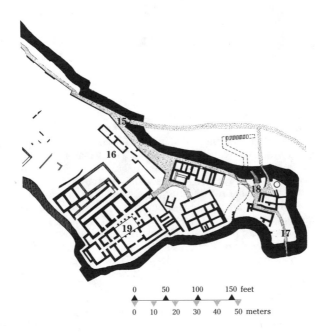

11. Palace Megaron
12. Guest Chamber
13. Grand Staircase
14. Archaic Temple to Athena
15. North Gate
16. Storage Areas
17. North Sally Port
18. Underground Cistern
19. House of Columns

Detail of the Lion Gate, Mycenae, showing the sacred column similar to Minoan architecture

tury BC, the walls were made of limestone. The present conglomerate walls were built over the limestone blocks around 1250 BC. At that time the walls were extended to bring Grave Circle A within the walls of the fortress. The decision to bring the grave circle inside the fortress speaks to the sacred importance of the graveyard and its valuable contents.

The Lion Gate presents the visitor with an awesome point of entrance. From a technical point of view, the Mycenaean engineers had learned that the huge lintel we pass under would not break if the space above it was in some way relieved of the weight of the wall. The resulting sculpture is, then, both functional and emblematic. The triangle relieves the weight on the lintel, and it also represents a sacred emblem of power. The Minoan column, an image of the goddess, stands upon an altar. The two lions, front paws on the altar, frame the column. The missing heads were not of the same stone as the rest of the piece, but were most likely carved of steatite. They were fastened to the bodies by dowels, the holes for which are still visible. Most likely the heads were lion heads rather than griffin heads, as some have speculated, in that the powerful modeling of the shoulders suggests a naturalistic representation of lions. The heads faced outward, looking right at the visitor approaching the gate.

The lintel itself, supporting this emblem, is a huge piece of conglomerate weighing 18 tons. It measures nearly 15 feet in length (4.5 m) and is 6 feet thick (1.98 m). The supporting doorjambs are 10 feet high (3.1 m), making the doorway nearly square. Thick double doors covered with glistening bronze once gave access through the gate. Pivot holes in the lintel show that the doors were mounted on beams fitted to the doorjambs. Holes in the jambs show that a large bar was used to lock the doors. This system of pivots and supports would have provided security against any attempt to use a battering ram to break the door.

Entrance and Grave Circle A

Inside the main gate, an area about 13 feet (4 m) square is marked out as an Inner Court. To the left is a small room whose position suggests a guardhouse, although the remains to the right form a more extensive set of rooms for that purpose, including stairs that gave access to the top of the walls. The room on the left may have been a shrine where persons entering or leaving the citadel marked the transition with prayer or offerings. However, Schliemann's excavations cleared these areas before more detailed studies could be done.

Grave Circle A was uncovered by Schliemann in 1876. Here, in several of the five shaft graves uncovered in that initial dig, Schliemann discovered the richest treasure in all of the history of Greek archaeological exploration. Among the gold cups, gold crowns, inlaid swords, and libation vessels were five gold burial masks, one of which Schliemann claimed as the death mask of Agamemnon (found in grave 5). Only later was it learned that the masks had been placed on the bodies of more ancient kings or nobles of Mycenaean history. Grave Circle A dates from the sixteenth century BC, the last interment taking place in about 1500 BC. Agamemnon would have ruled in the twelfth century. Despite the revision of history, however, the mask remains Agamemnon's in the popular imagination.

Grave Circle A is part of a large cemetery that extends past Grave Circle B, well outside the walls to the south. Circle A must have been regarded as very sacred to have been separated from the rest of the cemetery and drawn within the new fortification walls. Such veneration makes it clear that the memory of former kings and great heroes gave strength to the later dynasty and to their belief in divine support.

Nearly 92 feet (28 m) in diameter, the grave circle was an enclosure purposely designed to relate the geometric form of the circle to a sacred function, namely burial and ancestor worship. The graves were simple rectangular shafts sunk in the earth to various depths and not cut to any standard size. In Circle A, six shaft graves have been excavated, the sixth more recently discovered just to the right of the entrance. The circle was marked out by a low wall made of slabs, fitted vertically and horizontally. One horizontal slab to the left of the entrance shows the construction. Within the circle, a rubble wall snaked around the six shafts to mark the extent of the group in the circle and was later covered over. Reconstruction of the circle also suggests that vertical slabs looking very like modern tombstones were erected within the circle, possibly marking significant graves.

Exposed stonework of Grave Circle A, Mycenae, with shaft graves at various levels

In all, the grave circles represent an important focus of Mycenaean life. The similarities to Egyptian burial practices have not escaped scholars. In these graves, as in the *tholos* tombs much later, the soul of the deceased was given food, weapons, wealth, and magic totems to overcome the terrors of the unknown. Although no sense of any heavenly destination is known in the Mycenaean religion, some belief in the soul's immortality is represented by this elaborate burial cult. The open nature of the grave circles and their prominent position within the fortress also suggest ceremonial cult activity.

The Great Ramp

Extending from the Lion Gate and running alongside the grave circle is the sacred processional way of the citadel. The route of this major road within the fortress connects the Lion Gate to the North Gate and to the two gates to the most important areas in the citadel: the hilltop palace and the lower cult area meant for temple and shrine activity. Fifteen steps take the visitor up to the cobbled ramp and to the top of the first slope. Continuing to the east, straight ahead, the ramp descends to the cult center.

To the left the ramp climbs the slope and divides, the left branch going down and around to the North Gate and the right branch continuing the ascent to the palace. From the location of the supposed Propylon of the palace, it would appear that the official entrance was on the north side. Residents, however, would most likely have taken the right branch and entered the palace from the south, bypassing the Propylon.

Newly discovered cult area along fortress wall, Mycenae

The Cult Center

Recent excavation by Mylonas and his associates, including Lord William Taylour, have revealed a whole new world within the citadel of Mycenae. The area to the south of the palace, served by the processional way and by a series of formal ramps and entrances, is now understood to have been a cult center. Uncovered in 1968 and 1969, it strongly suggests a temple and shrine rooms where religious activity took place. This discovery is important because it is the first major evidence of Minoan-Mycenaean religious practice outside of the royal palace quarters. No doubt shrines existed in the hilltop palace in Mycenae as well, but here, below the palace, we find a separate area served by priests and designed for ritual and sacrifice.

The cult center is reached by following the ramp until it encounters scattered rubble that finally gives way to grass and becomes a worn trail snaking down to the retaining walls of the first buildings. The original ramp has been discovered and cleared. It was reached by a set of stairs and a door, the threshold of which still exists. The ramp turned back sharply to the west and then turned once again to the southeast. At this point the visitor may be stopped from further investigation, unless the Greek Archaeological Society has recently opened the site. But the nature of the area can be determined from this vantage point.

If the area is open, access to the so-called Temple is provided by a recently installed set of stairs. The rooms are quite complex in design, with several levels and small alcoves where many unique figurines were discovered. The most interesting of these was a tall (2-foot) clay goddess with raised arms and ugly demeanor, perhaps chthonic in character. She is hollow at the base. One suggestion is that these idols were designed to be fitted on poles and carried during ceremonies, but no evidence has yet appeared to show such usage.

Among the original finds of this area were also many clay snakes, quite realistically modeled, which supports the view that Mycenaean religious practice included the worship of household snakes, a common Greek practice in Archaic and Classical times. Snakes were associated with healing and with the mysteries of immortality. Thus, here in the cult center, where libation tables, idols, and other common cult features were found, scholars are also unearthing the connections between Mycenaean and later Greek culture. It is quite likely that this cult center was related to burial practices and that the character and position of the temples and shrines were meant to suggest earlier Minoan cave sanctuaries.

The Palace
Back on the processional way, the visitor may approach the palace from the north through the traditional Palace Propylon. Here the ancient visitor to the palace was directed into a narrow set of entrances and rooms that only after many turns and corridors lead to the Palace Megaron. Adjacent areas, no longer visible, were also accessible from this entrance. The porch of the Propylon was supported by a single column, and we are reminded of the West Porch entrance at Knossos and of the goddess whose image the column represented.

The Court
After the Propylon, a stairway to the left, now gone, gave access to a corridor and rooms adjacent to the Megaron. Another corridor went straight ahead, turned left, and led to the courtyard, the true beginning of the royal quarters. The open courtyard resembles a tower, in that it sits above the slope of the hill and commands a magnificent view of the valley to the west. To stand here and survey the Argive Plain is to feel the power possessed by the occupants of this citadel.

The conical hill across the valley is the cone of Argos. To the right, due west, is Mount Artemision, nearly 6,000 feet (1,770 m) high. The rugged land to the west is Arcadia, sacred to Artemis, whose anger at the House of Atreus caused its eventual destruction. The image of the reclining goddess, outlined by the receding hills, haunts the western horizon.

The Megaron
East of the court, entered through two porticoes, is the Megaron, the central room of the palace complex. The stone bases of two wooden columns remain to show the construction of the portico entrance. This main room measures 42 feet (13 m) long and 37 feet (11.5 m) wide. Typical of Mycenaean palaces, the center of the Megaron is taken up by a wide (11 feet, or 3.3 m) circular hearth, above which would

have been a chimney or roof opening to allow smoke to escape. The hearth is presently marked by a partial ring of stones in the floor. Note, too, the bases of four columns that supported the roof of the Megaron.

What remains of the Megaron has allowed some reconstruction of the appearance of the room. Fragments of frescoes depicting scenes of war were discovered on the northern wall. The king's throne stood at the center of the south wall. Custom suggests that similar thrones were provided for distinguished guests. Tables for food and stands for wine and other vessels for libation were carried in according to need. The floor was decorated with stucco, no doubt brightly colored. We have the oral tradition of Homer to tell us something of the interior of these resplendent *megarons*. In Book Four of the *Odyssey*, Telemakhos and Peisistratos are prepared for their welcome to the court of Menelaus at Sparta:

> What a brilliant place
> that mansion of the great prince seemed to them!
> A-glitter everywhere, as though with fiery
> points of sunlight, lusters of the moon.
> The young men gazed in joy before they entered
> into a room of polished tubs to bathe.
> Maid servants gave them baths, anointed them,
> held out fresh tunics, cloaked them warm; and soon
> they took tall thrones beside the son of Atreus.
> Here a maid tipped out water for their hands
> from a golden pitcher into a silver bowl,
> and set a polished table near at hand;
> the larder mistress with her tray of loaves
> and savories came, dispensing all her best,
> and then a carver heaped their platters high
> with various meats, and put down cups of gold.

Such was the splendor of life in the Megaron. When the feasting was finished and the hearth died down to glowing embers, guests went off to sleep in the *xenon* or Guest Chamber of the palace, which is preserved to the west of the Megaron on the other end of the open Great Court. The king would have retired to his private quarters, which were above the Megaron to the north. Both of these quarters were furnished with a private bath and a private open court.

The Archaic Temple of Athena
On the summit of the citadel are the foundations of the Archaic Temple to Athena erected during the sixth century BC. Doric in style, the temple was oriented to the northeast (more east than north) and probably was aligned with the rising of the Pleiades, the star cluster in Taurus that rises in the east with the sun to mark Athena's feast day. The importance of this temple for Mycenae is marked by its probable placement on the ruins of a hilltop shrine associated with the king's official function as chief priest.

The North Section

Too many visitors to Mycenae reach the palace and end their explorations there. But much more remains to be examined, in particular the impressive North Gate, the adjacent Storage Areas, the North Sally Port, and the famous Underground Cistern, one of the most remarkable pieces of engineering of the Mycenaean era.

The North Gate and Magazines

A well-worn path across the top of the citadel leads down toward the North Gate. On the right, in the eastern section of the complex, lie the remains of houses that were occupied by artisans. The closest ruins were workshops. The farther foundations are of a more elegant dwelling, with a peristyle courtyard. The latest speculation is that these rooms were part of the palace and were connected to the hilltop rooms. The so-called House of Columns might have been part of the royal household, perhaps the queen's *megaron*.

The North Gate, without relieving triangle, Mycenae

Continuing down the slope to the northwest brings us to the North Gate. Here is the same style of construction as the Lion Gate, except that the huge lintel stone is not relieved by a triangle above it. Rather, two stones were placed so as to leave a space just above the lintel and force the rock-splitting weight onto the two supporting posts. The modern double doors give some sense of how the originals were placed. The gateway is designed to prevent large numbers of invaders from converging on the wooden doors at one time. Inside the gate are a square court similar to the one at the main gate and again a small room on the left, serving either as a guardhouse or a shrine.

Nearby, partially hidden by the remains of the cyclopean wall, are Storage Areas, some still containing *amphorae* found during excavations. The area gives an indication of the relationship between the wall and storage rooms built into it all along the perimeter. These rooms would have been filled during times of siege and would also have stored the wealth of the citadel.

The Sally Ports and Cistern

At the eastern extreme of the citadel are the Sally Ports, two narrow doors cut into the wall. The arched design is called corbel vaulting. These doors were intended to be hidden from the outside and were evidently used to allow defenders to leave the citadel to confront attackers outside the walls.

At a time when long sieges were perhaps common and a regular water supply was essential for survival, the Mycenaeans dug beneath the wall and deep into the slope to the level of the groundwater, building there a secret cistern to serve the citadel. The engineering of this cistern is remarkable. It is still possible to descend to the level of the cistern, but a flashlight and steady nerves are both necessary. When Henry Miller made his visit to Mycenae just before World War II, he declined to visit it:

> We have just come up from the slippery staircase, Katsimbalis and I. We have not descended it, only peered down with lighted matches. The heavy roof is buckling with the weight of time. To breathe too heavily is enough to pull the world down over our ears. . . . I refuse to go back down into that slimy well of horrors. Not if there were a pot of gold to filch would I make the descent.

Miller expresses something of the foreboding felt in this descent into the underworld, still full of myth and power. But the actual facts of this tunnel and the wonder of its construction may overcome natural fears. There are three turns in the descent. The first cut is through the wall, down sixteen steps to a landing, then a left turn down twenty steps to another landing, then a sharp right turn for the major descent of fifty-four steps to the cistern. The well is 16 1/2 feet (5 m) deep.

THE THOLOS TOMBS

There are nine excavated *tholos* tombs in the vicinity of Mycenae, four of which may be conveniently visited. In the immediate area of the main gate are two tombs, one called the Tomb of Aegisthus and the other the Tomb of Clytemnestra. To the north of the Tomb of Aegisthus and across the road is the Lion Tomb. The most important and impressive of all the tombs, the Treasury of Atreus, is located farther to the south, down the main road. It should be noted

right away that these names have little to do with the tombs'
actual history. These are local names attached to the tombs
as a way of connecting the mythology of the citadel to the
tales of Homer.

The *tholos* tombs are later in construction and use than
the two grave circles in the ancient cemetery. In general the
tombs date from 1550 BC to 1200 BC. Since the tombs have
long since been pillaged, it is not known what family might
have laid claim to them. Burials did occur according to dynasty, and tombs were opened and closed several times in
order to bury members of one family.

Tomb Construction

These royal tombs were clearly part of the sacred traditions
of the Mycenaean people. Their roundness expressed the
sacred nature of the passage to a higher life for privileged
persons. The lesser chamber tombs that dot the countryside
are rectangular or are simply shaped to fit the terrain and
rock into which they were dug. The *tholos* tombs, however,
were dug into the rock in perfect form, overcoming the geological challenges confronting the builders.

The first step in building a tomb was to select a proper
place in terms of landscape features. The most important of
the tombs, the Treasury of Atreus, faces Mount Zara and is
itself a conical hill, creating its own sacred image. The builders fixed a point—the sacred act of locating the spiritual
center of the tomb complex—and inscribed the circle that
would be the diameter of the tomb. Then they dug down from
the top of the hill, carrying the dirt and rock away until the
level of the surrounding terrain was reached. This gave a
cleared area, perfectly round, with the entranceway, or
dromos, providing access for the sledging of the stones that
would form the beehive shape.

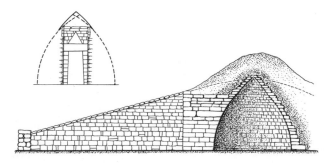

Fig. 17. *The precision of construction shown in tholos tombs, Mycenae.
Evidence shows almost no shifting of stones over three thousand years.*

The vertical shape of the beehive tomb was determined by placing a stake at the edge of the tomb circle, extending a cord through the center to the opposite edge (a diameter), and then inscribing an arc upward to a point above the center. This arc dictated the incline of the tomb as it rises, but only to a point several feet from the very top, where the peak would be formed. At this point the arc was surrendered to accommodate the support of the completed arch. Proper distribution of the weight required that a perfect triangle complete the roof.

By this method of construction the tomb was built within a cleared space, and scaffolding was used to raise each level. The huge lintel stone over the door of the Atreus tomb weighs at least 120 tons. The logical answer to the perennial question of how that stone was placed is that it was moved slowly into position up a ramp built into the side of the hill. In this sacred undertaking the stones would have been moved in the fullness of time and without strain.

The Tombs of Aegisthus and Clytemnestra

These two tombs differ only slightly in their specific measurements. The major differences between the two are in their age and condition. The Aegisthus tomb is the oldest of the four, and its collapsed condition may reflect a less advanced knowledge of construction. The tomb can be examined from the top, since its vault has collapsed. The process of final vaulting must have been a matter of experimentation over many years, perhaps centuries, until the correct balance between weight distribution and ceiling angle was reached.

The Clytemnestra tomb is the most recent in this immediate area, having been completed around 1250 BC, the same time as the Lion Gate and the expanded fortifications of the citadel. Some restoration work has repaired the vaulting in this tomb above the height of 28 feet (8.5 m). One notable feature of this tomb's construction is the band of wider blocks at the level of the lintel, which provides a firmer base for the rest of the vaulting. During the third century BC, the Hellenistic occupants of the area constructed a theater nearby, one row of which can be detected above the *dromos* of the tomb. The placement of the theater suggests that the existence of this tomb remained unsuspected until the nineteenth century, when it was discovered by the Turkish landlords then in power.

The Treasury of Atreus

Here we have the finest expression of the *tholos* tomb, the apex as well of Mycenaean sacred architecture. The construction of this tomb was so precise that in the three thousand years of its existence, it has not settled an inch, so firm are its foundations and fixed its vaulting. Like the fabled acoustics of the theater at Epidauros, the sound quality of this tomb seems quite magical. If the visitor is fortunate enough to be alone in the tomb or the group is asked to focus its attention,

Monumental stone set as foundation for the dromos of the tomb of Atreus, Mycenae

the acoustics can be demonstrated. A word whispered along the wall can be heard throughout the tomb because the structure functions like an amplifier. A foot simply turning in the dirt of the floor sounds like the grinding of huge stones. Whether or not this quality of sound had any significance or purpose is unknown, but chanting of funeral hymns in this space would have been imposing and very powerful.

The Dromos and Doorway

The entrance to the tomb, cut into the natural side of the hill of Panayitsa, is nearly 120 feet (35 m) long and 20 feet (6 m) wide. Some of the conglomerate blocks that line the walls are of monumental size. The stone on the right of the entrance, for example, is 20 feet long (6 m) and 4 feet high (1.25 m). The doorway, still in excellent condition, measures 17.7 feet high (5.4 m) and 8.8 feet wide (2.45 m) at the threshold and is slightly narrower at the top. The doorway was decorated with elaborate designs, fragments of which are in the National Archaeological Museum in Athens and the British Museum in London. As the column base on the left side of the door reveals, the door was framed by two half-columns cut of green stone and elaborately carved. Above the door, where the relieving triangle is now revealed, two more half-columns and a decorated panel once completed the facade.

The threshold to the tomb presents an interesting construction. Two pieces of conglomerate were placed against the doorjambs and then wedged into place by pieces of limestone driven into the space so as to press the conglomerate blocks out against the jambs. Also worth noting carefully is the subtle carving around the door, including the lintel stone, to fuse each individual block into the whole design.

The outer circle of the tomb measures 48 feet in diameter (14.6 m) and the height at the center measures just over

Dromos of the tomb of Atreus, with relieving triangle and trapezoidal doorway, Mycenae

44 feet (13.5 m). There are thirty-three rings of conglomerate blocks making up the corbel vaulting. Many of the blocks show holes where bronze nails were used to mount gold and bronze decorations—rosettes and spiral designs typical of Minoan and Mycenaean sacred architecture.

On the north side of the chamber is a side room 20 feet square (6 m)—a rare feature in *tholos* tombs. Some speculate that at the time of multiple burials the bones of earlier occupants may have been moved to this chamber in order to clear the main chamber for the new ceremonies and bodies. It has been suggested that the Mycenaeans believed that as long as the flesh clung to the bones, the soul remained with the body, but when the bones were bare, the soul had fled and the bones could be moved with impunity.

The Funeral Cult

If we imagine the Atreus tomb, newly prepared and open to receive its first occupant, we can fit the details into a general picture. The following account is given in Lord William Taylour's *The Mycenaeans* and was compiled from several sources:

> The great bronze doors with their gilded bosses would be swung back to receive the cortege, and in the dim light the vault with horizontal bands of bronze would gleam with a thousand gold rosettes. Spread out on the earthen floor was a carpet of gold to receive the body of the king, arrayed in his robes of state, crowned with his diadem, his seals of office attached to his wrist, and his favorite dagger at his side. Around him would be laid the vessels of food, the flagons of wine, jars of oil and

unguent, and all the necessities for the sustenance and care of the body on his last journey. Weapons of war would be added too: swords, rapiers. daggers, and spears, the mighty figure-of-eight shield, the well-stocked quiver, and the bow.

One rapier had a special task to perform. It is taken from the pile and to the words of a solemn incantation the blade is bent so that its spirit may be released and be swift to do battle for its master, should threatening demons bar his way. Then the signal is given for the slaughter of the horses that had drawn the chariot with the bier, and that have been fidgeting nervously, in the *dromos,* apprehensive of the doom that awaits them. There follows the slaying of the rams and other sacrificial beasts within the vaulted tomb itself. The fires are lit, the sacrifices roasted, and all partake of the funeral banquet. In the still glowing embers the mourners cast their last tributes to the dead, and then withdraw.

After the ceremony, the great door was sealed, using small blocks, and then the entire *dromos* was filled in, making the hill look natural once again. For subsequent burials, the dromos would be cleared and the door unsealed. Such labors occasioned the death of kings.

3
THE
TEMPLE
CULTURES

With the decline of the palace cultures of Crete and the mainland after 1100 BC, the Minoan-Mycenaean world went into eclipse. A darkness spread over the Aegean world for a period of four hundred years, and the territory that was to become Greece transformed itself from a land of palace cultures similar to other Mediterranean cultures into a wholly new world. During this so-called Dark Age, migrations from the north and east continued. The resulting brew of new ideas, new values, new gods, and new economic conditions spawned a new culture, but very little of the change was recorded and almost nothing of the transformation left its mark in the archaeological record.

The major development, the *polis*, or independent city-state, seemed to emerge whole as if from some obscure laboratory. Historians have been able to explain the development in general terms, but the mystery remains as to how the *polis* actually emerged as an idea and a fact of civilization. Some historians say that in the chaos that followed the destruction of the palaces, it was natural that aristocratic families joined together for defense, establishing settlements surrounding the important sacred sites that eventually evolved into city-states.

TEMPLES AND SANCTUARIES

The most evident changes during the Dark Age were the decline of the palaces as centers of religious power and the emergence of the temple sanctuaries in their place. The priest-king gave way to the invisible god, and the temple sanctuaries, which had been minor adjuncts to the palace, now emerged as the prominent feature of the acropolis, the sacred high ground of the city. The secular dwellings moved off the acropolis and became prosaic in design, although some country villas retained the old *megaron* form.

Since the temple was designed to house a god and not a priest-king and his retainers, the design features differed ac-

Engraving of the western facade of the Parthenon, Acropolis, Athens

cordingly. The temple was a holy sanctuary with areas of limited accessibility, the entire structure covered over with a wide roof supported by columns. The design and placement of temples reflected the persona of the god and, like cathedrals in medieval European cities or churches in town squares, were constant reminders of the presence of divinity in the lives of the populace.

THE NEW REALITY

The culture that emerged after the Bronze Age was in many respects modern. Iron was used to make weapons, household goods, and temple fittings. Cremation replaced elaborate burial of the dead, who lived on in private memory. The gods themselves became distant powers unrelated to daily life. Epic poetry described heroic deeds of a dim past not connected with present culture. Political power was held by aristocratic, landowning families who shared power and raised armies to protect their interests.

And yet there existed a minority view, a world in which the spiritual values and powers once so central to the culture were kept alive by a new elite. This group of priests, poets, architects, and aristocrats came to prominence as the philosophers and statesmen of the Classical Period. It is their monuments of language and stone that remain for us to examine and cherish. Their wisdom was preserved after the decline of the Roman Empire by the scholars of Islam, who with patience and dedication cherished the essential truth of the ancient knowledge until Italian Renaissance scholars discovered it once more nearly two thousand years later.

ATHENS

Modern Athens is hard to love, especially in the heat of a summer day, in the haze of car and bus exhaust, when this city of over three million swells to six in the height of the tourist season. Visitors in the hot months are advised to plan their tours in the early morning and late afternoon. Midday is for rest, boat trips to the close islands, or a visit to the National Archaeological Museum. But late at night in the twisting streets of the Plaka and in the restaurants set up in the small quiet squares—far away from the crowded, expensive tourist cafes in Omonia Square—the city turns on its charm and becomes not only friendly but inviting.

Life has always been a struggle for the Greeks. The land yields its fruit grudgingly, and each year the sprouting of new grain and fruit blossoms is greeted with religious celebration. To the devout, Easter affirms the hope of a new crop each spring. Because the countryside is grudging in its support, many Greeks have had to migrate to the city to earn a living, exchanging their attachment to the land for the demands of the service industries that support the tourist trade.

Without planning or restraint Athens has grown away from its acropolis to cover the surrounding hills and spill into the connecting valleys. Most of the construction consists of gray concrete with narrow balconies used on summer nights to catch a breath of breeze from the sea. Despite its sprawl and noise, Athens is still a Mediterranean city and has a slower pace hidden beneath its frantic struggle to find its place in the Common Market. On summer nights, when the business day ends, each neighborhood gathers in its square, tablecloths are spread on folding tables, and space is created for a more leisurely way of life. Supper runs very late, often past midnight, and it is always surprising to see the snarls of traffic on the roads so early the next morning as Athenians race to work after only a few hours of sleep.

THE ANCIENT SITES

The ancient treasures of Athens center on its Acropolis, where the Parthenon still sits gleaming after more than a decade of restoration. But a complete experience of Archaic, Classical, and Hellenistic Athens includes much more than an admission ticket to the Acropolis, and visitors are urged to schedule enough time to see and absorb the full spectrum of this remarkable ancient culture.

Surrounding the Acropolis, which contains the

The Acropolis, Athens, seen from below, with the Roman arches of the Odeion of Herod Atticus in the foreground

Parthenon, Propylaia complex, Erechtheion, and Museum, are the ancient Theater of Dionysos, the Asklepieion, the Odeion of Herod Atticus, the ancient Agora, the Areopagus, the Kerameikos (ancient cemetery), the Pnyx, where the debates of the Athenian democracy took place, and the Olympieion, sanctuary of the great temple of Zeus. To the north, outside the ancient Dipylon Gate, lie hidden the remains of Plato's Academy, seldom if ever visited and nearly lost in the winding commercial streets.

In addition to the Acropolis Museum, there are two other important museums containing ancient artifacts: the Agora Museum, beautifully situated in the renovated Stoa of Attalos, and the National Archaeological Museum, home of the major collection of ancient treasures in Greece.

HISTORY

The recorded history of Athens takes us back at least to Neolithic times, in the third millennium, before the Mycenaean kings and before any Minoan influence. Neolithic remains discovered on the slopes of the Acropolis point to continuous settlement of the hill from at least 2800 BC. Clearly, the earliest settlers recognized the advantages of this site, protected as it is by the surrounding mountains, elevated above the plain for defense, and provided with ample water from springs within the hill.

It should also be noted that unrecorded history places settlement in Athens as early as 9000 BC by a culture powerful enough to have attracted the attention of Egyptian historians. Plato recorded the legend that the Athenians of that era defeated the Atlanteans and thus saved Hellas from domination by that mythical kingdom. The historical record does show evidence of conflict as far back as 9000 BC. So Plato's account may have validity.

In Mycenaean times a palace stood on the hilltop, probably next to the site of the ancient Temple of Athena. The remains of this temple were discovered between the present Parthenon and the Erechtheion, which was named after Erechtheus, an early, legendary king of Athens. Evidence suggests that the early Temple of Athena was part of a sacred enclosure connected to the Mycenaean palace.

The last Mycenaean king of Athens, Kodros the Pylian, was killed defending the Acropolis against the Dorians, who never did win a complete victory over the Athenians. So, the identity of the Athenian stock that held on and merged with the Dorian invaders has always presented a mystery for historians and anthropologists. Those who claim kinship to the original clans and families who made up the earliest population seem to be at least partly indigenous, although very little evidence exists beyond certain linguistic clues.

RULE BY THE FEW AND THE MANY

The form of government in Athens that history records after the Bronze Age resembled an oligarchy. Authority rested with *archons*, officials who shared power and administered the business of the city. The *archons* were chosen from the leading families and served an indefinite time. In general, the *archons* divided their responsibilities into secular, religious, and military areas of rule. The effect of this form of divided authority was to remove leadership from sacred ground; hence the shift of power from the Acropolis to the Agora, which from the Archaic Period onward became the center of all secular and at least some religious life.

Oligarchy as a form of government served Athens throughout most of its history. Rule by the few, the *aristoi*, varied in its details and flexibility, sometimes leaning heavily on the people but more often tending to tyranny. Occasional periods of either full or limited democracy have characterized Athenian government from Mycenaean times to the present, but democratic impulses have always played an important part in Athens's struggles for independence.

INVASION AND DESTRUCTION

In the summer of 480 BC, the date that marks the end of the Archaic Period, the Persians overran Athens and destroyed the sacred buildings on the Acropolis before they in turn were defeated by the Greeks at Salamis and Plataea. This was not the first time the defenses on the Acropolis had been successfully breached. However, this defeat and subsequent destruction were deeply felt by those Athenians who survived the attack and then returned to view the desecration of their sacred shrines. They resolved to let the ruins stand as a reminder of this outrage, and they buried the beautiful sculptures that had adorned the sanctuaries. Many were subsequently discovered many centuries later when excavation began, and many now reside in the Acropolis Museum.

PERICLEAN ATHENS

What took place under the leadership of Pericles in the fifth century BC in Athens has already been described in the historical overview. This period was the apex of Athenian history, and what we see today around the Acropolis dates mainly from this period of monumental construction, war with Sparta, and artistic achievement. The Walls of Themistocles, for example, rose on the Acropolis to protect against further attack. Portions of former temples were also used, especially on the north side where column drums were fitted alongside regular blocks to form the wall. The Parthenon (447-438 BC), the Propylon, and the Temple of Athena Nike were completed during this time, and the Erechtheion was finally finished at the close of the century.

FROM ROMAN TO TURKISH RULE

Athens declined in power and influence after the fifth century BC, although it continued to be home to many of history's great minds, Plato and Aristotle being the most prominent. During the centuries spanning the rule of Alexander, the Roman invasions, and subsequent Roman domination, the Acropolis and the city surrounding it rose and fell with the whims and curses of conquerors. In AD 429 the Acropolis ceased to be a place where the Olympian gods were worshiped. Christian basilicas replaced the temples and the architectural profile of the hill changed forever.

After the fall of Rome, Athens fell victim to invader after invader until Greek independence was finally achieved in 1833. The Crusades passed through in 1204, followed by the Franks, the Turks, and the Venetians, who in 1688 damaged the Parthenon with a cannon shot that ignited gunpowder stored there by the Turks. Had this explosion not occurred, the Parthenon would be complete, or nearly so, today.

MYTHOLOGY

The mythology of Athens tells the moving story of a city and a people born to excel and fated to suffer and find redemption in acceptance of that suffering. It is a story of glorious deeds, ignominious defeats, and a unique spiritual destiny. The king Theseus is the hero of this myth, and his story is the story of the city. It seems certain that a Theseus did rule as king in Athens during the Bronze Age and did consolidate the towns in Attica into an expanded and powerful *polis*.

THE HERO AND THE SPIRITUAL PATH

Theseus was the son of Poseidon, the god whose power ruled the sea and whose separation from Zeus parallels the human separation from the divine. Theseus was the earthly son of Aegeus, king of Athens, but he was born secretly in Corinth through the magic of the sorceress Medea. Theseus grew to manhood away from Athens and without knowledge of his patrimony. Against the day when Theseus might be strong enough to undertake the life of a hero, Aegeus had hidden a sword and a pair of sandals beneath a huge rock, to be discovered and used if the young man was capable.

When Theseus visited Delphi as a youth, he demonstrated the necessary qualities to become a hero. Shown the rock that covered the spiritual symbols of his heroic quest, he moved it easily, took the tokens, and followed the road to Athens. On the way he met and destroyed various monsters, including Sciron, who bore a huge club for killing wayfarers. Theseus seized the club and, after killing Sciron with it, used it to fight his way to Athens. Substitution of the club for the spiritual sword signifies both a love for earthly power with its more sensual rewards and the hero's connection to the figure of Herakles.

As a guest at a banquet in Athens, Theseus drew his sword to slice a piece of beef and was recognized by Aegeus, who proclaimed him son and heir to the Athenian throne. The rest of the now familiar tale forms an important part of the mythology of Crete. The tale of Theseus and the Minotaur appears in the section on the mythology of Knossos.

The Athenian myth, with its blend of success and failure, shows the typical path of the hero seeking earthly and spiritual glory. Theseus is tempted by earthly fame and turns his back on true wisdom. His betrayal of Ariadne, who showed him the secret of the labyrinth, demonstrates the blinding effects of earthly fame and the inability to recognize and depend upon spiritual guidance.

THESEUS AND PERSEPHONE

The accounts of Theseus are extensive and powerful, full of his love affairs, military victories, and political triumphs. Another myth serves to show how his spiritual quest took him, as it does all true heroes, to the underworld where he had to encounter his own mortality. Since the abduction of prized possessions was a heroic pastime, guaranteed to incite warfare among neighboring city-states, Theseus and his companion-in-arms Peirithous set out to make new conquests. Their first adventure took them to Arcadia, where they insulted the Dioscuri, Castor and Polydeuces, who ruled Sparta, by carrying off the beautiful Helen, then just a child.

Some years later, seeking to know if he would ever marry Helen, whom he had hidden away, Theseus consulted an oracle of Zeus. The oracle trapped Theseus and his companion by suggesting that the adventurers seek instead to win the release of Persephone from Hades. Persephone's presence in Hades was a result of natural law, a union of chthonic and Olympian powers, resulting in her presence in Hades for four months of the year. Such an attempt by mortals was an outrage, and when Theseus appeared in Hades, he was confined to a stone seat, fused to it so that movement was impossible. He was, in effect, bound to the earth. Confinement to this stone seat, the Chair of Forgetfulness, signified his complete loss of spiritual awareness.

Theseus gained his freedom from this mortal bondage through the heroic intervention of Herakles, who literally ripped him from the stone seat to set him free. This rescue was another example of the special bond between Herakles and Theseus, a friendship that overcame many difficult trials. This theme of the special bond between those who have suffered is seen again in the story of Theseus and Oedipus, that suffering hero whose misery knew no bounds.

THESEUS AND OEDIPUS

When Oedipus was forced to leave Thebes after the revelations of his terrible deeds of patricide and incest, he wandered homeless with his daughter Antigone for twenty years, until one day he came upon the sacred grove of the Eumenides at Colonus. a small town just one mile north of the sacred gate into Athens. Here Oedipus vowed to remain, knowing in his newfound wisdom that the gods had destined him to die in this place.

His terrible appearance frightened the local elders, who called King Theseus to come to their aid and decide the terrible question of whether or not Athens should grant refuge to a man such as Oedipus. Theseus, in his wisdom, saw that this blind old man would bring a special gift, wisdom earned from unparalleled suffering, to the Athenian people. He pledged to honor Oedipus as a citizen by granting him an honored burial and eternal rest for his bones. This insight demonstrated the special knowledge achieved by the Athenians as a result of their collective suffering and their protection by Athena, goddess of wisdom.

These myths describe the struggles and suffering of Athens itself. The sense of adventure, the spiritual promise darkened by arrogance, the glorious victories tempered by the wisdom of moderation and justice, all reflect the history of this great city.

THE SITES OF ATHENS

THE ACROPOLIS

> *Not Magnitude, not lavishness*
> *But form, the site;*
> *Not innovating willfulness,*
> *But reverence for the archetype.*

> — Herman Melville

One always has the sense in approaching the Acropolis of Athens of being in the company of all mankind. It is one of the universal places where the collective mind and soul meet and gather in a unity. Even the most dull of heart have been transformed by this space. Being a sacred place, divinity was attracted and made manifest here. Athena was goddess of the city—protectress, source of wisdom, nurturer of greatness, and dispenser of justice.

There are three ancient monuments left standing on the Acropolis: the Propylaia, along with the delicate Temple of Athena Nike; the Erechtheion, supported by the famous Karyatides statue-columns; and most famous, the Temple of Athena Parthenos, more commonly called the Parthenon. In addition, though sometimes neglected by hurried visitors, there is the modern Acropolis Museum, which houses friezes from the Parthenon and many fine archaic statues from the period before 480 BC. One statue of a young girl in particular—the famous Almond-Eyed Kore, sculpted in 500 BC—is a highlight of a visit to Greece. The purity and grace of this statue demonstrate the highest standards in Archaic art.

EXCAVATION AND RESTORATION

Foundations of earlier temples, sections of wall, and carefully marked rows of marble blocks everywhere on the Acropolis attest to years of excavation and research. After Greece achieved independence from the Turks in 1833, restoration work on the Acropolis began. Initially, years of "foreign" construction had to be cleared away to expose the ancient ruins.

The first major piece of work was the restoration of the Temple of Athena Nike, which had been torn down in 1687 to strengthen the fortification walls.

Starting in 1885 archaeologists began clearing the hilltop down to bedrock. This standard technique of excavation sifts through the various levels of construction in order to establish accurate dating of building foundations and artifacts discovered at each level. During this period of investigation the rich finds of sculpture buried after the destruction of 480 BC were discovered. In 1895 actual reconstruction began on several monuments, particularly the Parthenon, which had been damaged severely by an earthquake in 1894. Work on the site has been continuous ever since, except during World War II.

Today a cooperative effort by many nations, institutions, and individuals continues the work of restoration and repair. The major concern on the Acropolis is the deterioration of the marble due to the acid content of the air in Athens. Automotive exhaust, held over the city by the bowl of surrounding mountains, is eating away the monuments that are outside and exposed. Some steps have been taken to minimize the damage. For example, visitors may no longer walk on or touch the Parthenon or the Erechtheion. The Karyatides have been removed from the Erechtheion, preserved in the Acropolis Museum, and replaced by reproductions.

THE SACRED WAY

Let us picture for a moment the Panathenaia, the celebration of the birth of the city, which took place every year in July, at the beginning of the Athenian year. Every fourth year it was replaced by the Greater Panathenaia to signify a Panhellenic cycle of the birth and death of kings. This festival formed in a great procession north of the Agora at the Dipylon Gate, then made its way through the Agora to the northwest corner of the Acropolis walls, past the Klepsydra Spring, and up a winding path to the main entrance to the Acropolis.

The rendering of the procession on the great frieze of the Parthenon showed the extent of participation by all elements in the city. Horsemen, elders, young boys, and especially the young girls of Athens processed, the last carrying the new robe, the *peplos*, for the statue of Athena. The sacrifice of many sheep and bulls at the great altar provided an unaccustomed feast of meat for the populace of the city, who gathered for the collective banquet in the Agora. The important moments of the celebration came with the approach of the procession up the Sacred Way to the Propylaia and then into the sanctuary of the Temple of Athena Parthenos.

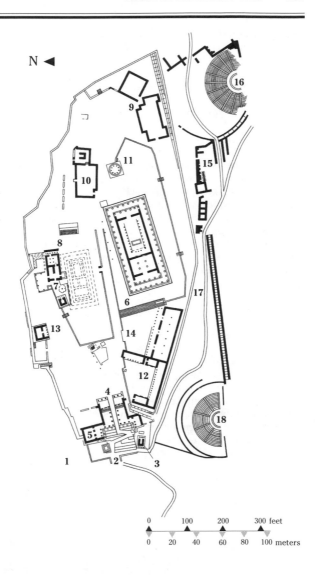

N ◄

Fig. 18. The Acropolis, Athens
1. Klepsydra Spring
2. Propylaia
3. Temple of Athena Nike
4. The Propylon
5. The Pinakotheke
6. The Parthenon
7. The Erechtheion
8. Karyatides
9. Acropolis Museum
10. Sanctuary of Zeus
11. Roman Temple
12. Sanctuary of Artemis
13. Cistern
14. Sacred Entrance
15. Asklepieion
16. Theater of Dionysos
17. Peripitos
18. Odeion of Herod Atticus

THE PROPYLAIA

The term *propylaia* refers to the group of buildings that make up the entrance complex. The term *propylon* refers to the actual entranceway through which one passes to enter the sanctuary. The modern visitor can approach the Propylaia as the ancients did by walking up the slope from Dionyssiou Areopagitou—the broad avenue used to reach the site—and continuing across the saddle connecting the hills of the Acropolis and the Areopagus. The paved walk goes down (to the north) beneath the Acropolis wall, through a gate to bring the visitor within sight of the fence surrounding the Agora excavations. To the right, along the Peripitos, the ancient road that runs around the Lower Acropolis, are the remains of the Klepsydra Spring, where the Panathenaic procession stopped for the ritual of purification.

The visitor, now following the route of the procession, can return up the path, turn left, and approach the massive Propylaia. The Propylaia served as a transition to another world, a sacred world in which human beings and gods met in communion. The purpose of the Propylaia was to still the mind, purify the thoughts, and prepare the body for the meeting with the goddess.

The sacred preparation was accomplished in several ways. First, the months of readying for the festival, particularly the weaving of the *peplos,* prepared the mind by focusing attention on devotions to the goddess. Second, the spectacle of the procession and the walk from the Dipylon Gate in the bright July sun brought an intense clarity to the mind. Third, the ascent to Propylaia stirred feelings of awe and respect and actually created the proper frame of mind for worship. Pausanius described his first approach to the Acropolis in the second century AD when the Acropolis was still well preserved:

View of the remains of the Great South Propylon, Acropolis, Athens

The Acropolis has one way in; it offers no other; the whole hilltop is sheer and strong-walled. The formal entrance has a roof of white marble, which down to my own times is still incomparable for the size and beauty of the stone.

From a man familiar with the monumental splendors of imperial Rome, this comment is noteworthy. What Pausanius encountered as he neared the Propylon were high monumental walls on either side of a temple facade of six Doric columns. The approach to this facade during the Classical Period would have been along a winding ramp, constructed so as to permit large numbers of animals to walk up the steep slope into the sanctuary. In Roman times stairs similar to the present ones gave access to the interior spaces. Some sense of the winding path still exists on the approach below the stairs.

Temple of Athena Nike
The ancient path was situated so as to provide at an eastern turning a dramatic view of a special temple of freedom. High on the right side of the Propylaia and separate from its monumental bulk is the small, exquisite Temple of Winged Victory, or Athena Nike. Designed and built by Kallikrates from 427 to 424 BC, this expression of freedom and triumph over adversity sits lightly upon its platform as if ready to take flight. The temple is amphiprostyle, that is, with columns front and rear, in this case in the Ionic order. A small frieze surrounded the building, depicting battle scenes in which Athenians eternally defeat the Persians.

The Propylon
The six Doric columns supporting the entrance introduce a general theme of patterns of six in the Propylaia. Six is the sacred number of creation, a feminine number of love and completion. Six anticipates the divine seven, which in turn suggests a desire to unite with the divine presence. Thus, the entrance sets the tone for the communion within. The roof of the Propylon was also supported by two rows of three slimmer Ionic columns placed on either side of the central passage. The high roof elements, some of which remain in the northeast corner, drew the attention upward and gave the worshiper a strong sense of stature, allowing the mind to expand into the space.

In other, less impressive sites, the pilgrim entering a sanctuary passed through a much simpler *propylon*, pausing to prepare for the experience ahead. At the Acropolis, the propylon itself resembled a temple, or at least was laid out like one. The pilgrim had the sense of entering an inner sanctum normally forbidden to anyone but the priests, in addition to the sense of rising, being drawn upward to the sacred space beyond.

To the left, or the north, of the Propylon was the Pinakotheke, or gallery of art, in which paintings done on

*View of the remains
of the North Propylon
and Pinakotheke,
Acropolis, Athens*

wooden panels lined the walls. None of the paintings has survived, but Pausanius reported scenes of Odysseus stealing the sacred bow from Philoctetes, Diomede carrying off Athena from Troy, and Orestes killing Aegisthus. Other heroic subjects carried out the theme of the journey of the hero in Homeric lore.

Once through the sacred gate of the Propylon, the visitor is greeted with the form of the Parthenon dominating the sanctuary. The procession bore to the right and passed along the northern colonnade of the temple and around to the eastern entrance, there to await entrance into the presence of the goddess.

THE PARTHENON

The Temple of Athena Parthenos means Temple of the Virgin Athena. Maiden goddess of Athens, she sprang full grown from the head of Zeus the Father. She was pure in mind, heart, and body, and was Wisdom incarnate. The Parthenon, like all temples in Greece, was an image of the god housed within and thus an icon of Athena's attributes. It was also designed to attract her spirit to the place, to embody her presence so that her worshipers might commune and feast in her presence and be united with her.

The Parthenon has attracted more attention from scholars, historians, archaeologists, architects, poets, and madmen than any other building in the world. It stimulates artistic and philosophical theories and expressions of adoration or loathing or even what seems like indifference. Pausanius, for example, who described so many Greek monuments in admi-

View of the Parthenon most treasured by pilgrims, from the entrance to the Acropolis, Athens

rable detail, wrote almost nothing of the Parthenon itself, attracted as he was by the sculpture on the pediments and the massive gold and ivory statue of Athena inside.

Siting of the Temple

From early Archaic times a temple dedicated to Athena has been located on the Acropolis, first on the northern side and later in approximately the position of the present temple. We can speak of three significant dates: the first, circa 530 BC when a temple stood to the north of the present site; the second, circa 480 BC, when an unfinished temple was destroyed by the Persians; and the third, in 438 BC, when the present Parthenon was completed. All three temples faced the east, but the third temple was shifted several points on the compass to the north, possibly to adjust to the shift in stellar movements over the years.

It was Francis Cranmer Penrose, former director of the British School of Archaeology, who while examining the site in 1891, first proposed that the Parthenon had been oriented to the rising of the Pleiades, the constellation also called the Seven Sisters, which is clustered in Taurus and which rose in the east every spring. Jane Harrison, in her book *Epilegomena and Themis*, points out that when the Pleiades rose twenty-seven days after the vernal equinox (about April 16 on our calendar), the Athenians celebrated the festival of the first harvest. From Frazer's *Golden Bough* we also learn that the final setting of the Pleiades in the fall marked the time of the fall planting.

Also, Scully points out that the Parthenon is oriented to the horned Mount Hymettos, seen from the Acropolis to the east as two gentle peaks rising at the end of the ring of mountains that sweep around from the south. Since we know that a Mycenaean palace was located on the Acropolis and that the earliest temple was adjacent to it, it is likely that the orientation to Hymettos was always a part of temple siting in Athens.

History of Construction

When the decision was finally made to rebuild the Acropolis after the destruction of 480 BC, it was Pericles as general and leader of the Athenian people who led the way. Pericles had been reared an aristocrat and tutored by Anaxagoras, the Ionian philosopher affectionately known as *Nous*, or Mind. As Plutarch tells us, Anaxagoras "was the first of the philosophers who did not refer the first ordering of the world to fortune or chance, nor to necessity or compulsion, but to a pure, unadulterated intelligence, which in all other existing mixed and compound things acts like a principle of discrimination, and of combination of like with like."

Pericles was very much the student of Anaxagoras. His life was a model of discrimination based on the principle of mind. Critics, including his enemy Thucydides, accused him of terrible excesses, particularly in the cost of building the Parthenon. However, they failed to understand Pericles' vision as manifested in rebuilding the Acropolis; namely, that the intense, focused labor of thousands of people working together to one end would produce a gathering of consciousness on that site that would recapture what had been lost through hundreds of years and several disasters. Mind, as his tutor had told him, was capable of creating a world, and Pericles saw his role as creator of a conscious *polis* dedicated to Wisdom.

In charge of the work was the sculptor Phidias, whose command of sacred geometry and architecture established a high level of work. The result was a unity of construction that we have come to call the triumph of Classical art and that Edgar Allan Poe described as "the glory that was Greece." The architects of the Parthenon were Iktinos and Kallikrates, and the temple they began in 447 BC and crafted for nine years was an expression of the Greek cosmos, a temple of the universe, and of divine and human proportion.

Sacred Number in the Parthenon

The architects had several aims in mind as they envisioned this new temple. First, they knew that it had to rise in approximately the same position on the Acropolis as the old one. The position was sacred, and the actual point on the ground from which the building would be generated was already known. Seond, they wanted the temple to be wider than the previous temples. The facade would present eight columns rather than six, meaning that the total number of columns in the outer colonnade would be forty-six. In the Pythagorean canon, integers of numbers larger than ten were added together to reflect sacred principle. Here, four plus six yielded ten, the number of divine revelation and perfection.

The number eight, seen in the facades of the temple, was

the octave—the One sounded again, only now as a new note, reached through the manifest world of growth and seeking. Eight is the highest feminine number and is the mark of completion in the creation.

Principles of Construction

There is disagreement about which geometric principles served as the basis for designing and building the Parthenon. The more prevalent view identifies the Golden Proportion as the starting point (see pp. 73–75). Another view sees the circle and its square as the basis of design. Whichever view is favored affirms that the Parthenon was designed according to geometric principle and number proportion (see Fig. 19).

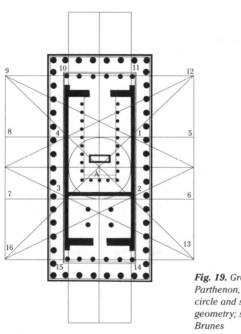

Fig. 19. Ground Plan of Parthenon, Athens, with circle and square geometry; system of Tons Brunes

According to the theory of the Circle and Square, the architects first locate the center or the point from which the form would generate. In this case, that point is now located directly behind the platform of the cult statue, shown in the diagram as Point A. A circle is inscribed, the diameter of which will measure the width (60 Greek feet) between the inside of the *cella* walls. From that circle the exterior square is constructed (1, 2, 3, 4) and from that square, ten more squares are added, making the larger square (9, 12, 13, 16). The base square (1, 2, 3, 4) gives the ruling dimensions of the building.

For the front, or facade, of the temple, the same basic

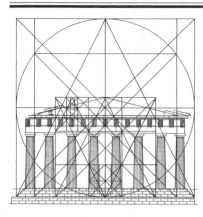

Fig. 20. Front of Parthenon with circle and square geometry: intersections dictate the placement of key temple elements

square is stood on end and used to determine the height of the peak of the roof and the spacing and position of the columns across the front. The doubled square also gives the width of the stylobate and the center point of the pediment. This design principle explains why the space between the two outside columns is smaller than the other column spaces in the facade. On the ground plan the division of the base square into nine smaller squares requires that the final space between the last columns be narrower to account for that geometric pattern, which also gives the edge of the stylobate.

This geometric theory allows a temple design to be generated from a single sacred point on the ground, evolving from unity to manifest form through the expansion of geometric relationships (see Fig. 20). In the case of the Parthenon, the stylobate is 100 Greek feet wide (the Greek foot measuring 12.16 inches relative to the modern foot of 12 inches), the diameter of the initial circle is 60 feet. Sixty marks the width of the *cella* and also the height of the pediment from the bottom step. Thus, the initial diameter fixes the controlling measurement for the entire building.

The other theory of design uses the principle of the Golden Proportion. In this design, the ground plan and facade design both conform to the laws of the Golden Rectangle. A circle is inscribed from the same central point, just behind the cult statue. The diameter of this circle, however, beomes the distance between the center of each exterior column adjacent to the center point. This diameter (which measures about 94 Greek feet) then forms the basis for inscribing an arc based on the square root of five (see Fig. 21). This arc fixes the center points for the four corner columns on the ground plan. This same circle (and its square) also fixes the dimensions of the facade of the temple.

Thus, we see two design principles at work in this structure. In fact, the two working together, the generative and regenerative, determine all the important dimensions of the temple as well as its overall harmony and power. The prin-

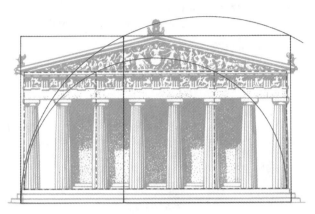

Fig. 21. *Front of Parthenon with Golden Proportions*

ciples of sacred geometry were arranged to produce harmonies that would manifest the qualities of Athena. Belief in the power of geometry meant that sacred knowledge could take form and bring the divine into communion with the human. The temple was the means of bridging the distance between the two worlds, and the bridge was designed using geometric shape, proportion, and number.

The confusion that all this geometry might produce in the mind, whichever plan was used, dissolves in part when we appreciate that a building of this elegance and magnitude was designed using the simplest of tools: a compass, a straight edge, and a line. Of course nothing would have come from simply playing with these tools. The laws of sacred science had to be applied by individuals long exposed to those principles, which had been passed down through the millennia from the temple priests of Egypt and before that from dim origins in the East. In later years these same principles were followed by the architects of the Gothic cathedrals of Europe.

In addition to the geometric arguments, there are also elaborate theories about the Parthenon as an expression of astronomical principle. When Penrose measured the building in 1846, he determined that the two ends of the building measured 100 Greek feet, which corresponds to many ancient descriptions of the building as a *hekatompedon*, or a hundred-foot temple. Penrose then went further. Based on knowledge gathered from Egypt concerning the astronomical measurements of the Great Pyramid as a guide to dimensions of the earth, he determined that the width of the stylobate of the Parthenon was equal to one second of one degree of arc of the circumference of the earth. This correlation is controversial and rejected by many scholars, which speaks to the extraordinary difficulty in duplicating these measurements and the disagreement about the degree of sophistication of the temple builders.

Materials and Decoration

The next step in making the bridge between the divine and the human was the use of appropriate materials and the arts of decoration. The Parthenon is made of the purest white marble, quarried ten miles away on Mount Pentelicus. The marble was checked three times on delivery: for color, for damage in transit, and for grain or natural flaws in the stone. The estimate is that over twenty-two thousand tons of marble were quarried for the Parthenon.

The decoration of the Parthenon was the most ambitious of any temple before its time or afterward. Although the design was essentially Doric, which called for simpler decoration, the architects designed the entablature of the interior colonnade to include a frieze, normally a feature of the Ionic order. The frieze ran around the entire building 40 feet (12 m) above the floor, and was in relative darkness all of the time. Many observers have questioned the common sense of placing a frieze high on an interior entablature where its details could barely be seen. This concern from the human perspective fails to appreciate the sacred intent. The frieze contributes to the whole, to a divine purpose. The temple was Athena's home. It was the gods who saw.

The frieze portrayed the sacred procession in honor of Athena. The idealized subject matter was essentially the same on both long sides and included relief sculptures of horsemen, chariots, elders marching on foot, musicians, tray bearers, and animals for sacrifice. At the west end, horsemen prepared to join the procession, and at the east end, over the entrance, the final presentation of the *peplos* was pictured, in the company of gods, leading citizens, priests, and young maidens. Fragments of the frieze are in the Acropolis Museum, the National Archaeological Museum, and the British Museum in London.

Engraving of frieze section from the Parthenon showing Panathenaic procession

The Parthenon had ninety-two *metopes* (pronounced met-o-peze), or sculpted panels, each measuring 4 feet by 4 feet (1.2 m x 1.2 m). The technical problems of placing the *metopes* were great because they had to be raised and fixed in place on the frieze before the roof elements were set. This arrangement meant that they had to be completed quickly in order to be ready at the right moment, so as not to slow the rest of the work. The estimate is that they were carved between 447 and 442 BC and raised in the latter year. If the work was not completed, a blank marble block was raised and the sculpting was done in situ.

Such a volume of work meant that a large group of artists was involved in the sculpting. The *metopes* were more than reliefs; most were full sculptures of striking detail. A few of the pieces, such as #32 on the north corner, remain in place. The others were removed, some by the infamous Lord Elgin of England while Turkey ruled Greece, and others to preserve them from damage. The Acropolis Museum has one *metope* on view (Room VII, #705).

Although very few *metopes* have survived, we know that the subject matter for most of them was the Battle of the Centaurs. This piece of Athenian legend pitted Theseus and Peirithous the Lapith against the drunken Centaurs, whose coarse actions had disrupted a wedding feast. The subsequent defeat of the Centaurs represented a victory of human aspiration over lower human nature, a victory for the spirit in the fight to control human desire, in this case with help from the gods.

The Pediments

In all probability the last task in completing the temple was the carving and placement of the pediment figures. The record of payments to artists suggests they were completed later

The Parthenon seen from the east, its sacred entrance, Acropolis, Athens

than the other work—in fact they may not have been started until 438 BC. Since these colossal statues were placed individually, there need not have been any pressure of scheduling for their completion.

There were about fifty individual sculptures done for the pediments, an equal number for each end. The western pediment presented the struggle, won by Athena, between the goddess and Poseidon for possession of Athens. The other figures were legendary Athenians, such as Erechtheus and his ancestors. The eastern pediment illustrated the birth of Athena, with Zeus and Athena sharing the central positions and the other Olympians arrayed in harmony on either side.

The artistic achievement of the pediment sculptures can be partially seen in the remaining figures of the eastern pediment. Still clinging to their narrow perch are horses and Helios, the sun god. The figures rest easily and yet spill out of their confined space as if they were not to be restricted to the architectural limitation of a narrow triangular shelf. The effect of so much movement and harmony is to lift the building up and away from its own weight. Other fragments of pediment sculpture may be found in the Acropolis Museum and the National Museum.

Details of Design

As the visitor moves around the Parthenon, absorbing the life of this bridge between two worlds, noticing subtle details can help the attentive observer appreciate the overall effect of grace and harmony. One such detail is the *entasis,* the slight bulge in the circumference of the Doric columns (a third of the way up) as they rise toward the entablature. This bulge, hardly visible to the eye, compensates for the optical illusion of concavity present in perfectly straight columns (see pp. 85–86).

Detail of Parthenon roof construction, showing interlocking tiles, Acropolis, Athens

The columns lean inward slightly just as the roof elements overhang to compensate for the illusion of the columns leaning outward if they were to stand exactly vertical. This slight inward tilt all around means that the blocks that make up the interior walls are ever so slightly trapezoidal—shorter at the top than at the bottom. Thus the building is not "square" in our mechanistic sense of that term.

Separating the *metopes* are triglyphs, marble carvings that suggest patterns of three columns cut in relief. The triglyphs appear to relieve the weight of the frieze as it sits above the architrave. The triglyphs give the illusion of vertical support in a horizontal element. On the top and bottom of the triglyphs are *guttae*, or drops, which suggest pegs or nails. These relieve the harshness of an otherwise uninterrupted horizontal line at the top of the architrave. Finally, along the southern flank of the temple, visitors may examine a display of roof tiles set in position as they were in ancient times.

The archaeological evidence tells us that although the Parthenon was essentially white or the natural color of the marble, the decorative elements were painted in vivid primary colors. The pediment background was red, as was the trim above the architrave and under the frieze. The triglyphs and guttae were deep blue. Our conceptions of so-called "Classical" art should not remain fixed on the faded ivory tones of weather-beaten marble.

The Cult Statue of Athena

When the participants of the sacred procession of the Panathenaia reached the eastern entrance to the Parthenon and entered the huge doors of the *cella,* they were greeted by the colossal cult statue of Athena, sculpted by Phidias and dedicated in 438 BC. The statue was surrounded by colonnades of twenty-three Doric columns, one set on top of the other, making a total of forty-six columns.

Set on a platform 26 feet wide (8 m) and 13 feet deep (4 m), the gold-and-ivory statue rose over 39 feet (12 m). The figure was supported by a huge wooden armature set through the platform into the temple floor. Athena was presented in her long *peplos*, helmeted, holding in her left hand the huge shield and sacred snake. In her right hand, supported by a single column, was a small statue of Winged Victory. Her face and arms were done in ivory, imported from Africa and carefully molded in strips to cover the wooden base. The gold, which was closely guarded and accounted for, was beaten into thin millimeter sheets and inlaid. The gold remained on the statue until 296 BC, when it was removed by the tyrant Lachares to pay his army.

THE ERECTHEION

An important element in the sacred life of the Greeks was the existence and care of the *xoanon*, the ancient cult statue of a patron god. For the Athenians the *xoanon* of Athena Polias,

Engraving of the Erechtheion, showing multilevel design and use of Ionic columns, Acropolis, Athens

the patron goddess of the city, was not the great statue in the Parthenon, but most likely, a small Archaic figure of a sitting goddess carved from stone. The *xoanon* was housed in a place regarded as highly sacred, an ancient sanctuary on the Acropolis now occupied by the Erechtheion.

In the myths of Athens both Athena and Poseidon vied for patronage of the city. One myth tells that Poseidon offered the horse as his gift, and Athena offered her sacred olive tree. The horse reflected the god's power, grace, and swift victory in battle. The olive reflected growth, renewal, and immortality. The olive tree was sacred because it was self-sown and because after the great conflagration of the Persian invasion, the olive sprouted leaves and fruit again after fire had destroyed the Acropolis. Thus, in the courtyard of the Erechtheion Athena's tree stood, walled about in sacred ground.

When Pericles and Phidias planned the new Acropolis, they were greeted with a genuine problem on the site of the Erechtheion. Because of its ancient sacred history, the site had to serve at least four major functions: sanctuary of the *xoanon* of Athena, temple of Poseidon, tomb for Erechtheus, and altars for Zeus Hypatos (a local cult) and Hermes. There were also minor functions. Room had to be made for the olive tree and for altars to Hephaistos and to various heroes.

Principles of Construction

Ralph Waldo Emerson once said, "The pleasure a palace or a temple gives the eye is that an order and a method have been communicated to stones, so that they speak and geometrize, become tender or sublime with expression." The architect of the Erechtheion, perhaps Mnesikles, who also designed the Propylaia, solved the problem of the sloping northern site and the multiple use of the sanctuary by working in several levels and by keeping the structure very "light." That is, he chose the Ionic order with its slim, graceful columns and its unique use of statues as columns, also slim and graceful in their supportive function.

The entire building, which is accessible from four levels and four directions, is held together in geometric harmony through the equilateral triangle. The numbers of columns used throughout the building also create symmetry in an otherwise unbalanced configuration. For example, looking from the west (or from the Propylon) the viewer sees two tall, slender columns supporting the north extension, the four columns of the main temple, and two Karyatides, or *kore* columns, supporting the south porch and balancing the entire side view.

The Karyatides

The six statue-columns that make up the south porch of the Erechtheion represent a brilliant fusion of the arts of architecture and sculpture. Here is an example of the vision of sacred intent worked out in innovative design and individual genius. Because the statues were suffering damage from modern pollution, they were removed in the 1970s and placed in the Acropolis Museum, where they may be admired at close range. The present copies on the site nonetheless allow the visitor to see just how these graceful figures were integrated into the design of the building.

The different levels of the foundation from east to west made it unsuitable to run a colonnade down the southern side of the main temple. The solution of a south porch permitted a softening of the harsh lines of the unrelieved *cella* wall, and the Karyatides were reminiscent of the young girls of Athens who passed by during the Panathenaic festival carrying the *peplos* for the goddess. It appears quite impossible that these slight figures should be able to support the porch roof. Theirs is a graceful power in the service of Athena.

Karyatides columns on the south porch of the Erechtheion, giving the illusion of effortless support of the porch

THE NEW ACROPOLIS MUSEUM

The newly renovated museum sits almost out of sight in its hollow at the southeast corner of the Acropolis and does not draw attention from the Parthenon or obstruct the view of the surrounding landscape. So hidden is it, in fact, that visitors often miss its numerous treasures. The museum houses some of the finest examples of Archaic sculpture in the world, plus several pieces from the Parthenon friezes, *metopes*, and pediments.

The museum provides the observant visitor with an excellent opportunity to appreciate the differences between Archaic and Classical sculpture. The pieces from the Archaic Period, particularly the sixth century BC and early fifth century BC, portray the ideal of spiritual attainment and reality in the human form. As the exhibits move into the Classical Period, the figures become more naturalistic as aspects of individual personality emerge. These changes reflect a shift in the ideas of soul, mind, and consciousness held in the culture during the Classical Period.

Archaic Displays

The first four rooms (marked I-IV) of the museum display remains of Archaic temples and early votive sculpture. The Archaic pediments in Rooms I and II give a vivid picture of the importance of the serpent in Greek religious belief. The dragon was a favorite image of the early Archaic Period and appears again and again in myth and sculpture. The early pediment in Room I, for example, pictures Herakles battling the Lernaean Hydra, a mythical serpent of great power and importance. The Hydra seems to refer to the demonic fertility rites that were brought under control by the labors of Herakles and through the worship of Athena. In more general terms, the dragon stands as a symbol of vanity, which if unmastered will destroy but if mastered serves the hero on his spiritual journey.

The Calf-Bearer, #624 in Room II, is dated to 570 BC and illustrates a sacrifice to Athena. The large figure stands in an attitude of worship with the calf, expressing in his whole being devotion to the goddess. The smile, so typical of the Archaic period, indicates a beatific state. The other Archaic votive sculptures, particularly the *korai* in Room IV, exhibit the same beatific attitude. They are exemplars of devotion and were meant to lead worshipers by their example to the desired state.

The famous Almond-Eyed Kore (#674) in Room IV, like the Kritios Boy in Room VI, stands as a remarkable fusion of Archaic and Classical genius. Her expression, the gentle draping of her garments, the patina of the marble, all indicate loving attention from the artist. Dated to 500 BC, she stands at a critical juncture in the sacred life of the Athenians, which was also a special moment in the history of sculpture. Here is goddess and individual woman, an archetype and also a

Detail of the marble statue of the Almond-Eyed Kore, 500 BC, Acropolis Museum, Athens

person. In the aftermath of the Persian invasion of 480 BC, this and other statues were buried, literally given funeral rites, as a recognition of the sacrilege committed by the invaders. This *kore* lay in the earth for more than two thousand years before it was discovered, along with others, in 1885.

More than any other sculpture in Greece, this *kore* represents the embodiment of spirit in matter. She is both a specific woman and an abstraction. She is the expression of consciousness in a human being, caught by the sculptor's art in a moment of grace. It is a tribute to the museum that she is placed so that visitors may view her from all sides.

The Classical Displays

The break from the so-called idealized strong style of the Archaic Period and the shift to the "severe" style of the early Classical are nowhere more dramatically displayed than in the Kritios Boy, #698 in Room VI. So named because it is most likely a statue by the sculptor Kritios, this figure marks a new vision of being in the spiritual life of the Greeks. The slight break in the right knee drops the right hip, introducing a touch of naturalism. The facial expression of this transitional figure (dated at 485 BC) still holds something of the Archaic idealism, but there is also an emerging individuality that betrays a loss of contact with the spiritual vision and idealism of the Archaic Period.

While the new Classical style seems to reflect a loss in spiritual presence, it marks an interesting shift in consciousness. The new philosophy emphasized the development of the human soul and a more interior journey to divinity. Fresh interest in public debate and intellectual discussion focused more attention on the powers of the human mind *(nous)* and the structure of the human soul *(psyche)*. As has been noted elsewhere, the works of Plato marked the culmination of this

Poseidon, Apollo, and Artemis, from the east frieze of the Parthenon, Acropolis Museum, Athens

new definition of consciousness. The new sculpture began to emphasize the human form as the temple within which more modern ideas of God would be found.

A vivid example of the new style is found in Room VIII of the museum. A panel from the east frieze of the Parthenon shows three gods sitting in human poses. Poseidon speaks to Apollo, who turns to hear what he is saying. Artemis holds

Nike untying her sandal, from the Temple of Athena Nike, Acropolis Museum, Athens

One of the original Karyatides, showing sculpting of hair and clothing elements to accommodate weight-bearing requirements, Acropolis Museum, Athens

her robe over her breasts in maidenly modesty. The naturalism of these figures brings god and human being together. This scene could easily be an aristocratic gathering or a symposium of philosophers.

Also in Room VIII is a lovely, flowing sculpture from the parapet of the Temple of Athena Nike. The graceful, winged figure is pictured untying her sandal, a very human but also devotional act. She is fully draped but still exposed through the transparency of her garment. As a servant to Zeus and to Athena, with whom she is always found, Nike was a transitional divinity, that is, immortal but servant to the gods. She was a beloved figure even through Roman times, perhaps because of her accessibility, situated at a midpoint between the divine and human conditions.

The Karyatides

The last display in the museum is the new home specially created for the Karyatides, which were removed from the Erechtheion south porch to preserve them from the ravages of polluted air and the vibrations of passing aircraft. These column-statues were carefully designed in order to meet contrary needs: to reflect feminine grace and to support tons of entablature. One solution to that problem was to increase the bulk at the neck by the addition of thick plaits of hair, which despite their bulk still fall gracefully down the back. From the front, however, the statues appear to support weight without effort, an effect enhanced by the falling of the chiton in front to expose the neck.

THE THEATER OF DIONYSOS

Beneath the southeast wall of the Acropolis, carved into the hill, lie the remains of the world's most famous theater. Here, during the fifth century BC, the plays of Aeschylus, Sophocles,

Theater of Dionysos, as seen from the wall of the Acropolis, Athens

Euripides, and Aristophanes were performed (see historical overview). Visitors to the Acropolis cannot gain entry to the theater site without leaving the hill and returning to the main avenue, off of which is the gate. After paying the small fee, visitors will appreciate the relative peace and quiet among the trees and ancient stones of this sanctuary, called the Precinct of Dionysos Eleuthereus.

The present remains of the Theater of Dionysos are mostly Roman. However, careful attention to the earlier remains will gradually expose the Classical theater and, earlier than that, the sixth century BC remains of a temple and dancing ground. When dramas were first performed, the stage was a cart that was rolled into place in the Agora, where small audiences could watch the new art form. It is most likely that the first primitive plays, developed it is now believed by the actor/producer Thespis in 534 BC, were performed in the marketplace and were not associated with the worship of Dionysos, at least not with his cult located at the present site.

What took place in the precinct of Dionysos Eleuthereus in the sixth century was probably related to the Dithyramb, the hymns of praise and invocation devoted to Dionysos and performed during his festivals. In particular, the Greater Dionysia was held each year during the month of Elaphebolion (March-April) to celebrate the release from the bondage of winter and the gifts and powers of new life. Groups of young men sang and danced in honor of the god on the dancing floor, which was a large circle 66 feet (20 m) in diameter in its earliest form. It had an altar at its center. The smooth dirt floor was carved from the hillside and supported by a terrace.

Behind this dancing floor stood a small temple of Dionysos. A few *poros* stones from that temple form part of the later Periclean hall. This small temple, built *in antis,* faced to the east and measured 44 feet (13.4 m) long and 26 feet

(8 m) wide , with two columns at the entrance.

Beginning with the plays of Aeschylus in the 470s BC, the theater as we know it made its debut. The early "cart dramas" and the sacred Dithyramb were combined to create a new, powerful art form. To accommodate this new form, just behind the circular dancing floor (now called the orchestra) there must have been a modest scene building (or *skene*), which provided the actors with a place to change costumes and masks and a place to portray interior scenes.

The audience sat on the terraced hillside on wooden benches or wooden planks set into the hillside. The orchestra with its central altar was simply packed dirt, and the modest wooden scene building provided the necessary backdrop to the action. Behind the *skene* could be seen the small temple of Dionysos, also modest in its appearance.

When the Acropolis was renovated during the time of Pericles, the theater also received attention—a measure of the high regard in which drama was held. The orchestra had to be moved north, toward the Acropolis walls, to provide for the new scene building, which was deeper and wider than the previous and may have had three doors with a deeper raised stage supported on a stone foundation. The *skene* was provided with a device called an *ekkyklema*, a platform that could be rolled out of the central doors to reveal an interior scene—usually the bodies of those who died offstage. The *skene* also had a roof that supported the *mechane*, a sort of a crane that revealed and sometimes lowered gods to the stage from above. From this crane came the Latin term *deus ex machina* to refer to godlike solutions to insoluble human problems.

Thus, at the height of Classical tragedy, the theater had a wooden scene building with a raised stage, three sets of doors, a round orchestra with central altar, and an auditorium of wooden seats rising up the hillside toward the Acropolis wall. It was in this theater that the great tragic poets developed their craft and the comic poets hurled insults at all the noted figures of the time, including the great lover of wisdom himself, Socrates.

Pericles also built the Odeion, the remains of which can still be located to the east of the theater above the auditorium. Greek engineers are currently renovating this site. The huge square building was modeled after the famous tent of the Persian king Xerxes, who was defeated by the Greeks and whose opulent shelter was a prize of war. The Odeion measured over 200 feet by 225 feet (62 m by 68 m), and the centrally peaked roof was supported by an inner colonnade. During the Greater Dionysia, the Odeion was used for musical contests in honor of the god.

During the time of Lycurgus (338 to 326 BC) further work was done on the theater. The stone auditorium was constructed at this time, essentially as we see it today except for the later Roman additions in the front rows. The retaining walls on either side were built and the seating area extended up the slope to accommodate audiences of over fourteen thousand.

In the late Hellenistic period (the late second century BC), a permanent stone *skene* was constructed, most likely of two stories, the second set back so as to provide a wide stage for the actors. On the ground level three doors opened onto the orchestra. There is a good deal of earnest debate on the subject of raised stages in the Greek theater. The physical evidence for them is scarce because any wooden elements would not have survived anyway, but the plays argue well for their use from the fifth century BC onward.

The many changes during the Roman period have been difficult to trace. During the Imperial era the orchestra was paved and cut off to accommodate an expanded scene building. One inscription dates this work at AD 61. The new skene and *proskenion* (proscenium) construction presented a high, elaborate facade, now partially echoed in the backdrop of the Odeion of Herod Atticus nearby. Many of the marble carvings scattered about the site belong to the Roman period.

An indication of the desecration of the theater and abandonment of its sacred and religious function during the Imperial Period is the evidence of stone and cementing work ringing the orchestra, which made the area watertight in order to accommodate sea battles and other spectacles popular during that time. The neglect of this important site is partially explained by its Roman character. Some day, perhaps, a restoration of the Classical original may be attempted.

THE SACRED LIFE OF DRAMA

The importance of the Theater of Dionysos lies in the genius of its first poets, those who understood that this new form called tragedy could serve a spiritual purpose. The myths employed by Aeschylus, Sophocles, and Euripides were transformed into experiences designed to move people and to lift them away from the deadening habits of ordinary life. The plays spoke the truth of human existence and sang of the cost in suffering for those who sought wisdom and justice without the aid of the gods.

The plays written between 450 and 400 BC were approximately fifteen hundred lines long and lasted under two hours. They were composed in verse of varying meters and lengths. With a few exceptions the thirty-three complete tragedies we have left of the thousands that were performed have certain fundamental unities. The action took place in one day, in fact often in a few hours, close to the actual running time of the play. They took place in one setting, usually before the king's palace but sometimes on an island or on the beach at Troy. The plays were structured in patterns of dialogue and choral odes intended to lead the attentive listener through an emotional, intellectual, and spiritual *agon*, or conflict, resulting in catharsis.

This purging of the emotions, accomplished by watching a tragic figure struggle with his or her growing understanding of the world and the ways of the gods, was religious in the very best sense. To effectively achieve these ends, actors were trained in music and movement. They each played several characters during the course of the play, now a king and now a prophet, spinning out the beautiful rhythms of Greek speech and sounding the cries of agonized self-knowledge. To magnify their work, the actors stood in high boots and wore vivid masks that had built into them a sort of megaphone to project the voice to the ten thousand or more spectators in attendance.

The tragic plays were performed from sunrise to sunset over three days during the Greater Dionysia, a genuine marathon of drama. Three tragic poets were chosen each year to produce three plays each and were assigned actors and chorus by the *archon*, or festival leader, for the year. The chorus members rehearsed for months and were supported financially by wealthy citizens of the city. Judges awarded first, second, and third prizes based on the overall quality of the three plays presented. On the fourth day the comic poets had their turn, releasing the tensions of the previous three days with bawdy, raucous plays that celebrated freedom from the necessities of a difficult life and often satirized the absurdities of politics.

VISITING THE SITE

Although difficult to find, the remnants of the Classical theater do exist. Just within the gate on the right, for example, is the foundation of the altar at which offerings were made to the god. On the left are the foundations of the later Temple of Dionysos built in the Classical Period. Behind it, along the walls of the early Classical hall, are a dozen or so stones from the Early Archaic temple, including a cornerstone at the northwest corner.

In front of the foundations of the Roman scene building, on the right side of the orchestra near the water channel that drained the theater, is an arc of six stones of the wall that supported the terrace of the earliest dancing floor. From this point the observer is able to sense how far back from the present orchestra the original one must have been. On either side of the present orchestra are the retaining walls from the Periclean construction. These walls indicate where the entrance ways, called *paradoi*, were located.

The throne-like marble chairs are from the Roman period but are most likely accurate copies of similar chairs of honor from the fourth century BC. There were originally sixty-seven such thrones in place. The center throne was for the priest of Dionysos and was elaborately carved. We are able to make out two satyrs, two griffins, and several human figures. The other thrones were for various dignitaries whose names were inscribed on the backs.

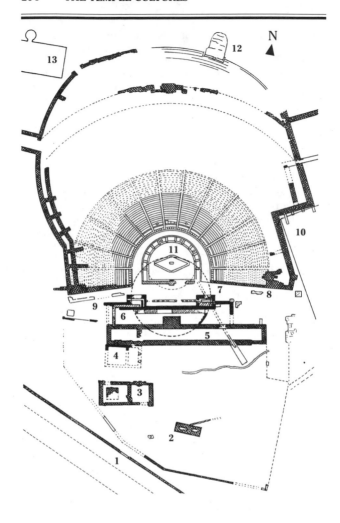

Fig. 22. *Theater of Dionysos, Athens*
  1. *Entrance to Site*
  2. *Altar*
  3. *Later Temple*
  4. *Archaic Temple*
  5. *Hall*
  6. *Skene*
  7. *Circle of Classical Orchestra*
  8. *East Parados*
  9. *West Parados*
  10. *Odeion of Pericles*
  11. *Roman Remains*
  12. *Monument of Thrasyllos*

LATER MONUMENTS

High up in the orchestra, carved into the Acropolis rock, is the Monument of Thrasyllos, erected in 319 BC to celebrate the victories in the Dithyramb won by the poet. The placement of this monument marks the extent of the stone auditorium of the Late Classical Period. To sit for a few moments at this height gives a sense of the size of the ancient theater and the size of the actors' task to communicate by voice and movement the content of the plays. In 270 BC the son of Thrasyllos, named Thrasykles, celebrated his own victories in drama by building bases for victory tripods. Later still, during Roman times, the two tall columns were erected for the same purpose.

Cutting through the upper rows of the auditorium is the main road that circles the Acropolis. Called the *peripatos*, this road passed through the upper retaining wall and down a fairly steep ramp to the Asklepieion. The modern visitor must scramble around the ruins of the wall and climb up the slope to reach the road.

THE ASKLEPIEION

In 419 BC a private citizen named Telemachos gave funds for the purchase of land and the construction of a modest Asklepieion, or healing sanctuary, near the sacred spring that for years had provided fresh water for this site. Telemachos must have been a friend of the poet Sophocles, whose interest in healing and willingness to house the sacred snake of Asklepios have been documented. Sophocles knew that there was a close relationship between drama and healing. The intent of drama was to heal, to bring the individual to a unity of body, mind, and spirit through the movements, speech, and rhythms of the play.

The Asklepieion as seen from the Acropolis wall, Athens

The Temple of Asklepios within the sanctuary of the Asklepieion, Athens

At that time, the cult of Asklepios had been firmly established in hundreds of centers throughout Greece and the Aegean. Here in Athens, the establishment of a minor Asklepieion near the theater was a natural enough culmination of the ancient connection between the healing arts of drama and the cult of Asklepios.

The original fifth century BC Asklepieion was made from wood and probably included only the bare minimum necessary to provide for the rituals of purification, sacrifice, and healing.

Later, in the fourth century BC, more substantial stone buildings were erected. These included temples to Asklepios and Hygieia (goddess of health), an altar, a *propylon,* and the important *abaton,* where patients slept to induce healing dreams. The *abaton* was a two-storied Doric stoa and was an ambitious structure for this site, enclosing as it did an ancient spring and a sacred offering pit, which suggests something of the chthonic qualities of this cult.

The sacred spring is now enclosed behind a wall that probably dates from the sixth century AD, when a Christian basilica was constructed right over the former temple and *abaton.* The Christian church continued the tradition of healing, however, as it was dedicated to the *aghioi anargyroi*, or doctor saints.

The visitor to the present site will have little difficulty finding the various remains. They are indicated clearly by stone markers. The only obscure site may be the *propylon,* which is along the road to the west. Today, during quiet times, usually early or late in the day, it is not surprising to find Greek pilgrims beneath the sheltering trees close to the sacred spring, sitting in meditation. This area still has aspects of holiness, and visitors are urged to approach "in a sacred manner."

OTHER MINOR SITES

THE ODEION OF HEROD ATTICUS

Brief mention here should be made of the amphitheater that dominates the southwestern slope of the Acropolis. As the *peripatos* winds around the rock from the east, it passes through a huge stoa, the remains of which extend almost to the Theater of Dionysos. This is the Stoa of Eumenes II of Pergamon, who built it in the second century BC. Connected to it is the Odeion, built by Tiberius Claudius Herodes Atticus much later, in the second century AD. Atticus was a Greek orator, amateur philosopher, and possessor of great wealth. In his admiration for Athens he gave some of his wealth for the construction of the Odeion, which still serves the public as a theater and concert hall.

THE AREOPAGUS

To the west of the Acropolis across the saddle that now is crisscrossed with paved walks and refreshment stands is the Areopagus, the small hill where the ancient Council of Areopagus met to rule on matters of justice. It was here in legend that Orestes pleaded his case before the council and won acquittal by the tie-breaking vote of Athena. It was also here in AD 51 that Saint Paul preached the new gospel to the Athenians.

In Archaic and early Classical times the Council of Areopagus was very powerful. Its life members, the Areopagites, were chosen for their good character and judgment. To the Greeks of this time the issue of justice, or *dike,* stood before all other questions in the life of the *polis*. The word encompassed a broad spectrum of concerns, including the nature of divine justice as well as issues of social behavior and fairness. Within the concept of *dike* was contained the meaning of human action, divine retribution, and immortality.

A walk around the hill today is like a stroll in the country. Paths wind through the trees, caves invite curious investigation, and the hilltop rock yields a fine view of the Acropolis and Agora. Little remains of any construction, and archaeologists still debate the locations of key buildings. We do know that during the Bronze Age the Areopagus was a burial ground. Several Mycenaean chamber tombs have been discovered, the contents of which are now displayed in the Agora Museum. The tombs were refilled after excavation because of the instability of the rock and surrounding slope.

THE PNYX

A ten-minute walk from the Areopagus is the Pynx, the next hill to the southwest, where the Athenian Assembly met to debate questions of public policy. Only the stone steps of the place of assembly still remain, but the hill affords a fine view

Funeral stele from Athens, called the Ilissos. These stele are similar to tombstones and were either inscribed or sculpted.

of the Acropolis. It is from this site in the summer that the Light and Sound Show is performed. This tourist attraction yields little but dramatic lighting effects and explains why visitors to the Acropolis encounter junction boxes, cables, and instruments in awkward places.

THE KERAMEIKOS

To the north of the Pnyx and the Agora lies the Kerameikos, the ancient cemetery of Athens. This site is especially interesting on two counts. First, it is the location of the important Dipylon (or double) Gate and of the Sacred Gate, the beginning of the Sacred Way to Eleusis. Second, it is the main source of information about ancient burial practices after the Bronze Age.

With the decline of the Mycenaean palaces, the practice of building and maintaining family tombs also declined, to be replaced after the Dark Age by single burials and cremation. We have learned from excavation at the Kerameikos that about two-thirds of the burials involved cremation urns. The pattern, especially in Classical and Hellenistic times, was for the family to place a *stele* (stee-lee), or decorated marble plaque, over the burial mound, which was usually a simple pit lined with stone. The cremation urns were also buried in similar pits. Some of the *stele* are fine examples of relief sculpture and are on display in the small museum on the site.

Although family tombs were no longer in use after the Bronze Age, there remained in the culture a strong emphasis on family mourning, with expensive funerals and elaborate honors for the dead. So excessive were these funerals on occasion that laws were finally passed regulating expenditure, number of mourners, and lavishness of monuments. Such laws indicate the excesses to which some families extended themselves to promote the family name and position in Athenian society.

Visitors to the Kerameikos pay a small fee at the entrance, which gives access to the grounds and to the museum. The view to the south (facing the Acropolis), or toward the remains of the Dipylon Gate, reveals as in no other place the magnificence of that Gate, the main entrance to the city. Next to the Dipylon Gate is the Sacred Gate, used only for formal processions and particularly for the mass march to Eleusis for the Mysteries. For those interested in the details of the Kerameikos area, a detailed map is available at the ticket booth.

THE TEMPLE OF OLYMPIAN ZEUS

The area known as the Olympieion is an enclosure that includes the Arch of Hadrian, the Temple of Olympian Zeus, and the remains of many ancient buildings that once lined the famous Ilissos River, which now runs underground through the modern city. The Temple of Zeus was the largest temple built on mainland Greece. Measuring 362 feet (101.4 m) by 143 feet (43.5 m), the temple had 104 Corinthian columns, 13 of which remain standing. The great temple was begun by the Peisistratid tyrants in 515 BC, although nothing of their particular effort now remains.

In 174 BC, King Antiochus IV of Syria sought to complete the temple, changing the design to include the Corinthian order. After ten years work ceased, not to begin again for several hundred years. Completed in AD 131 by Hadrian, the temple finally achieved its purpose, although late and without strong association with Greek culture. The record indicates minimal enthusiasm for the project.

Engraving of Temple of Zeus, with the Parthenon in the background, Athens

THE AGORA

> *Look upon the dance, Olympians,*
> *Send us the grace of Victory, ye gods,*
> *Who come to the heart of our city*
> *Where many feet are treading and incense steams;*
> *In sacred Athens come to the Market-place,*
> *By every art enriched and of blessed name.*

— Pindar, *Spring Dithyramb*

Whereas the Acropolis has always represented the spiritual soul of Athenian life, the Agora, or ancient marketplace, has represented her mind and body. After the Bronze Age, as Athens emerged from the Dark Age, the Agora gradually became the center of daily life. Here the laws were written and displayed, commercial goods and crafts bought and sold, and the democratic spirit born and nurtured. In the poem above we sense something of the special spirit of the Agora, which lived in the hearts of the Athenians.

A visit to the Agora captures more of the life of ancient Athens than can be found anywhere else. Although the area is much overgrown with trees and shrubs these days, the diligent seeker will still find treasures here. The site may be reached from three different directions: from Plateia Theseiou to the west, from Hadrian Street to the north, and from the southeast. We will begin from the southeast entrance just below the Acropolis wall, an easy walk down the path from the Propylaia. The American School of Classical Studies at Athens runs this excavation and has prepared excellent guides to the area. Our purpose will be to focus on the Archaic and Classical Agora and to indicate something of its sacred life.

HISTORY

The history of this small area has produced a rich source of archaeological records. As is the case in most excavations in Greece, the record begins in the Neolithic Period, about 3000 BC. Chamber tombs from that time were discovered in the Areopagus slope. Further digging in this area revealed Mycenaean grave sites, plus graves from the later Geometric Period (900-700 BC).

In the Archaic Period the area just below the future site of the Temple of Hephaistos developed as the center of Athenian civic and economic life. Ground plans for the Agora in 500 BC show the area beneath the small hill called Kolonos Agoraios to be devoted to civic and religious buildings. In addition to a large square building called the *bouleuterion,* or council house, there were small temples to Meter (another name for the Earth Mother) and to Apollo, a shrine to Zeus, and farther north the Altar of the Twelve Gods and the royal stoa. Also were to be found the first *heliaia*, or law court, and the ancient fountain house.

In the fifth century BC growth in the Agora was rapid, with many additional buildings constructed to meet the needs of the growing city. The Temple of Hephaistos was begun in 444 BC and completed around 415 BC. The Tholos, or round temple, was constructed, as was a new council house. New and commodious stoas and a circular orchestra appeared in the center of the grounds in a space later to be occupied by a temple to Ares.

During the Roman era the appearance of the Agora began to reflect the authority and values of an alien presence. Buildings were erected to glorify various Roman emperors or governors, as well as Roman deities. Because of general crowding, construction shifted to the east, where the Roman Agora has now been excavated. Beginning in AD 267 a series of destructive attacks leveled most of the buildings with the exception of the Temple of Hephaistos, which fortunately for us has managed to survive almost intact. From the Byzantine era on, the Agora slowly became a residential area until serious excavation began in 1931, when over three hundred private houses were torn down to permit work to begin on the site.

ARCHAIC AND CLASSICAL REMAINS

Beginning at the southeast entrance to the Agora site (see Fig. 23), the visitor is greeted with the long stretch of the Panathenaic Way, the route of the procession of the major religious festival in the Athenian year. The road enters the Agora from the north at the Dipylon Gate in the distance, where the procession formed. The Panathenaic Way is not the same as the Sacred Way to Eleusis. The two roads more or less converge at the northern boundary of the Agora, where

Remains of the Eleusinion sanctuary in the Agora, Athens

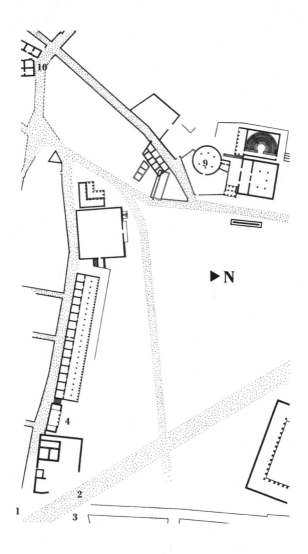

Fig. 23. *The Agora, Athens, fourth century BC*
1. Southeast Entrance
2. Panathenaic Way
3. The Eleusinion
4. Southeast Fountain House
5. Altar of the Twelve Gods

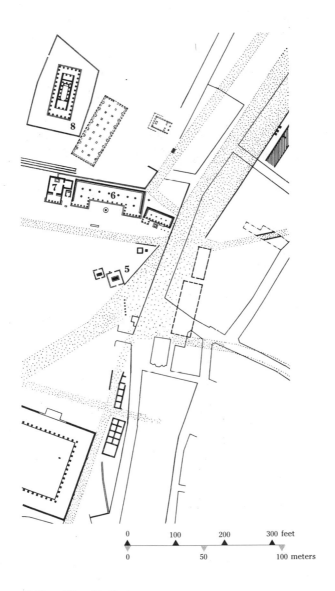

0   100   200   300 feet

0   50   100 meters

6. *Stoa of Zeus Eleutherios*
7. *Temple of Apollo Patroos*
8. *Temple of Hephaistos*
9. *Tholos*
10. *State Prison (suggested)*

the Panathenaic Way becomes the main road through the ancient city. Ancient records indicate that the Athenians may well have used this road for horse racing during the festival games.

The Eleusinion

A most sacred structure in the Agora was the Eleusinion, the sanctuary devoted to the Lesser Mysteries in Athens (see Fig. 24). Each year, sacrifices were made here to Demeter and Kore (Persephone), and sacred objects were stored for a time before the procession to Eleusis began on the nineteenth day of Boedromion (September 27 or 28) in celebration of the Greater Mysteries. Records indicate that the Council of 500 met at the Eleusinion on the day following the Mysteries when the initiates had returned to Athens.

The sanctuary is on the east, or the right as the visitor looks down the road into the Agora site. A break in the wall with a stone threshold marks the position of the ancient Propylon. Since very little work has been done on this site recently, the foundations of the temple are obscured by deep grass. Evidence points to the early fifth century BC as the likely date of construction of this small temple. Though small, it was well placed and could easily be seen as a dominant feature even though it sat in the shadow of the Acropolis. As the plan indicates, below the temple was a lower sanctuary con-

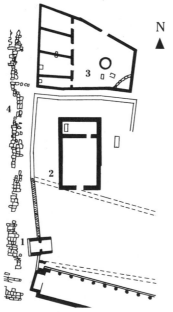

Fig. 24. Eleusinion, Athens
1. Propylon
2. Temple of Demeter
3. Priests' Quarters
4. Panathenaic Way

taining a building with four rooms and a round pit or altar. The lower building may well have been designed for the storage of objects sacred to the Mysteries and for the use of the priests.

Some of the mystery surrounding this sanctuary is reflected in the reference to it from Pausanius. As he passed through the Agora toward the Eleusinion, Pausanius began a story of Eleusis, in particular the lineage of Triptolemos, but he stopped his account in deference to the sacredness of the Mysteries:

> I wanted to go on with this story and describe the contents of the Athenian sanctuary called the Eleusinion, but I was stopped by something I saw in a dream. I must turn to the things it is not irreligious to write for general readers. In front of this shrine, where also is the image of Triptolemos, you see a bronze steer being led to sacrifice. Epimenides of Knossos is there too, sitting down. They say he was out in the country one day and went into a cave to sleep, and sleep kept him there until he had slumbered away for forty years, and afterwards he wrote poems and purified cities, Athens with the others.

In the Agora Museum visitors will find remnants of a *stele* discovered in the Eleusinion on which are inscribed the details of the sale of property belonging to Alkibiades, the infamous aristocrat and student of Socrates who was exiled in 415 BC for sacrilege to the Eleusinian Mysteries. He was probably discovered serving the sacred drink, the *kykeion* (about which we shall have more to say), in violation of the priests' control over its use. The confiscation of his property and subsequent vilification are indicative of the sacredness of these ceremonies and the beliefs that lay behind them. That a number of *stele* were erected in the Eleusinion in silent witness to this event indicates the concern of those in power that no further mockery of the Mysteries take place.

The Southeast Fountain House

Visiting the Agora is much like walking around inside a puzzle, particularly if the seeker wishes to find those hidden pieces that are the most ancient. The archaeological method is to work down through the layers imposed by years of shifting debris, disasters, deliberate rearranging of elements, collapse from one level to another, recording what each inch reveals. After that process is completed down to bedrock the guesswork begins. What was found? What should be left in place? What are the dates? Is the information reliable? What corollary evidence is there to support identification of a find?

In the case of the fountain houses in the Agora, there have been many arguments. The literary record indicates that a fountain house of sacred importance was situated in Athens, and archaeologists have supposed that it was located in the Agora. In the 1930s the square fountain house in the southwest corner of the Agora was identified as the one in question.

Twenty years later, however, the Southeast Fountain House was uncovered and subsequently has been identified as the important one.

We can say now that what Pausanius describes as "nine-springs" is located just behind the Church of the Holy Apostles on the left just down the road. Nine-Springs was in use from Archaic times as a source of water for daily use and a place where those who wished for special blessings went to bathe.

The foundations of the Fountain House are difficult to distinguish. They show it to have been a rectangular building 60 feet (18 m) long and 23 feet (7 m) wide. Its northern entrance was framed by three columns. Although in early times the fountain was no doubt fed by a natural spring, later, when the demand for water was greater, a pipeline ran to it from a more plentiful source. A large earthen pipeline, still visible, ran beneath the Panathenaic Way, past the Eleusinion, and fed the nine spouts, which if urn drawings are accurate, were in the shape of animal heads.

Altar of the Twelve Gods

At the end of the Panathenaic Way is the northern entrance to the Agora. One of the site plans of the Agora is located there for the convenience of visitors. The plan of the northern section reveals that from Archaic times an Altar to the Twelve Gods and the *eschara*, or underground altar, were located here. The famous Altar of the Twelve Gods will be hard to locate since its foundations now rest mostly within the railroad right-of-way, but a corner of it may be found near the retaining wall. This altar was important in ancient times not only for its dedication to the Olympians but also because from this spot all distances to other cities and important sites were measured.

Temple of Hephaistos

Hephaistos was the crippled god, cast out by Hera from the beauty and perfection of heaven to dwell in the caverns of the sea, where he transformed the substance of the earth into that selfsame beauty and perfection. He was the god of the artisans, a role he shared with Athena as patron of artists. For the worship of both gods the Athenians erected this temple (444–416 BC), known also as the Theseion, for Theseus, legendary king of Athens. The Temple of Hephaistos has survived for over two thousand years because, like the god it represented, it continued to serve the masters who possessed the Agora from age to age until, ironically, it survives as the least crippled temple in Greece.

Approximately half the size of the Parthenon, the Temple of Hephaistos is of the Doric order, with six columns on the short sides and thirteen on the long, following the usual formula of the long side having twice the columns of the short side plus one. The total number of columns is thirty-four, which in Greek numerology equals seven, the sacred number

Temple of Hephaistos seen from the point of approach, the Agora, Athens

of divine completion. The placement of the temple makes it clear that it was designed to be approached from below, in front of the eastern facade. When completed, the Temple of Hephaistos contained cult statues of Athena and Hephaistos made by Alkamenes. The temple featured *metopes*, but more modest ones than those in the Parthenon, and they were made only for the eastern facade and the near panels on the north and south, again confirming the limited perspective planned for the building. The carvings were of the nine labors of Herakles, plus four featuring Theseus. Inside the peristyle above the *pronaos,* the frieze also featured the labors of Theseus, the dramatic nature of which resulted in the temple

Side view of the Temple of Hephaistos, showing its excellent state of pres-ervation, the Agora, Athens

becoming known in its time as the Theseion.

As visitors descend by the southern path from the temple, they may wish to stop at the Agora plan thoughtfully provided at this slightly raised location. It affords an opportunity to locate prominent features and to try to imagine what the site might have looked like in the Classical Period. Unfortunately, tall trees and numerous bushes now obscure many features of the site.

The Tholos

It is not surprising that the Classical Greeks would establish their seat of government in a round building. As mysterious as these round buildings are to us—here, in Delphi, and at Epidauros—it seems clear that they were always regarded as sacred. The functions associated with them include sacrificial pits and cult centers for local heroes and gods. It was in the Tholos that the ruling council met to eat, to be paid, and to sleep, so that someone of the ruling council would always be available in emergencies.

Attentive visitors will find several foundation stones of the Tholos plus three bases of the six interior columns that held up the peaked roof. In addition, there are the remains of an Archaic *tholos* to the south of the Classical site, which also included several other important buildings, all devoted to the administration of the city.

The State Prison

Of particular interest to lovers of Socrates and Plato is the site of the State Prison in the Agora, where Socrates was confined for a month between his conviction by the Athenian Assembly and his death in 399 BC. Tentative identification of this site was made only recently, using as evidence the age, size, and structure of the building, the supporting literary evidence from Plato's dialogue *Phaedo*, and the discovery in one of the rooms of thirteen small vials typical of those used to contain poison.

The supposed prison site is located in the southwestern corner of the Agora. The ruins are now merely foundation stones just above the ground, and the building is located just below and to the west of some prominent Roman ruins. In the northernmost room there is visible the rim of a large *amphora* which might have been used as a bathing tub by prisoners, as we note in the *Phaedo:* "When he had spoken these words, he arose and went into the bath-chamber with Crito." After his bath, late in the afternoon, as the sun touched the western hills, Socrates drank the portion of hemlock and soon died, saying, "Crito, I owe a cock to Asklepios, will you remember to pay the debt?" It was the custom for those cured of an illness to pay the priests of the healing god Asklepios a cock. Having been cured of the disease of life, Socrates cleared his debts and departed for the next world.

The Agora Museum

The Stoa of Attalos was an important addition to the Agora in the second century BC, a gift of King Attalos II of Pergamon. Restored completely by the American School, it now houses many valuable finds from the Agora excavations and serves as well as the center of archaeological research and storage at the site. Visitors are welcome to visit the main exhibit area on the ground floor and the colonnade of the upper floor, where models are exhibited of the Acropolis and Pnyx. The second floor also affords a comprehensive view of the site and is a pleasing vantage point from which to conclude a visit to the Agora.

The obvious delight of a visit to the Stoa of Attalos is simply the reward of being in a completely restored ancient building: to sense its comfortable size, to feel the expansive luxury of its openness, and to experience the movement of light and air through its colonnades. Here is a building designed for human use that gives its inhabitants the stature idealized in sculpture and immortalized in images of the gods.

The museum contains a chronological ordering of artifacts from Neolithic to Turkish times—a span of nearly four thousand years. There are sixty-three exhibits in the main gallery, plus the sculptures in the ground floor colonnade and the terrace.

One of the notable finds in the Agora was the monumental marble Apollo Patroos (unearthed in 1907), the cult statue from the small temple located below the Temple of Hephaistos. The Apollo is one of the few larger-than-life sculptures extant in Greece and, despite its fragmentary condition, still communicates a sense of power. Also in the colonnade is the lovely marble Nereid, which may well have come from the Temple of Hephaistos. This graceful female figure shows the movement possible in sculpture, in particular for those pieces placed high on temple pediments where their garments were eternally ruffled by the breeze.

In the main gallery are the various burial displays from the Mycenaean Period and displays of changing burial practices through the Archaic Period. Also of great interest is the mold for a bronze statue in Case #23. This exhibit was carefully reassembled from a molding pit found at the western edge of the Agora, and it shows the various stages and difficulties encountered by those artisans who worked with metals. Case #36 contains a particularly beautiful bronze of Nike dated between 420 and 415 BC as an example of the art of casting. Far from being lapses in technique, the channels visible in the bronze work were provided as anchors for gold and silver sheets that covered the head originally.

THE NATIONAL ARCHAEOLOGICAL MUSEUM

A visit to this impressive collection of treasures demands both time and focused attention, the latter in particular because the exhibits are close together, and some can be missed simply in the profusion of riches. As is true of all the sections on museums in this guide, the purpose here is to mention just some of the high points of the collection. The museum has a number of impressive full-color guides to the complete collection, all reasonably priced.

The museum is laid out in wonderful symmetry. The central hall, Room #4, contains the impressive Mycenaean collection, including the famous Schliemann gold treasures: masks, cups, and jewelry. On the left is Room #5, the Neolithic collection, and to the right is Room #6, which contains the Cycladic collection. Beginning in Room #21 and moving in both directions (Rooms #7-31 and 34) are the Archaic, Classical, and Hellenistic collections of sculpture. Rooms #36–40 house the bronzes, and Rooms #41–43 the Roman sculpture.

ROOM #4, THE MYCENAEAN COLLECTION

In Case #1 in Room #4 are important items of gold and silver found in Mycenaean tombs. Of special interest are the gold seal-rings, which give us glimpses of religious and secular life. The Minoan Pantheon, item #992, shows four female figures, one either a goddess or priestess, surrounded with Minoan religious symbols, including the double ax, the sun and moon, the figure-eight shield, and poppies. It is from small but vivid portraits such as these that we have gained our very limited knowledge of Minoan religious belief.

The gold bull with disks and the bull rhyton illustrate the practices of sacrifice in Mycenaean and Minoan culture. The sacrificial animals were elaborately decorated in gold. In particular, the horns were often gilded. Also in this case is a grave *stele* from Mycenae inscribed with the typical and important spiral designs so often seen in room decoration. The spirals evoke images of the labyrinth and the initiatory rituals of Minoan religious practice.

In Case #3 are the five gold death masks found by Schliemann at Mycenae. These masks reflect the wealth of the palace cultures and the importance of the cult of the dead in Mycenaean religious ritual. The mask wrongly identified by Schliemann as Agamemnon's is #624. Subsequent study has dated this mask nearer 1550 BC, a date much earlier than the period when Agamemnon would have occupied the throne of Mycenae.

The fresco fragment in Case #14 is an outstanding example of Mycenaean artistry. Close examination of the black lines that outline the figure show that the artist worked the wall with great control. The line of the upper arm, for example, moves in one perfect curve from elbow to the tip of the index finger. Such control is extremely difficult, particularly in fresco

The gold death mask attributed by Schliemann to the body of Agamemnon. This mask, however, belongs to a much earlier period.

painting. The attention to the task here demonstrates a high degree of sophistication, which is sometimes lost in our fixation on the representational in art.

Both the quality and the delicacy of the work on view in this room support the assessments made of the advanced state of Mycenaean culture. One can see in these artifacts the great care and precision that resulted in structures like the beehive tombs and the other monumental architecture left to us at Mycenae. Here was a culture of sensitivity and depth as well as military power and grandeur.

ROOM #6, THE CYCLADIC COLLECTION

The Cyclades are those islands in the Aegean Sea that form a rough circle around the sacred island of Delos, traditional birthplace of Apollo. "Cycladic culture" refers to the period between 3200 and 1100 BC, when most of the artifacts in this collection were produced. Much disagreement centers on the nature and significance of the female figurines in this room. The controversy is over their possible identification with the Earth Mother cults that probably existed elsewhere in the Neolithic Period and the function and use of the figurines in connection with those cults. Some observers believe that these figures are simply primitive in execution, the "best" that artisans could accomplish.

Those who argue that these figures represent divinities or sacred subjects point out the emphasis upon geometric principles in the design: the triangular heads, torso, and genitalia and the circular patterns on breasts and hips. Since greater realism was certainly possible, they argue, the abstract qualities of the design suggest divine qualities rather than human features. Abstraction of form points to function rather than feature.

A compromise position suggests that these figures represent human beings in various postures of worship. The folded arms remind us of the frescoes from Knossos showing worshipers during religious rituals. And since many of these figurines were found in graves, there is the logical conclusion that they were placed as tokens to guide the deceased on to the next world.

These early examples of sculpture point out once again the extraordinary skill and power of so-called primitive work. Time spent in this room softens a little our modern arrogance. The clear superiority of this work over most representative modern art suggests that human beings have lost touch with certain principles and forgotten the power of abstraction.

ROOMS #7-13, ARCHAIC SCULPTURE

A short detour back through the lobby (keep your ticket stub handy) will bring you to the Archaic collection, a jump of five hundred years but only a step in conception and brilliant articulation. Special attention should be given to the various *kouroi*, one of the finest collections in the world of these idealized male youths.

One sees the powerful symmetry in these visionary expressions of humanity. Our eye lingers on these figures because they so clearly express the laws of balance and symmetry in the one form we know so well: our own. The finest example of geometric and sacred principle applied to a *kouros* is in Room #13, the Kouros of Croesus (#3851), dated at 520 BC. We see here balance, power, serenity. unity, and wholeness. The figure does not represent a particular individual, even though it was dedicated to a real youth named Croesus who died in battle. The figure transcends personality while typifying the ideals of human achievement.

ROOMS #14-21, CLASSICAL SCULPTURE

Room #15 contains two of the great treasures of the Classical Period: the bronze Poseidon (#15161) and the relief of the Eleusinian Mysteries (#126). The Poseidon bronze is dated to 460 BC and was recovered in 1928 from the sea off the coast of Euboea. Comparison of the Kouros of Croesus with the Poseidon, an idealized portrait of a god, shows the development of sculpture from the Late Archaic to the Early Classical Period. Poseidon has individuality and is recognizable as the god. He is pictured in action, throwing his trident, whereas the Kouros stands in perfect stillness.

The famous Eleusinian relief showing Demeter on the right and Persephone (Kore) on the left giving a shaft of grain to Triptolemos is a brilliant example of relief sculpture. The figures appear quite full even though they protrude only slightly from the background. The two goddesses look with great affection at the boy who will bring the Mysteries to humanity. Demeter's motherly gesture in touching

Triptolemos, probably in benediction, brings a focus to the work that tells us this is a Classical piece. Artists of that period concentrated their attention on the balance and structure of the whole work and not merely on a single figure.

Of note in Rooms #19-20 is the Roman copy of the famous statue of Athena housed in the Parthenon and sculpted by Phidias. This copy, called the Athena of Varvakion (# 129), gives us informatio about the monumental original without, certainly, competing with it artistically. We are able to see details of the *peplos*, the small statue of Winged Victory in Athena's right hand, and the helmet adorned with a sphinx and two griffins. Also evident is the great serpent coiled behind the shield. Similar copies of the monumental statue must have been fairly common throughout the ancient world.

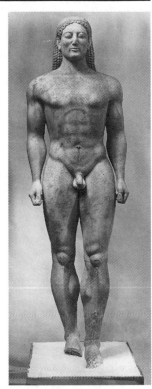

Famous Kouros of Croesus, 520 BC; excellent example of idealized Archaic man, National Archaeological Museum, Athens

Marble relief of Demeter, Kore, and Triptolemos, found at Eleusis and emblematic of the Eleusinian Mysteries, National Archaeological Museum, Athens

ELEUSIS

Queen of fragrant Eleusis,
Giver of Earth's good gifts,
Give me your grace, O Demeter.
You, too, Persephone, fairest,
Maiden all lovely, I offer
Song for your favor.

— Homer

The Mysteries celebrated at Eleusis from Mycenaean to Late Roman times were part of a long tradition of initiatory rituals among the Greek-speaking peoples. Some of these rituals and their elements must have been inherited from Near Eastern sources going back another four or five thousand years and transmitted through Crete and the Minoans in the Bronze Age. Other elements arrived from the north from as early as Paleolithic times in the rituals of the nomadic hunting tribes. Purification, procession through a labyrinth, sacrifice, isolation in the darkness, and final epiphany in the light are all characteristic of initiatory rites.

The Mysteries were rituals of death and rebirth, both seasonal and personal. The *mystai* (or initiates) "died" to the old self just as seeds "die" awaiting germination in the earth, and then, like the sprouting grain, the new souls were reborn into the company of those who had gone before *(epoptai)*. In the rebirth was an implicit affirmation of immortality, a hope closer in concept to the Christian belief than to the traditional Olympian system. In fact, in the Mysteries the virgin mother bears the savior for mankind. The Mysteries were also bound up with the lunar and solar cycles—with the dying of the sun in winter and the rebirth of the light in the birth of the son.

Another major difference between the Eleusinian Mysteries and traditional beliefs was the focus at Eleusis upon the worshiper rather than upon the god who is worshiped. The *mystai* were the center of attention, and the great Telesterion where the final secret was unveiled, probably with the aid of an entheogen, or mind-enhancing drug, was a space specially designed for a carefully controlled mystical experience. The purpose of the ceremony, then, was not so much to invoke an epiphany of the goddess within the ceremonial space, but rather to induce an internal epiphany in the participant, to recreate the myth of Demeter-Kore for the individual. Therefore, in its internal sense, the great secret of

Eleusis was, as Kerenyi has said, *arrheton* (ineffable), which means unknowable as well as "under the law of silence." Ineffable though it may have been, the experience was very real, and its reality has made the ceremony an event of considerable interest and importance throughout subsequent history.

HISTORY

In the ancient world, Eleusis was the site of the Greater Mysteries, that secret ritual of initiation that for nearly two thousand years was so central to Greek life. So important was it that in AD 364, when the Emperor Valentinian ended all so-called "nocturnal rites," he was persuaded to lift the ban on the Eleusinian Mysteries on the grounds that life for the Greeks would end without them. The Greeks believed, in fact, that the Mysteries held the universe together, that without them the cycle of birth, growth, decay, death, and rebirth would cease. If the Olympian gods were too remote, even indifferent to human suffering, the Mysteries revealed a compassionate and immediate Mother who promised eternal life to the initiate.

The origins of the Mysteries at Eleusis are obscure. This much is known: settlement on the slopes of the hill of Eleusis has been traced back to the eighteenth century BC, or the Middle Helladic Period, prior to the domination of the Mycenaean culture. The early structures appear to have been simple houses, and no temple or sanctuary has been located. Later, during the Mycenaean Period, about 1500 BC, a simple *megaron* was built on the spot where much later the famed Telesterion, or ceremonial chamber, appeared. The *megaron* seems to have been designed and built for ritual purposes and may mark the beginnings of the annual rites, but no other evidence has emerged of early initiatory activity.

ARCHAIC AND CLASSICAL TIMES

Gradually, from at least Homeric times onward, the Eleusinian Mysteries developed into a Panhellenic rite celebrating the divinity of Demeter and her daughter, Kore. In the seventh century BC, when Solon the lawgiver was influential in Athens, the sanctuary at Eleusis was greatly expanded, indicating the growing number of people who took part in the annual rites. From this period up to the Persian invasions the sanctuary continued to grow and was under Athenian control.

During the great period of building and expansion under the leadership of Pericles in mid fifth century BC, the sanctuary of Eleusis was further expanded, repaired, and transformed into an international center for transmission of the Mysteries to a much broader range of participants. After the fall of Athens in 404 BC, Eleusis fell from its position of splendor for a time but maintained its rites and physical integrity. No power would commit the sacrilege of harming the inner sanctum, regardless of the animosities aroused or the allegiances involved. Thus, through the Macedonian period and the chaos of the Late Hellenistic times the sanctuary remained relatively unharmed.

RISE AND FALL UNDER ROME

The Romans showed a great interest in Eleusis, mostly because its rites were so universal and the secret of its initiation so appealing. The early emperors were lavish in their support of the sanctuary and made many changes in the design of the site. Many of the remains we visit now are Roman, but despite a general tendency to overwrought design on the part of Roman architects and builders, the remains at Eleusis retain a Classical Greek flavor. No doubt the priests of the sanctuary held their sacred ground when it came to extensive changes in the character of the site.

The later Roman period, when the first Christian emperors took control of the empire, saw the first signs of the end of the sanctuary. As indicated, the beginning of the end came in AD 364, when the Emperor Valentinian put an end to all nocturnal rituals as anti-Christian, presumably because they were considered of the Devil. Such a conclusion was natural enough, since for years the Mysteries had been associated with the worship of Dionysos, and they were chthonic in nature. But Valentinian amended his edict when it became apparent that Greek spiritual belief was so bound up with the rites at Eleusis that an end of the Mysteries would mean an end to the Greek people. Initiation meant life itself.

Only thirty-two years later, however, in AD 396, Alaric the Goth swept down upon Eleusis from the north and destroyed the sanctuary. The Mysteries might have survived even this physical destruction had it not been for the internal subversion by the Greek priesthood, who permitted and perhaps even encouraged the destruction, so perverted had the rites become by that time. As with many of the ancient sites in Greece, the modern period saw general desecration and neglect until the nineteenth century AD when excavation began and a great world treasure was once again revealed.

MYTHOLOGY

Although there is evidence of a pre-Homeric myth of Demeter from Crete, most of the mythology upon which the Eleusinian Mysteries are founded has come down to us from one source, the Homeric *Hymn to Demeter*, which was written in the eighth century BC, probably not by Homer. The elements of the myth were woven into the general patterns of initiatory ritual to form the unique character of the Mysteries.

The myth is based on the story of the two goddesses, Demeter, or Mother Earth, and Kore, the Maiden, also known as Persephone, goddess of the underworld and wife of Hades. The name "Persephone" was seldom used because it was considered part of the secret of the Mysteries and was not to be uttered lightly. A similar practice in the Jewish faith is writing "G-d" to keep the name of the Lord sacred and pure.

THE MYTH OF TWO GODDESSES

Demeter was the daughter of Cronus and Rhea, and the sister of Zeus. She was worshiped as the Earth Mother, giver of life and provider of grain and the other fruits gathered from cultivation. Demeter had one daughter, Kore, by Zeus, her brother. One day Kore was gathering flowers with her companions. It was a day of great beauty, full of sun, welcome breezes, and new flowers. She wandered from her friends, attracted by the beauty of the narcissus *(narkissos)*:

> It was a thing of awe whether for the deathless gods or mortal men to see; from its root grew a hundred blooms and it smelled so sweetly, so that all wide heaven above and the whole earth and the sea's salt swell laughed for joy. And the girl was amazed and reached out with both hands to take the lovely toy; but the wide-pathed earth yawned. . . .

Hades, god of the underworld, emerged in his chariot, seized Kore, and bore her to his home below. There he made

Detail of the Well of Demeter, preserved through the ages as a sacred place, Eleusis

her queen of the dead, confined to rule forever in the darkness. In the depths, Kore refused to eat or to accept any advances from the lord of the dead. Meanwhile, Demeter mourned the loss of her daughter and roamed the heavens for nine days searching for her. Finally, she gleaned from the all-seeing sun what had transpired, and in a rage she left the company of the deathless gods and came to the earth, to Eleusis, where she appeared as a crone, alone and in mourning.

She sat in sadness beside a well until she was approached by the four daughters of King Celeus of Eleusis. She was invited to the palace, where she was received by Queen Metaneira in the great hall. The grace and bearing of the old woman was such that Metaneira urged her to stay and become nurse to her newborn son, Demophoon. Demeter, still mourning the loss of her daughter, agreed to nurse Demophoon, who under her care grew strong and noble.

Demeter's care of the young prince included the slow process of making the boy immortal by placing him at night in the burning coals of the hearth. The queen, curious as to how her son was growing into such a godlike figure, stole one night into the nursery, only to see the boy being placed onto the coals. She screamed, whereupon Demeter revealed herself in all her immortal splendor and said, "You mortals are thoughtless and unknowing; you cannot distinguish between evil and good." The goddess then left the palace and demanded that a great temple be built for her nearby, where she would be worshiped.

Because Kore remained with Hades, Demeter caused the earth to dry up and freeze and remain barren throughout the year. No grain grew, no olive or fig trees bloomed, and no animals could feed or reproduce their kind. The gods were without sacrifices from human beings. All was dead. Knowing this could not continue, Zeus dispatched Hermes to command Hades to release Kore and thus restore the fruitfulness of the earth. Hades appeared to agree and relinquished his bride, even returning her in his chariot. But before she left the underworld, Kore ate one seed from a pomegranate, an act that sealed her union with Hades.

In the power struggles among the gods, rights and privileges must be maintained. Laws must be honored. All-powerful Zeus is all powerful only to a point. Demeter demanded the return of her daughter. Hades demanded his due. Because Kore ate the seed, sealing her union with Hades, she had to serve her husband as queen of the dead for one-third of the year. For the other two-thirds she returned to her mother.

Thus, the earth remains barren for four months and is fertile for eight. Demeter restored the fertility of the earth for those eight months of the year. She also celebrated her partial victory by teaching her rites to humanity, initiating all who desired to know her mysteries. As a final gift, she selected one of the noble youths of Eleusis, Triptolemos, and instructed him in the arts of cultivation, so that human beings could settle in one place and enjoy the fruits of agriculture.

Spiritual Meanings of the Myth

Modern interpreters of the myth of Demeter-Persephone fall into three categories: those who see the myth in terms of nature and seasonal cycles of growth and decay; those who see the myth primarily in human terms—both cycles of birth, death, and resurrection and psychological cycles of separation, initiation, and return; and finally, those who see the myth in spiritual terms, as a description of the triumph of consciousness over repressive subconsciousness, or the sublimation of the soul's struggle with earthly desire.

The Classical understanding of the human soul, or *psyche,* as a unique and structured entity within each individual was developed by Socrates (as related to us by Plato). He taught that the soul was the center of life, the reason for being, and the object of philosophical and spiritual attention. The soul had a structure, just as an individual did. It had a body, a mind, and a spirit, just as an individual did. And as this soul was vital to existence, it became important to discover the nature of the soul and the laws by which it operated.

The myth of Demeter-Persephone is related to these Classical ideas about the soul in that the Mysteries, which grew out of the myth, were intended to be the initiation of the individual soul into the company of the saved. The soul struggled just as the individual did to deal with its earthly and divine situation. It sought release through the perfection of its divine attributes, striving for rhythm *(eurhythmia)* and harmony *(eurharmostia)* with the gods.

Although the myth has agricultural connections and can be read at that level and also has psychological connections that can be applied to physical and mental existence, the most important interpretations have to do with spiritual transformation. Certain themes that have become associated with the Eleusinian Mysteries and its Homeric myth appear again and again in the history and conduct of the rites. The first is the marriage of the Olympian sky gods to the chthonic gods of the underworld, or the marriage of conscious and subconscious forces and the resulting containment and transformation of the latter. Demeter is the Olympian spirit of the earth, a force of conscious spiritual power. Hades is an underworld god, king of the dead, keeper of souls, a symbol of subconscious power, but as brother to Zeus is still a spiritual force. Persephone is the innocent maiden abducted to the underworld against her will. She is a savior of mortals, queen with Hades and yet virgin (pure spirit) on Olympus, where she lives eight months of the year with her mother. Her return is the affirmation of immortality possible in the purified soul of a human being.

The second theme of importance in the Mysteries is the initiation ceremony and its spiritual significance. Here the themes of spirit (consciousness), earthly desire (subconsciousness), repression (separation and denial), and sublimation (transforming subconscious desire into consciousness) are played out in the myth. Persephone is innocent earthly desire, attracted to the sensuous narcissus and swept underground to marry Hades (repression). If she eats the food of death (the pomegranate provided by Hades), she will forever repress her desires and become captive to them, unable to transform them into conscious spirit. Because she represents the human condition in this myth, Persephone eats a seed from the pomegranate taken from Hades' orchards and appears condemned. She has something within her that must be sublimated and transformed. Demeter represents spirit unblemished by earthly desire, which has the power of transformation.

As the result of intervention by Zeus (Bright Consciousness), Persephone is permitted, despite having eaten the fruit of death, to return for most of the year. She is thus able to transform her state through grace and through her mother's power over nature. To sublimate rather than repress desire means to keep a pure spirit and heart in spite of contrary desires and to be obedient to the spiritual powers who are working on behalf of salvation. Thus, the key to this mystery is the difference between unhealthy, destructive repression, and healthy, life-enhancing sublimation.

Repression means to cover, to separate, to deny, to hide. It means to internalize to the point of spiritual stagnation. It is the route of cynicism, the path of darkness, and it produces destructive guilt. Sublimation, on the other hand, means to transform, to uncover, to join, to affirm, to open. It involves trust and conviction, and it is the path of light. To know the difference when faced with earthly desire is to know the proper path to enlightenment. To be able to exercise the will to follow that path is to know enlightenment. To accept help from spiritual guides and gods is to understand the nature of human limitation; it is the key to successful sublimation.

The Sacred Rites

The old Archaic myth of the two goddesses became ritual in the two major celebrations associated with the Mysteries: the Lesser Mysteries in Athens and the Greater Mysteries in Eleusis. There appeared in the rites an additional element from the Orphic tradition in which Persephone gives birth to a male child, the result of her abduction by Hades. The child is identified frequently with Dionysos, particularly in Classical times. The cry "Iakche" (ee-a-kay), which is associated with the Mysteries and with other celebrations of Dionysiac revels, refers to Iakchos, a demigod often identified with Dionysos himself.

Candidates for initiation into the Mysteries had to be adults—slave or free, citizens of Athens or aliens—who presented themselves as pure of hands (no murderers, for example) and able to speak or understand Greek. The language requirement seems to have been based on the need to understand the instructions and the ability to sing the various hymns and call out the sacred words that were so important a part of the ritual. Although only adults were initiated, one boy was specially chosen each year to take part, presumably to represent the figure of Iakchos or Dionysos in the ceremony. The boy and his family would be much honored that year.

The Lesser Mysteries took place in Athens in a sanctuary called Agra near the Ilissos River. This sanctuary dedicated to Artemis should not be confused with the Eleusinion in the Agora. The Agra site is located on the Arditos Hill near the present site of the modern Olympic Stadium. The date for the Lesser Mysteries was the twentieth of Anthesterion (in mid-February), and the candidates for initiation, the *mystai,* gathered at a small temple of Meter, mother of the gods, for purification and sacrifice. This ceremony was a necessary part of the initiation and could not be missed if the initiate wished to participate in the Greater Mysteries seven months later.

Little is known of the details of the Lesser Mysteries, except that the candidates were "consecrated" at this time as proper *mystai* through purification rites in the *myesis,* or beginning of the ritual of initiation. In all probability, one of the elements would have been the acting out of the abduction of Persephone into the underworld. According to the late poet and scholar Robert Graves, the Lesser Mysteries enacted a marriage between Dionysos and a minor goddess, Thyone (or Semele). Many commentators suggest the working out of sexual themes as central to these rites.

THE GREATER MYSTERIES

The Greater Mysteries began on the fourteenth of Boedromion, which in the modern calendar generally falls on September 22, and lasted for nine days, corresponding to the wanderings of Demeter in search of Kore. On this day the officials from Eleusis, including the high priestess, the Hierophant (high priest), and the Dadouchus (torchbearer), left the sanctuary at Eleusis and marched along the Sacred Way to Athens, a distance of just over 12 miles (20 km). The procession was met by youths from Athens assigned to conduct the official party to the Eleusinion in the Agora, where the cult objects *(heira)* were deposited temporarily.

The fifteenth (*heira*) of Boedromion (September 23) was regarded as the first official day of the Mysteries. On this day the officials of the Athenian *polis,* including the *archon basileus,* the festival leader, whose task it was to maintain the Athenian religious calendar, met with the Eleusinian party to inaugurate the Mysteries. Sacrifices were made on the Acropolis to ask Athena for her blessing, and a ceremony took place in the Agora to bless the *mystai.*

The Pig Sacrifice

On the sixteenth of Boedromion (September 24), early in the day, throughout Athens the cry was heard, "*Mystai* to the sea." A procession formed in which each initiate took a sacrificial pig to the sea, washed both it and himself, sacrificed the pig, and then buried the body in a deep pit. This sacrifice enacted a symbolic death for each initiate—a letting of blood and a burial in which the personal self or ego died so that the new, greater self could be born at Eleusis during the secret nocturnal ceremony.

The sacrifice of the pig was a significant act. The death of the animal, especially on such a personal, individual basis—one for each participant—created a genuine psychological space within the initiate, an emptiness that had to be filled or replaced with something else. The intention was that the space would be filled with light, signaling the birth of a new life for the soul. The death and burial of the pig forced the initiate to strip away the old, material view of existence and to live with the resulting emptiness until it was filled, more than a week later, with a new spiritual realization.

Preparation and Procession

The next two days were spent in preparation for the procession to Eleusis. Additional sacrifices were made and the participants from the different cities were gathered together. A special celebration for Asklepios was held, honoring the god of healing and affirming the ancient practice of allowing special dignitaries to enter late into the ritual as, legend had it, Asklepios himself had done. It is also worth noting that Asklepios in his capacity as a healer was associated with Hades, god of the dead. As one having power over life and death but also a compassionate god, Asklepios was an integral part of the ritual.

On the nineteenth of Boedromion (September 27) all the participants gathered for the procession to Eleusis. The day was known as *agrymos,* the gathering. This day marked the beginning of the rule of secrecy. As a result, the details from this point on are both sketchy and intriguing, since we realize that the rule of secrecy meant that what was regarded as *arrheton*, or ineffable, contained within its awesome aspect the power to create a mystical experience among the *mystai.*

The procession formed at the Eleusinion in the Agora. The officials from Eleusis, including the priestesses carrying the sacred objects in baskets on their heads, led the *mystai* and a whole crowd of celebrants through the Agora, through the Kerameikos, and out the Sacred Gate. At the head of the procession a priest carried a wooden statue of Iakchos, the boy god whose birth would be a culminating event in the secret ritual.

Myrtle leaves were woven into the hair of the initiates and each carried a myrtle bough, sacred to Dionysos and symbolic of the death of the old life and the birth of the new. (The myrtle, for example, was carried by Greek colonists when they left their home to start a new home in a distant land.) The participants also sang hymns along the way and chanted sacred words and phrases, all designed to keep the mind fo-

cused on the object of devotion, in this case the statue of
Iakchos.

One of the familiar aspects of any initiation is the
so-called hazing or mockery that greets the candidate who
desires inclusion into a secret society. This mockery is usually intensely personal and is meant to humiliate and to reveal
for the initiate the folly of his or her gross existence. The
procession to Eleusis included such mockery. As the line of
initiates crossed the Kephisos River in Athens, on the bridge
spanning the river groups of mockers greeted each initiate
with insults. Thus exposed, the old self literally died for
shame.

After the *gephyrismoi*, or "bridge jests" as they were
called, the procession began the long climb up to the pass at
Daphni, where ritual stops were made at temples sacred to
Apollo and Aphrodite. In Euripides' play *Helen* we learn that
it was Aphrodite who managed with beautiful music to relieve Demeter's mourning during Kore's confinement with
Hades. Gifts of this kind and the power to relieve sadness
were celebrated during this solemn procession. At this point,
too, the procession came in sight of the twin peaks of the
island of Salamis, which to *mystai* of the Classical Period
would have suggested the great victory over the Persians and
the miraculous advent of the mystical *mystai* on that occasion.

Some archaeologists locate the bridge-jesting ceremony
closer to Eleusis, at the crossing of the Eleusinian Kephisos
River, where a Roman road and bridge have now been uncovered on the left side of the National Highway leading into
Eleusis. The weight of evidence, however, seems to place the
bridge in question closer to Athens.

As night fell on the procession, the torches were lit as
the throng came down the pass and approached the sanctuary of Eleusis. The darkness must have matched the mood of
the participants, who by this time were tired, thirsty, and
hungry, having fasted all day. During the Archaic Period, a
large dancing ground outlined the famous Well of the Beautiful Dances, where initiates or specially chosen dancers
enacted in ritual movements the arrival of Demeter in Eleusis
after her nine days of fruitless searching.

The Nights of the Mysteries

As the initiates arrived in Eleusis and entered the sanctuary,
they came, as had Demeter, searching for Kore, which in their
case meant searching for the return of an innocent "soul" from
the ravages of the underworld. The actual events of the next
two nights are obscured by the rule of secrecy. What is available to us now are unconnected details: descriptions from
literary accounts, illustrations from pottery and sculpture,
and interpretations based on archaeology and anthropology.
In addition, new evidence for the use of a hallucinogen during the ceremony is capturing greater attention.

In the abstract, the initiates were now exposed to the

Sacred Precinct of Plouton, a natural cave with an altar, regarded as the entrance to the underworld, Eleusis

horrors of the underworld—to its darkness, uncertainty, fear, and loneliness. Even in a crowd, this experience must have left each participant feeling isolated and empty from this temporary but vivid separation from all that was ordinary and familiar. For the next two days the individual was exposed to the drama of the Demeter-Persephone myth.

Before the candidates entered the Telesterion, they took part in further sacrifices and rites of purification, both at or near the ancient well and at the Cave of Hades, or as it was known then, the Precinct of Plouton, god of the underworld. At the entrance to this cave was an *omphalos,* or world navel, which marked the transition from the world of light to the world of darkness. The *mystai* had prepared for this moment by fasting (to what degree is uncertain) and the twelve-mile march. This moment and this place marked the symbolic descent by Kore into the underworld, the place of death from which only the purified may return to "live again."

Within the Telesterion, the huge building specifically designed for this ceremony, the participants moved among a grove of columns in dim light provided by torches and then sat, huddled together, on the rows of narrow steps that line the sanctuary. In the middle of the Telesterion was another small building, the *anaktoron*, entrance to which was reserved for the high priests and priestesses and from which a great fire would burst at the crucial moment of the ritual.

A Christian writer, Hippolytos, wrote that at a crucial moment in the ceremony the high priest shouted out, "The Mistress has given birth to a holy boy; Brimo has given birth to Brimos; that is, the Strong One to the Strong One." Piecing together the evidence has led to the conclusion that it was here that the young boy, representing both Demophoon in the Homeric myth and Iakchos in the Orphic tradition, played his part in the ceremony. Ringed by torches, the boy emerged in a fiery birth from the womb of the returned goddess. The transformation sought by the *mystai* is here represented by the birth of the new soul in fire, a burning away of the old self and the birth of the new out of the ashes. There is evidence of cremation near the Telesterion, which would also connect the sacred fire with ceremonies of death and rebirth.

During this drama, which may well have involved symbolic or actual intercourse between the high priest and priestess, the participants enacted ritual movements with the sacred objects that had been carried to and from Athens in baskets the week before. The baskets contained sacrificial cakes, sheaves of grain, and perhaps phallic objects that were used during the ceremony by each initiate to mimic implanting the seed of life into the fertile goddess of the earth.

Just prior to the fiery manifestation, the priestesses passed through the crowd and distributed in small bowls the *kykeion,* or sacred drink, which was composed of barley, water, and mint. Emerging research from scholars who have devoted years to the study of entheogens, or revelatory stimulants, strongly suggests that the priests of Eleusis had mastered the art of using ergot (a fungal growth from barley) and a particular wild grass growing in the Rarian Plain near Eleusis, to make an effective hallucinogen.

Ergot was isolated by Albert Hoffman, a Swiss chemist working for the Sandoz Corporation. In 1943, while studying the effects of ergot, he isolated LSD and sampled some, with the effects now well understood. To illustrate the relationship between the rites in the sanctuary and Hoffman's experience, the following excerpt from his notes in 1943 may be instructive:

> Everything in my field of vision wavered and was distorted as if seen in a curved mirror. I also had the sensation of not being able to move from the spot. . . . The dizziness and sensation of fainting became so strong at times that I could no longer hold myself erect. My surroundings had now transformed themselves in more terrifying ways. Everything in the room spun around, and the pieces of furniture assumed grotesque, threatening forms. They were in motion, animated, as if driven by an inner restlessness. . . . Even worse than these demonic transformations of the outer world, were the alterations that I perceived in myself, in my inner being. Every exertion of my will, every attempt to put an end to the disintegration of the outer world and the dissolution of my ego seemed to be a wasted effort. . . . At times I believed myself to be outside my body. . . . Now, little by little, I could begin to enjoy the unprecedented colors and plays of shapes that persisted behind my closed eyes. Kaleidoscopic, fantastic images surged in on me, alternating, variegated, opening, then closing themselves in circles and spirals, exploding in colored fountains. . . . It was particularly remarkable how every acoustic perception . . . became transformed into optical perceptions.

Remains of the Telesterion, with Mycenaean remains in the foreground, Eleusis

Such images may well have been the sensations of the *mystai*, contributing to their experience of what followed. At the close of the ceremony, to the awesome sounds of a huge gong or drum that must have filled the Telesterion and the surrounding countryside with thunder, a great light burst forth from the *anaktoron* and in a moment of epiphany the Kore appeared. Her appearance at the crucial moment of the ritual affirmed the content of the myth and the hope of the *mystai* for a renewed life.

After the rites in the Telesterion, the newly initiated poured out of the great hall into the darkness, led by torchlight, and gathered in the nearby meadow. Chanting, dancing, and feasting released the tensions of many days of intense anticipation. The release was also an affirmation of life and must have also brought with it a sense of renewal. Seeing daily existence in a different light was quite literally an aim of the ritual, and this different "seeing" began as the moon rose over the celebrants and they experienced the release from what may have seemed a lifetime of darkness.

The Secret of the Mysteries

Demeter, as Mother Earth, gave the secret of agriculture to human beings, establishing the gift of divine aid and suggesting tangible divine presence. It is through this myth that a connection to divinity is maintained and the hope is sustained that human beings may yet become reunited with the gods. In the myth the barren conditions wiped out the natural fruits of the earth upon which life depended. Certainly the last glacial period and numerous droughts remained in human memory to fuel such myths.

The Demeter myth describes these events quite accurately. After Demeter successfully wins the return of her daughter from Hades and settles for keeping her for eight months out of twelve as an expression of the laws of Nature, human beings are able to see the connection between the natural law and the divine presence for which they long. The Eleusinian Mysteries provided a ritual through which the Greeks could reenact the shift from nomadic to agricultural life, acknowledge the real loss of their gods in a period of glacial darkness, and be reunited (or forgiven) once again. This ritual pattern is the source of all initiation mysteries.

The secret of the Mysteries is the moment of reunion, the appearance of Persephone as she emerges from the underworld, with the experience aided by the entheogen. At this moment the initiate experiences the emotional and psychic release from the dark night of the soul and is reborn to the light. The journey of the maiden is the human journey from its grain-gathering nomadic ways to the paralyzing darkness and cold of the underworld only to return again into the light and fecundity of earthly paradise, a Garden of Eden still occupied by divinity. Human beings need to know that they have not sacrificed union with the gods for the seeming comforts of civilization. Demeter is the forgiving mother, nurturing her children and providing for them the means to return to her bosom after life is over.

This level of meaning helps to explain why, in AD 364, the Roman Emperor Valentinian was persuaded to allow the Mysteries to continue. To fail to reenact the ritual would be to bring the darkness back to the earth once more. The guilt for having created civilization (a state of being known only to the gods before Prometheus stole fire for human beings) could only be assuaged by this ritual. To offend Athena might result in the destruction of Athens, but to offend Demeter would destroy life itself—forever.

The Nature of the Secret

In the ninth discourse of the Bhagavad-Gita, it is said that the great secret of the universe, of life itself, has several characteristics that mark it as a true secret. First, the secret has to be intuitional, that is, capable of being known by anyone wishing to know it and not dependent upon outside teaching or being revealed by an adept. Second, it has to be righteous, that is, consistent with cosmic law. And third, it has to be pleasant beyond measure, that is, the secret has to be life-enhancing and exceeding the pleasures of earthly existence.

These principles suggest that any great cosmic secret, such as that of the Eleusinian Mysteries, has to be available to all, full of light (and thus goodness), and must exceed all the pleasures of the earth in its greatness. After all, if the great secret of the universe did not exceed the greatest joys of the earth, seekers would not care very much what it was, but would strive for the ultimate earthly delights as the true aim of life.

The secret of Eleusis was the miraculous experience of

the event, the miracle of which would remain valid only if the secret was kept. The labyrinthine journey from Athens, the fasting and sacrifices, the terrors of the darkness, the drama of the birth from fire, and the return of the beloved goddess from the underworld under the influence of a carefully prepared agent of illumination worked together to do in ritual what for many could not be done by philosophical inquiry and devotion alone. As Hoffmann wrote of his experience, "Exhausted, I woke the next morning refreshed, with a clear head, though tired physically. A sensation of well-being and renewed life flowed through me. . . . The world was as if newly created. All my senses vibrated in a condition of highest sensitivity, which persisted for the entire day."

THE SITE

The journey today from Athens to the site at Eleusis still has some of the aspects of the ancient course: the taunting jests, the dusty trek, the sense of labyrinth in which the spirit shrinks from its lofty intention and fears for its very existence. All these sensations may be experienced as the modern pilgrim tries to follow the Sacred Way and appreciate the vitality and importance of the annual rite for the ancient Greeks.

The National Highway heading north out of Athens passes through typical twentieth-century urban sprawl. Except for the relief felt at the pass at Daphni, where the natural beauty of the landscape and the heritage of the site have been preserved as a public park and campgrounds, the twelve-mile route demonstrates the denial of spirit so notable in modern life throughout the world today.

The site of the Eleusinian sanctuary itself has been cramped and nearly obliterated by the steady encroachment of a cement factory and the inexorable growth of the local port facility. The smokestacks of the factory seem for just a moment like columns against the dusty sky, and it takes a determined eye to see beyond them to pick out the ancient landscape features that directed the original founders of the sanctuary to establish the Mysteries on this particular acropolis.

After the journey out of Athens or along the highway coming in from Corinth, the relative peace and quiet of the site itself are a pleasant relief. Seldom do crowds arrive in tour buses or large numbers of tourists descend on the site all at once. One usually has an opportunity to gather oneself for a focused tour of a place blessed with two thousand years of continuous occupation for a single sacred purpose, a purpose quickly felt as features like the ancient well, the Cave of Hades, and the remains of the great Telesterion itself greet the attentive eye.

It is possible to enjoy a relaxed lunch or afternoon coffee in the small town that serves the sanctuary, and the modest museum at the site offers several important artifacts for inspection, including several marbles showing early representations of Demeter and Kore.

ORIENTATION

There are two ways of approaching a visit to Eleusis. One is to approach as an initiate might have, by locating the ruins of the Sacred Way to the left of the modern entrance and proceeding past the sacred well, through the Roman *propylaia*, past the Precinct of Plouton, up the Sacred Way, and into the Telesterion. The other is to seek a higher vantage point initially in order to grasp the general pattern of structural elements before attempting a closer examination.

Because the site is such a maze of ruins from Mycenaean to Late Roman times, it may be more useful to sacrifice the pilgrim's approach initially and choose the higher vantage point, which is available on the top of the ancient acropolis where now the Church of Panayia dominates the scene.

From here the visitor is able to grasp a sense of the development of the site over the years. The remains of the Telesterion, the center of the sacred site, are down to the right. The Telesterion was created by cutting into the rock of the acropolis to the southeast to level the ground for the massive foundations of the great hall. It was in this space that the first Mycenaean cult center was built. For the most part the natural features of the eastern slope were left alone in order to frame the cave where tradition has placed the descent to the underworld.

The Sacred Way, from the entrance to the Lesser Propylon, Eleusis

To the left, or north, where the entrances were built, the level ground accommodated several temples. In Roman times the massive *propylaia* and stone terraces, which now dominate much of that area, were added. To the east are ruins that are primarily Roman, including a triumphal arch, baths, and a retaining wall. Beyond the Telesterion to the east and south are the remains of the massive walls built during the Classical Period under the direction of Pericles. These walls guaranteed that no unwelcome visitor would invade the ceremonies and no invading army would overrun the sanctuary.

THE SANCTUARY

The visitor may now begin where the ancient *mystai* made their entrance to the site, at the point where the Sacred Way enters the sanctuary. The area has some modern facilities, mostly work areas and bathrooms for visitors, but here is where the ancient road from Athens ended. The first feature of interest is the Archaic well, still preserved, where tradition has it that Demeter sat when she arrived after her nine-day journey. Over the years the well has been preserved by walls and was included in the general terracing done by the Romans.

To the right, or north, are the ruins of a temple of Artemis built by the Romans, now evident only as a dim foundation. Next to it are the remains of an *eschara*, or underground altar, at which offerings were made to the gods of the underworld. The outer court, which earlier would have been the dancing ground, focuses the attention upon the Great

The Greater Propylon, showing in the background a square floor with the bases of four rows of three columns each. The porch is the light area in a rectangular shape. The procession angled to the left after passing through this gate, Eleusis.

The Lesser Propylon, a much smaller entrance. The remains show door grooves in the marble floor. The file of initiates narrowed at this point before entering the Sacred Way, Eleusis.

Propylaia of Roman construction, marking the spot where the *mystai* made their formal entrance to the sanctuary.

The Greater and Lesser Propylaia

The remains of the Greater Propylaia are sufficient to give a clear impression of the magnitude of this entrance way. Six marble steps approached a portico supported by six columns and leading to three doors that give way to a rear portico supported by six more columns. The Greater Propylaia directed the initiate toward the Lesser Propylaia and the Precinct of Plouton, before which sacrifices were made.

The Lesser Propylaia also had three doors, but the center door was larger and framed by two Corinthian columns. The interior of the Lesser Propylaia featured another large doorway framed by two Karyatides, named Kistophoros by the Greeks because they carried on their heads the baskets containing the sacred elements for the Mysteries. One of these priestesses may be seen in the Eleusis Museum (#5104 in the collection).

The Precinct of Plouton

Certainly one reason for the location of the Mysteries on this site was the existence of this cave. The associations with the Demeter-Persephone myth are rich in detail, and tradition has it that here Persephone was seized by Hades and taken to the underworld. The cave, then, was the point of transition. The *mystai* must have prayed here, entreating the dark god who dwelled below that they would return from their dark journey into the light once more and that Persephone would be permitted to return to the living.

In addition, there is archaeological evidence of the foundation of a platform that some observers suppose supported

The eight stone steps of the Telesterion, carved out of the natural hillside, Eleusis

an *omphalos,* represented by a pile of ash that covered and protected the coals of the hearth.

The Telesterion

In the time of Pericles, the Telesterion was rebuilt under the direction of Iktinos, builder of the Parthenon. The new, much larger building measured 170 feet by 174 feet (51.8 m by 53 m) and had a peaked roof supported by forty-two columns—six rows of seven columns each. Surrounding the central cult building and the columns were rows of eight steps on all sides. The initiates probably sat or stood on these steps during the ceremony. Their vision of the ritual would have been blocked somewhat by the columns, but the effect did not depend on clear sight lines anyway.

In terms of sacred numerology we can see that the patterns of six and seven columns represent both the creative principles of the ritual and the divine number of completion. The eight steps remind us of the eight steps of baptismal fonts, reflecting the idea of a new birth for the initiates. The nearly square shape of the building suggests the manifest world out of which will arise a spiritual unity, in fire bursting forth from the center, at the climax of the ritual. The same concept lay behind the construction of all square-based pyramids in Egypt and Central America.

The Telesterion in the Classical Period would have held over three thousand initiates. Access to the building was gained from two side entrances opening directly onto the Sacred Way. There were entrances also on the eastern and southern sides. On the eastern side of the square a stoa was constructed of white marble in the fourth century BC. It had twelve columns across the front and three on the sides. This Stoa of Philon, as it was called, seems to have been added during a period of aesthetic decoration of the sanctuary.

Outside the Telesterion

Since the sanctuary of Eleusis functioned throughout the year and was maintained by a council and a priesthood, there was need for several auxiliary buildings both within and outside the enclosure. To the south, built into the Classical fortification wall, was a *bouleuterion*, or council house, where the ruling council met to administer the affairs of the sanctuary. Its remains are indicated by the half circle of stones near the south gate. In front of the Bouleuterion are the remains of the wall erected in the fifth century BC when Iktinos was architect of the sanctuary. The massive wall behind the Bouleuterion was built by Lycurgus a hundred years later.

The ruins outside the sanctuary to the south include a gymnasium of Hellenistic construction and a Roman building devoted to the cult of Mithra, the Middle Eastern religion associated with Zoroaster. This cult was popular with the Roman troops who garrisoned the outposts of the empire. Mithraism had its roots in bull sacrifices, which were associated with pledges of immortality for the initiates. It was also one of the important mystery religions, which made it natural that its cult would appear at Eleusis during the Roman Period.

THE MUSEUM

The modest Museum of Eleusis offers several important artifacts excavated at the site. In Room #1, for example, a fine *amphora* of the Archaic Period (650 BC) illustrates on the neck of the vase the binding of Cyclops by Odysseus and on the body the myth of Medusa. The Fleeing Kore, #5235, is a marble pedimental sculpture depicting one of the friends of Persephone fleeing the scene of the abduction. A marble piglet, #5053, is emblematic of the sacrificial pigs that were sacrificed as part of the Greater Mysteries.

In Room #2 is a copy of the Eleusinian Relief of Demeter, Kore, and Triptolemos, the original of which resides in the National Archaeological Museum in Athens (see p. 223). The marble Demeter (#5076) from 420 BC is typical of the Late Classical style and depicts the goddess as Mother Earth in her capacity as nurturer.

Room #3 has a fine example of the attributes of Dionysos done in white marble (#5091). This Roman copy of a Classical piece shows the god as mortal, languid, amoral, almost careless in aspect. There is a decadent sexuality here that is both masculine and feminine, but there is also a distance that does not encourage intimacy. He has long hair entwined with ivy and leans on a vine-covered support, his hand gently touching the grapes.

Room #3 includes a statue of a girl holding a marble basin for water (#5140). Two of these basin bearers stood at the entrances to the Telesterion and were used by the initiates to wash their hands just before entering the hall. The large hole in the center held the support for the large basin. Also worth noting in Room #3 is the headless sculpture of

Asklepios (#5100), god of healing, which was found to the north of the sanctuary with other artifacts, suggesting the existence of an Asklepieion associated with Eleusis.

Room #4 contains two models of the sanctuary executed by Travlos. The first presents the site as it might have looked in the sixth century BC when the Telesterion was much smaller. The second model represents the site during the Roman Imperial Period. Of particular interest is the emphasis in Roman times on the outer court and the formality of the entrances to the sanctuary.

Room #5 holds the Karyatid (#5104) referred to earlier as one of two such columns framing the central door of the Lesser Propylaia. Tradition has it that this figure remained half buried through much of modern times and was revered by the local people, who associated it with Demeter and offered prayers to it for good harvests. Notable in this sculpture are the Gorgon head on the breast after the manner of Athena and the basket or *kiste* on the head, decorated with sacred rosettes.

In Room #6, the Vase Room, there is a fine collection of pottery from all periods of Eleusinian history. The earliest pieces are Neolithic (in Case #1) and date from 2500 BC and earlier. Of importance in Case #5 is a stirrup jar dated from the Mycenaean Period containing an inscription in Linear B script. In Case #21 are two *kernoi,* or headpieces, used to carry offerings to the goddess. Cup-like receptacles held grains or oils. The *kernoi* are pictured in vase paintings depicting the procession to Eleusis.

EPIDAUROS

*At Epidauros, in the stillness, in the great peace that
came over me, I heard the heart of the world beat.
I know what the cure is: it is to give up, to relinquish, to surrender, so that our little hearts may beat
in unison with the great heart of the world.*

— Henry Miller

Epidauros is much more than the site of the greatest theater
in Greece. It is a sanctuary of Asklepios—a man, a myth, and
a tradition worshiped throughout Greece as the god of healing. The cult of Asklepios focused more on individual worship
and healing than on collective worship at the level of the *polis*.

Of the hundreds of local sanctuaries associated with
Asklepios, the one at Epidauros was the largest and most
important. Renowned throughout Greece, it was the site of
major Panhellenic festivals in honor of the god. A smaller sanctuary is nestled in the hillside just above the Theater of
Dionysos in Athens, and another sits just below the Temple
of Apollo at Delphi. The connection of the cult to drama, in
particular, was notable in Greek culture. In the very best sense,
drama was a healing art. It purged the viewer of unholy
thoughts by the power of its subject matter and the patterns
of the performance. At Epidauros the magnificent fourth century BC theater is powerful enough even today to purge the
viewer of the ills of civilization, even without the benefit of a
play.

HISTORY

The history of this site tells the story of the Greek concept of
health, the idea of which was originally connected to worship, to "right thinking," from which come physical, emotional,
and spiritual well-being. When the Olympian gods came upon
the scene, Apollo became the god of the soul and its health
within the body. In the worship of Apollo the Greeks acknowledged the need for moderation in all aspects of life. A balanced
life was conducive to the health of the soul, and part of that
balance was the proper and measured worship of Apollo and
his son Asklepios, whose compassion for the human race
made him a major cult figure.

Theater at Epidauros, showing the circular orchestra and the theater's near-perfect condition

Asklepios was worshiped as a god and was also thought of as an historical figure. His approach to medicine had the same dual nature. The cause of illness lay in the *psyche,* and the manifestations were both physical and spiritual. If a person was not "thinking straight," he or she was not capable of relieving the physical symptoms of illness. First the mind had to be aligned to the mind of Apollo, then the body might recover its balance and health.

HIPPOKRATES

In the history of Greek medicine the figure of Hippokrates is central. It is no coincidence that this famous physician was born on the island of Cos, which was an ancient site for the worship of Asklepios. Hippokrates was born somewhere around 460 BC and thus belonged to the Classical age. He was present in Athens during the crisis of the Peloponnesian War, where he was an important figure both in philosophy and medicine. He died in Thessaly in 377 BC. Aside from his famous oath, his greatest contribution was his theory of "humors," based on the laws of internal secretions, or hormonal controls, operating in the body and affecting almost every aspect of physical and mental functioning.

We also understand now that the flow of hormones in the brain is responsible for the state we might refer to as "right thinking," that is, the balance of secretions within the body controlling mental as well physical health. It is in this area of modern medical research that we are coming closer to understanding the relationship of physical, mental, and spiritual well-being in the human organism. Drastic fluctuations in human behavior caused by uncontrolled desires or the excessive gratification of basic needs can so disrupt the system that illness results. For the ancient Greeks, the worship of Apollo was the first step in establishing a proper sense of life so that desires and needs were kept in balance and harmony. Asklepios entered the picture when there were signs of physical or mental illness, in which case the symptoms were treated first. But there was always the principle and purity of Apollonian worship in the background—or in the foreground if the patient was truly aligned with the laws.

THE HISTORICAL RECORD

Pausanius tells us that the recorded history of this site began with the worship of Apollo of Malea, a name indicating that the god is associated with a local cult and its site. Apollo's sanctuary is on top of Mount Kynortion, which rises just behind the theater. This site dates at least from Mycenaean times and was certainly in continuous use from that period. Pilgrims to the Asklepieion frequently made the ascent to Apollo's sanctuary to make a preliminary sacrifice before entering the main sanctuary.

The Asklepieion itself dates from the sixth century BC and was in use well into the fifth century of the Christian Era. Even a thorough sacking by the Roman Sulla in 86 BC failed to end its useful life. In its prime, in the fifth and fourth centuries BC, the sanctuary was a brilliant example of the Greek vision of human health and spiritual well-being. Pilgrims arrived continuously for specific cures at the hands of the temple priests, but there were also festivals, the principle one being the Great Asklepeia, which took place every four years in the spring. The festival lasted for nine days, and over the years the activities displayed the full range of human expression. There were games of athletic skill in the stadium in which participants showed their prowess in sprints, boxing, wrestling, broad jumping, and discus throwing. Both musical and dramatic competitions were added in later years.

True to the spirit of all festivals in Greece, the Great Asklepeia had a sacred intent. In the very best sense, the purpose was to reestablish for the pilgrim his or her proper place in the hierarchy of nature, which, of course, included the gods. This intent was both abstract and practical. It shows once again that the great contribution of the ancient Greeks to Western culture was to articulate at the very limits of human understanding and knowledge what it means to be a part of the cosmos.

MYTHOLOGY

The myth of Asklepios originates deep in the Greek past with the Earth Goddess. Both share the symbol of the snake as a sign of rebirth and eternal life, and it is this connection to the more ancient beliefs of the Earth Mother cults that gives

Asklepios his closeness to the common people and makes him a nurturing, sympathetic god. There is even evidence now that early images of Jesus closely resemble Asklepios, thus connecting the latter in the Greek mind with the transition to Christianity. Asklepios is also associated firmly with the Olympian sky gods, which enhances his importance in formal rituals and festivals. Today his ancient associations with healing, the snake, and the sky gods live on in the familiar symbol of the caduceus, the physician's staff with two entwined snakes and two wings at the top.

Pindar tells us that Asklepios was the son of Apollo and a beautiful young virgin named Coronis, daughter of King Phlegyas of Thessaly. The unfortunate Coronis, already bearing the "fruit of the love of the bright god," made the fatal mistake of falling in love with a mortal. At Apollo's jealous urging, Coronis was killed by Artemis, but not before the baby was saved and sent off to be raised by the wise and gifted centaur Chiron, who, among other things, taught the young Asklepios the art of healing. When he reached manhood, Asklepios began his work. He was known for his great skill as well as his compassion.

Because he bridged the animal and the human realms, being half horse and half man, as a healer Chiron can be seen to symbolize the secularization of medicine in Greece; that is, the gradual change from medicine as a sacred science to medicine as a skill in the hands of professional practitioners. And since Asklepios was taught medicine by Chiron, Asklepios in turn became a symbol of a blend of sacred and secular medicine. The same idea is expressed in the role of Epidauros as a center for the simultaneous practice of spiritual and physical healing.

Central to the popularity of Asklepios among ordinary people is the account of his death. Out of his compassion he brought a human being back to life. Zeus struck and killed him with his lightning bolt because to bring a mortal back to life transgresses divine law and is punishable by death. Zeus thus reminds us that it is spiritual life that is important, not immortal life in the body.

THE LOCAL GOD

Pausanius, our faithful guide to Greece, repeats another tale from his travels through Epidauros. The warlike Phlegyas, bent on conquering the whole Peloponnese, brought his retinue, including his pregnant daughter, Coronis, to Epidauros and was occupied in counting the population when his daughter gave birth to the young Asklepios. She took the child to the top of what may now be Mount Titthion, or "the teat," where the child was suckled by a goat and protected by the goatherd's dog. This "natural" start in the god's life indicates his affinity with the earth and with the healing arts.

The mythology of Asklepios, then, emphasizes his position relative to the gods and mankind. On the one hand he was the son of Apollo, the bright but distant god of Olympus, and on the other his mother was a mortal. He was raised by Chiron, a centaur, whose associations with the earth and animal existence give him a common touch. He understood the suffering of human life in ways that Apollo could not.

THE SITE

The natural environment of Epidauros is ample, gentle, and protective. From any point in the sanctuary the surrounding hills offer the viewer an undulating horizon line, a gentle blending of earth and sky. It is peaceful here, and the feeling of peace is created by a unifying of natural elements. The architecture of the site exhibited similar principles of harmony through the use of geometry and number for the purpose of stilling the mind, focusing the attention, and inspiring reverence and confidence to effect the desired cure. Each building within the sanctuary had a purpose and an appropriate design within the larger context. The key buildings were the Temple of Asklepios, the Tholos, the Abaton, and the Great Altar of Asklepios. Nearby were the ancient Abaton and the smaller Temple of Artemis (see Fig. 25).

However, the sanctuary was only part of the total effect

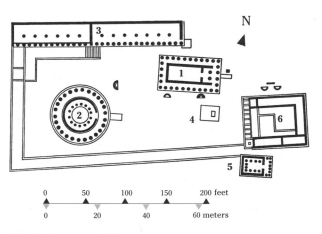

Fig. 25. *Sanctuary at Epidauros*
1. *Temple of Asklepios*
2. *Tholos*
3. *Abaton*
4. *Great Altar*
5. *Temple of Artemis*
6. *Ancient Abaton*

of the complex of Epidauros. Also included in the curative environment were the stadium, where games of skill and athletic contests tested human endurance and strength; the gymnasium, where lectures and philosophical discussions enlivened the mind; and the theater, where plays were performed as part of the cathartic process so vital to physical, mental, and spiritual health. These elements were added gradually to the site over a long span of time that really had its beginnings in the prehistoric period.

ARCHAEOLOGY AT EPIDAUROS

Archaeological work began on the site at Epidauros in 1881. At that time the theater and several temples, the gymnasium, and connecting buildings were uncovered. This work, conducted primarily by Kavvadias, ended in 1927. After World War II work was resumed in the sanctuary and on Mount Kynortion, to the south, where a temple to Apollo was excavated. Most of these finds date from the Archaic Period. The beautiful temples in the sanctuary date from the fourth century BC, when the cult was enjoying a resurgence of devotion and support. Excavation below the fourth century BC level revealed prehistoric remains dating from the Early Helladic Period (c. 3000 BC). Human and animal figurines from the Late Helladic Period (c. 1400 BC) indicate cult activity during the Mycenaean era.

This early habitation shows that from the beginning there was a continuous theme of veneration of the figure of Asklepios beyond the immediate concern for cures for specific illnesses. As we recognize the sanctuary as the heart of the site, we understand that for the Greeks, even in the earliest eras, the world of spirit came first. Beginning with purification, followed by sacrifice, and ending with thank offerings, the activity of the site centered on religious belief and practice. Attached to this central concern, however, were the games, the music, the orations, and the drama—all expressions of the very best of Greek culture. Seeing the theater, the stadium, and the gymnasium, it is easy to conclude, as many have, that Epidauros was nothing but an elaborate spa for the wealthy of Greece, a place to dry out from the excesses of good living where the guests were entertained and pampered by doctors, priests, actors, and athletes. Such is our own history after all, our decline and fall.

The evidence, however, suggests otherwise. During the Archaic, Classical, and early Hellenistic Periods, the cult of Asklepios at Epidauros was a source of renewal and strength for the Greek culture. The games, music, and drama at Epidauros demonstrated the full range of the human instrument put to regenerative purpose. The speed, agility, strength, lyricism, eloquence, harmony, and passion all elevated the spirits of the ill and weak, not to mention the depressed and cynical. In these contests and concerts the best were raised up as exemplars of achievement; they were honored above all others for having risen to such heights. In this honor was the aspiration of the human race standing before its gods.

The Propylaia

Visitors to Epidauros will arrive at a parking area to the south of the sanctuary. The modern entrance to the site leads directly to the museum as a starting point, but the ancient pilgrim entered from the north. To follow this traditional approach means a walk across the site directly away from the theater to the northern boundary of the excavation. The ancient Propylaia is at this northern extremity and was approached by crossing a small stream, now unfortunately quite dry and fenced off. The present ruins date from the fourth century BC and are located at a point where two major roads converged, one coming from the ancient village of Epidauros on the sea and the other from the direction of Argos.

Over 65 feet (20 m) in length, the Propylaia was like a small temple, approached by a ramp that is still in evidence. Across the front entrance six Ionic columns supported the entablature, on the architrave of which were inscribed the following verses:

Pure must be he who enters the fragrant temple.

Purity means to think nothing but holy thoughts.

The Greek inscription ends with the words *phronein hosia,* a phrase that carries more meaning than the sense of the English translation "think holy thoughts." Included in that phrase is the idea of lawfulness, of turning one's attention away from the world and its temptations and toward the spiri-

Site of the North Propylon, original entrance to the sanctuary, Epidauros

tual path, or "straight thought." What made the pilgrim ill in the first place was bound up in the neglect of lawfulness. Too much of the world, of the pleasures and demands of daily life, usurped the proper place of the divine within the individual, with the result that the body became ill and the mind was clouded with scattered dreams and irrational fears. The emotional or psychological state was out of joint and needed correction.

In the strictly religious sense, purity also meant to be free of pollution. The admonition was made not to enter the sanctuary for ignoble purposes or ridicule the healing process or rob the sanctuary of its treasures. Obviously, the whole life of the sanctuary would be threatened by anyone entering without proper respect for its holiness. Even today in Greece, the casual visitor is watched carefully to make sure that proper respect in dress and behavior is observed in the sanctuary.

The modern pilgrim will not experience much of the desired effect of entering the Propylaia and seeing the enclosure ahead. Today trees have replaced the six Corinthian columns that once lined the inner passageway. Since columns take their history and meaning from trees, the substitution is not entirely inappropriate, but the sight lines are obscured by the present vegetation. Enough of a view remains, however, to suggest something of the intent when entering the sanctuary from the north. The Sacred Way lies ahead, up a gentle incline.

The Sanctuary

Our goal along the Sacred Way is the sanctuary proper, or *heiron,* of Asklepios, where the central activity of healing took place. To reach it the modern pilgrim passes along the Sacred Way past Roman ruins on the left outside the once-restricted portion of the sanctuary. Just outside there was a small temple of Aphrodite, where one could pause to make a sacrifice and to pray for healing. As the detail map shows, the main buildings within the *heiron* were six, the most important being the Temple of Asklepios, a fourth century BC construction probably built on the remains of an older temple of Apollo. We know that from the late fifth century BC onward the site was devoted to Asklepios himself. This shift from Apollo to Asklepios illustrates the change in the perception of healing during the Classical Period. Later, as we shall see, the function of the *abaton* fell from favor and further secularized the practice of medicine at the site.

The Temple of Asklepios

The Temple of Asklepios was oriented to the east to face Mount Titthion, the rounded hill sacred to his birth. We are also reminded of the birth of Asklepios as we look to Titthion's sister hill to the west; although he is the son of Apollo, from whom all healing arts arise, there is also the organic matter out of which the human substance is formed and which re-

Bust of Asklepios, fourth century BC. This image was often used in statues of Jesus in Christian times, National Archaeological Museum, Athens.

quires the healing arts.

As we learn from the archaeological record, the Temple of Asklepios was in the Doric order and was peripteral—with six fluted columns at the ends and eleven columns on each side. The ground plan measured 76 feet (24.5 m) long and nearly 55 feet (13.2 m) wide. Its decoration was elaborate and brightly colored. In the *cella* (or *sekos*) the gold and ivory statue of Asklepios, carved by Thrasymedes of Paros, was of gigantic size and elaborate design. The god was portrayed holding the healing staff of life in his right hand and placing his left hand in firm control over the head of the serpent. The serpent represents the life force to be harmonized and controlled. So also, in the brilliant structure of the Tholos, the art of Asklepios brought the power of the serpent under control for the benefit of mankind, just as Apollo mastered the python in the mythology of Delphi.

The decoration of the throne of Asklepios carried through this theme. The hero Bellerophon is pictured killing the monster Chimera, symbol of powerful and destructive imaginings. Perseus is also pictured with the head of the Medusa, whose demonic aspect turned men to stone. Paul Diel put it this way: "The ancient Greeks made use of an infallible talisman against all kinds of illness. This was the Gorgonian, a medal showing the severed head of Medusa. Thus, mythical inspiration deemed the condition of inner harmony, victory over guilty vanity, to be the supreme protection against illness not only of the soul but also of the body." Thus, the pilgrim gazes upon the symbolic figure of the god in his representation as the conqueror of human vanity and unchecked desires, two of the major causes of human illness. To worship him was to sublimate (or make sublime) these desires, to give over control to a spiritual power.

Foundation of Tholos temple, showing recent excavations, Epidauros

The Tholos

At the westernmost point of the inner sanctuary are the remains of the most impressive and beautiful building at Epidauros. The Tholos, or round building, was designed by Polykleitos in the fourth century BC and served a central purpose in the curative practices of the sanctuary. Pausanius offers important information about the Tholos when he reports that he saw in it many inscriptions, or *stele*, giving the names and particulars of men and women cured by the god. He also describes some of the decorative murals in the building, including one of Eros playing the lyre and another of Drunkenness holding a wine goblet.

Recent excavations have revealed that the Tholos was built over a labyrinth of three concentric stone circles with openings. This small labyrinth was accessible from a trapdoor in the *cella* floor, which had a black-and-white spiraled mosaic design. The exterior design of the temple must have been most impressive. A circle of twenty-six Doric columns supported an entablature sparsely decorated with rosettes sculpted in the center of the *metopes*. The inner structure was supported by fourteen beautifully fashioned Corinthian columns, one of which can be seen in the museum.

The sculpting of these columns reveals a harmonious symmetry unmatched in ancient Greece. The design exhibits a startling control over natural growth, a perfecting of nature in grace and movement.

The purpose of the Tholos has been much debated. It is clear, however, that its symbolic purpose was to represent spiritual control over natural forces. The perfect circular shape is the circle of divinity—the unity of body, mind, and spirit. The exterior of the building is the perfection of Apollo, the form of the spirit embodied in geometric expression. It is also an expression of the imposition of spirit over the potentially destructive, repressed desires of human nature,

Detail of Tholos—the labyrinth of three rings of stone, with narrow gates leading to center, Epidauros

symbolized by the labyrinth beneath the building. In effect, the labyrinth marks recognition of the reality and power of the forces of the underworld, and the upper structure caps and sublimates those lower forces.

The Greeks expressed this relationship as that of *nomos* to *physis*, law in relation to nature. The *nomoi* were those laws, both spiritual and secular, that controlled the forces of *physis,* the part of human nature seen as something like a volcano ready to erupt. The Tholos, in its circular design with the natural imagery of plant life and with its labyrinth of human passion, expresses the imposition of *nomos* over the labyrinth of *physis*—the triumph of control, the containing of turbulence. The whole building illustrates the human being properly aligned, with spirit over mind and mind over body. It is also a vision of perfect health, and the inscriptions within the temple remind the pilgrim that those who came before have found health in this setting.

The actual function of this building is unclear. Pilgrims might have been led into the labyrinth in a ceremony of the underworld, passing through the dark night of the soul before emerging to the light and perfection of a new life. Another theory is that ceremonial snakes might have been kept in the labyrinth, again a symbolic statement of control of natural forces. We do know that geometric form was for the Greeks a means of articulating forces and powers, and so there must have been a symbolic purpose and a spiritual intent for this beautiful building as a central part of the life of the sanctuary.

Recent excavations at Eutresis on the island of Euboea have revealed a round pit used for burnt sacrifices. The pit is 20 feet (6 m) in diameter and 10 feet (3 m) deep and contained ash, animal bones, and pottery. Imposed over this pit, which has been dated in the Early Helladic Period, was a later sanctuary containing a libation table and round hearth. It is

Remains of the Abaton, where sleep cures were induced, Epidauros

certainly possible that such a structure was a sacrificial precursor of the later *tholos* buildings.

The Abaton

North of the Tholos lie the remains of the Abaton. Shaped like a long stoa, or narrow colonnade, the Abaton was a place for curative sleeping and was reserved for those whose cure called for this special ritual. The remains reveal two levels, the higher one reached by sixteen steps. The entire structure was 158 feet (70 m) long and 49 feet (9.5 m) wide. During the extensive archaeological digs many tablets describing miraculous cures were found in the Abaton. Now on display in the museum, some of the descriptions reveal clearly the Abaton's very special role.

The sleep cure was called *enkoimisis*. The patient prepared carefully for this process, undertaking rites of purification and sacrifice before entering the Abaton. Certainly, there was some sense in which the god entered the patient in this sleeping state and effected a cure, or through the medium of dream indicated what steps should be followed for a cure. The myth of Asklepios includes accounts of snakes approaching the patient and actually licking or touching the affected area to accomplish a cure. This part of the myth once again points out the importance of spiritual influence in bringing the body back to its natural state of health.

Examples of Cures

The *stele* found at the Abaton describe various cures involving *enkoimisis*. Stele 1 reads in part:

> Cleo was with child for five years. After she had been pregnant for five years she came as a suppliant to the god and slept in the Abaton. As soon as she had left it and got outside the temple precincts, she bore a son

who, immediately after birth, washed himself at the fountain and walked about with his mother. In return for this favor she inscribed her offering: "Admirable is not the greatness of the tablet, but the divine power. Cleo carried the burden in her womb for five years, until she slept in the Abaton and the god healed her."

Another stele reads:

> A woman from Athens called Ambrosia was blind in one eye. She came as a suppliant to the god. As she walked about in the temple, she laughed at some of the cures as incredible and impossible, [that] the lame and the blind should be healed by merely having a dream. In her sleep she had a vision. It seemed to her that the god stood by her and said that he would cure her, but that in payment he would ask her to dedicate to the temple a silver pig as a memorial of her foolishness. After saying this, he cut the diseased eyeball and poured in some drug. When day came, she walked out of the Abaton completely sound.

The silver pig was a symbol of vanity and doubt, an expression of the refusal to acknowledge the spiritual element within. Blindness in one eye is a further sign of denying the divine reality. Thus, sleeping in the Abaton can cure spiritual blindness and also restore physical health, or full sight. A five-year pregnancy might reflect a refusal to acknowledge the presence of the god within. Once it is recognized, the spirit lives as a natural part of human life.

On the other hand, we may be reading here literal descriptions of miraculous cures, although a five-year pregnancy defies medical possibility. There are many descriptions of lesser cures that are clearly the correction of actual illnesses through spiritual intervention.

As the visitor will see in the museum, the priests and physicians of the Asklepieion also employed surgical instruments and what we would call standard medical practice to effect cures. This evidence comes from a later period when Epidauros had lost much of its purely spiritual power. The whole archaeological record at Epidauros, however, is a history of the development of medicine and the story of the role of spiritual faith in restoring health.

THE THEATER

Nothing else like the theater at Epidauros remains in Greece. It is as if the perfection of its design and construction and its placement in the landscape have effectively shielded it from the ravages of humanity and time. Pausanius praises it in his own understated fashion:

> The Epidaurians have a theater in their sanctuary that seems to me particularly worth a visit. The Roman theaters have come far beyond all the others in the

whole world: the theater of Megalopolis in Arkadia is
unique for magnitude: but who can begin to rival
Polykleitos for the beauty and composition of his architecture?

This great structure is not the theater of Sophocles and
Euripides, although their works played here in the fourth
century BC as they do today in summer revivals. This theater
does not so much evoke memories of great drama as it does
visions of great design. Nowhere in Greece is the power of
sacred geometry made so accessible. In the fourth century
BC the wealth and fame of the sanctuary of Asklepios attracted
the best artists and builders in Greece to begin extensive renovation of the existing structures and to build new structures
like the theater. Among the most gifted of the builders was
Polykleitos the Younger, whom we know already as the builder
of the Tholos.

From the evidence we can be certain that Polykleitos
was well versed in the principles of sacred geometry. At the
time that the theater was designed and constructed, Plato
was teaching philosophy in his Academy in Athens. Over the
entrance to the Academy was inscribed, "A credit in geometry is required." One of Plato's favorite sayings was "God is
always doing geometry." The meaning of such a saying is seen
in this theater, which in its perfection embodies spiritual
knowledge brought to light, made manifest. It is knowledge
to be touched, walked on, sat in, enclosed by, experienced
fully.

The acoustics are stunning. As all the tour guides are
delighted to demonstrate, a person standing in the center of
the orchestra, at the site of the ancient altar, can tear a small
piece of paper—such as an admission ticket—and the sound
will carry to the last row of the Upper Cavea, 55 rows away.

Approach to the theater, with monumental western parados, Epidauros

Why this is the case no one can articulate in terms of principles of sound, but since geometry made this theater, we can suppose that geometry creates the acoustical effects.

Geometry and Number

The basic unit of measurement for the theater—and indeed for many of the fourth century BC monuments—was the Pheidonian ell, which corresponded to one and a half Doric feet, or 19.3 inches. Laid out flat, the radius of the outermost circle of the theater is 120 ells. The radius to the inner circle, or Diazoma, is 80 ells—which is probably the extent of the fourth-century BC construction. Indications are that the Upper Cavea of 21 rows was added in the second century BC, no doubt following through the geometric implications of the original design. The final construction creates a seating arrangement in which the Upper Cavea has 21 rows and the lower 34.

The ratio of 55 (the total number of rows) to 34 is 1.618, which is the ruling number of the Golden Proportion. The same is true of the ratio of 34 to 21. Sacred numerology reveals several remarkable relations: 55 is the sum of the first ten digits added together, with 21 the sum of 1 through 6 and 34 the sum of 7 through 10.

As Doxiadis pointed out in his analysis of architectural space in Greece, planners used either a ten- or a twelve-part system in designing and placing a given building on its site. At Epidauros, the base was ten in all measurements. The aisles of the theater, for example, radiate out at an angle of 18 degrees (360 degrees divided by 20, or base ten). The resulting design focuses our attention on the center of the orchestra very much the way a magnifying glass focuses the rays of the sun upon a burning point. During the dramatic competitions, the emotional and intellectual attention of the viewer would

Central aisle of the theater, showing size of actors from last rows, Epidauros

have been easily focused to a unifying spiritual intent.

It is still possible to experience something of this effect today, as dramatic performances of Greek plays are held here during the summer months. It is worth the effort to arrange to stay in Epidauros for the evening, or to drive out from Athens for a production. Even if you do not understand Greek, the sounds of the language in the night air arrange themselves musically and reflect some of the ancient power. The movements of actor and chorus are also beautiful to see in this space. Sitting high up, perhaps near the seats of honor at the Diazoma, the viewer can watch as the action is shaped to a larger design than is usually experienced in secular theater.

As a last note, during the day, when the theater is open and is relatively quiet—since even schoolchildren remain somewhat controlled in this space—it is possible to sit still for a time. Meditation goes well here, and it is never surprising to see still, erect figures blending into the sacred geometry of Epidauros.

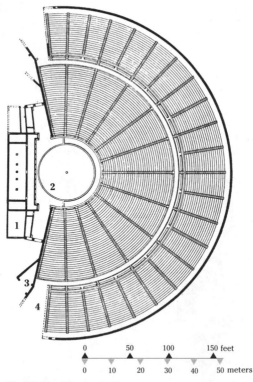

Fig. 26. *The Theater, Epidauros*
1. *Skene*
2. *Orchestra*
3. *Diazoma*
4. *Upper Cavea*

DELPHI

*And they met together and dedicated
in the temple of Apollo at Delphi
as the first fruits of their wisdom
the far-famed inscriptions
which are in all men's mouths,
"Know Thyself" and "Nothing Too Much."*

— Plato, *Protagoras*

Delphi was the spiritual center, the navel, of the ancient Greek world, its influence radiating out to include the civilizations which had formed around the Mediterranean Sea and the mountainous territories to the north. The natural setting of the sanctuary evoked the Earth Mother, her body carved out of the southern approaches to Mount Parnassos by earthquake and rock fall and opening out onto the valley of the Pleistos River, which wound like a snake to the sea. As a cult center and sanctuary, Delphi established itself early as a place where revelation became manifest and where the gods spoke to human consciousness.

Through most of Delphi's history, Apollo ruled there. The son of Zeus represented the harmony of human desires, the Logos or Word of the Father, and the Logos was delivered through the mouths of specially chosen women who had demonstrated receptiveness to oracular power. Their utterings were formed into hexameters by temple priests for formal communication to the faithful. Delphi was thus a spiritual matrix, a place where spirit took form and was heard. In that sense Delphi is still a sacred place, revered by many Greeks and others in the world, although it is silent, no longer expressing the divine laws except as pilgrims are able to embody the sense of them in themselves from the power of the setting and the ruins so lovingly attended.

HISTORY

THE EARTH MOTHER CULTS

The history of the sanctuary of Delphi tells the story of the development of Greek culture and religion. Prior to the Archaic Period and the final sweep of the Dorian invasions,

The Temple of Apollo with restored columns and monumental foundations, Delphi

Delphi was the center of a cult that worshiped the Earth Mother deity, an underworld deity known as Ge or Gaea, whose name means simply the Earth. Bronze Age remains at Delphi have yielded limited but firm evidence of Mother Goddess shrines and figurines. Finds at the Korykeion Cave on Mount Parnassos have also confirmed Earth Mother worship and oracular activity.

The legends of this early period tell of the sibyls, the inspired prophetesses who gave oracle on the great rock at Delphi and whose utterances were both wondrous and terrible. Oracles were also unpredictable, coming only during certain seasons and usually without warning. Sibyls were fairly common throughout the Mediterranean and were usually associated with sacred rocks and springs. This cult activity was a remnant of the knowledge possessed by prehistoric peoples of spiritual activity present at or near various features of landscape. At Delphi we are in the presence of the body of the goddess, the great clefts corresponding to the birth canal, above which rests the *omphalos*, navel of the world.

From 1500 to 1100 BC, Delphi was a Mycenaean village. The site of the present temple was probably the location of the *megaron*, within which the cult center for the worship of the Earth Mother Goddess was located. Sacrificial pits have been identified at the point where the inner sanctum or *adyton* of the temple was later placed and also within the sanctuary of Athena Pronaia. These common areas of worship suggest a continuous history of religious activity at very specific places within Delphi.

THE WORSHIP OF APOLLO

The history of the site suggests that the worship of Apollo may have begun around 1000 BC, when the god arrived from Dorian Crete or with the northern tribes of Thessaly. With the development of the *polis* and the arts of civilization, Apollo grew in stature and became the dominant god of prophecy. This shift in the image of prophetic power from the feminine to the masculine and from the nomadic to the settled was a function of two related developments.

First, the emphasis on the *polis,* with its new laws and customs, gave rise to a new attitude toward prophecy. The will of Zeus was sought out to affirm decisions made by rulers for the *polis.* Thus, prophecy and civilization became connected in the person of Apollo. It is noteworthy in the history of Greek culture that prophecy achieved such a high place in the official state religion. In many cases no important decision could be made without advice and consent from Delphi.

Second, and of greater spiritual importance, the desire to control and harmonize all oracular activity was accomplished by the invention of the temple, the "machine" by which human vision and genius formally invoked the presence of the gods. In the case of Apollo, the temple was the sanctuary where oracular activity took place. The *adyton* held the sacred *omphalos* and the tripod—a three-legged stool— upon which the priestess sat to receive her revelations. The temple controlled access to the place of prophecy, allowing the priests at a later time to give form to the proceedings, and, as it were, to make rational the raw material of inspiration.

Apollo had replaced the Earth Mother and her sibyls at Delphi after the Mycenaean Period. Later, perhaps in the eighth century BC, a modest temple of mud brick and wood was erected on the present site. The priests who assumed control of the sanctuary at that time retained the services of sibyl-like priestesses—usually peasant girls who had shown intuitive powers of utterance. The "divine madness" exhibited by these women was given form by the priests, thus providing measure and harmony to the utterances.

It was known and accepted among the Greek peoples that divine utterance was accompanied by fits of frenzied behavior that marked the point where divine and human consciousness converged. The human instrument was taken over by the god. The low-pitched voices of the women seemed to emanate from the abdomen (hence the ancient term "belly talkers"), and the utterances were always couched in the first person, so that it was clear that Apollo himself was the speaker. At such times the women were said to be *en theos* or "with the god." The English word "enthusiasm" is derived from this phrase—a fact that gives fresh meaning to Emerson's comment that nothing great is accomplished without enthusiasm.

Early in the history of Delphi the worship of Dionysos was introduced in conjunction with that of Apollo. This blend of the rational and irrational elements in religious belief and practice was probably in recognition of the natural forces present at Delphi and of the local beliefs that had accompanied the worship of the Earth Mother. Dionysos was the natural force of creative energy and enthusiasm recognized by the Greeks as an important part of spiritual life. His presence at Delphi with the rational god Apollo demonstrated awareness of these forces and respect for them both as necessary and vital to self-knowledge.

THE POLITICAL HISTORY

During the Archaic Period the administration of the oracle came under political and religious control. Twelve ancient families agreed upon the formation of a council that would have authority over the shrine. The administration included the temple hierarchy as well as secular leadership. The federation was named Amphiktyonia, and the ruling group was named the Amphiktyonic Council. The council met twice a year and established policy and a festival calendar for the shrine, including administration of the Pythian Games.

In 448 BC, the Spartans, Phokians, and Athenians each sought to increase their power. The ensuing conflict finally resulted in the agreement of 421 BC, as part of which Delphi emerged as an autonomous entity, uncontrolled by any *polis,* although influenced by the political power of the moment. The Spartans achieved prominence in the councils of the Amphiktyonia, for example, after their victory in the Peloponnesian War. Their influence continued into the fourth century BC, when the temple had to be rebuilt after earthquake damage to the sanctuary.

In 346 BC the Macedonians in their turn asserted control over the sanctuary. Philip II, father of Alexander the Great, became president of the Pythian Games and was the most powerful member of the council. During the next two hundred years the oracle declined in influence but remained active. Delphi dropped out of the historical record as politically influential, but the Neoplatonists gave it new spiritual significance as a source of revelation.

During the Roman Era Delphi enjoyed a political renaissance of sorts, being favored by a series of emperors who built impressive monuments and *stoas* on the site. In 86 BC, however, it was sacked by Sulla, which also left it vulnerable to further attack. Indeed, the sanctuary was plundered on a regular basis after that, sometimes on a massive scale. Nero, for example, removed over five hundred statues during his reign. Many remained, though. It was reported that during the time of Pliny the Elder over three thousand statues filled the sanctuary.

Legend has it that the Roman Julian the Apostate tried

to revive the oracle in AD 360 but received the following message from Delphi: Tell the king the fair-wrought hall has fallen to the ground. No longer has Phoebus a hut, nor a prophetic laurel, nor a spring that speaks. The water of speech even is quenched.

MYTHOLOGY

The myths of Delphi are twofold. They tell of Apollo's mastery of the oracular shrine, and they tell of the purification of the shrine from pollution. These two lines of myth parallel one another and describe the shifting beliefs in gods as oracles and the changing character of humans as the beneficiaries of those oracles. Like other sacred places, the ethos of Delphi has to do with the mysteries of divine epiphany. What is special about Delphi begins with its sacred setting and its geographic isolation from any major *polis,* so that in the end the site had a unique and universal quality. This is quite unlike Eleusis, which had always been closely connected to Athens and her history and which was without a powerful natural setting to enhance its oracular power.

To the Greek mind Delphi was the center of the world. Some took this quite literally and were then ridiculed as naive by the likes of Herodotos, but others understood this centrality in a different sense. Delphi was the source of oracular wisdom, the center of revelation, and therefore of divine knowledge. To acknowledge Delphi as the center was to accept faith in the gods as the source of life, fate, wisdom, and justice. Thus, Delphi was the point from which the greater circle of Greek culture, religion, and philosophy was inscribed.

THE MYTHS OF APOLLO AT DELPHI

Apollo was born of the goddess Leto, who was the daughter of Titans and rival to Hera. Hera tormented Leto during her pregnancy and pursued her throughout the world until at last she found peace on the lonely, windswept island of Delos, center of the Cycladic world. There she gave birth to Apollo and his sister Artemis. While still a baby, Apollo demanded bow and arrows and with them sped to Mount Parnassos, where he sought out the great serpent Python, enemy of Leto. Overmatched, Python fled to Delphi, to the security of the shrine of the Earth Mother, but Apollo disregarded the sanctity of the shrine and slew Python, polluting the sanctuary and offending the Earth Mother goddess.

Apollo then went either to the Vale of Tempe, a dramatic gorge and valley to the north beneath Mount Olympus, or to Crete and was purified of the crime of murder and the pollution of holy ground. The divergence in the myths at this point reflect the various claims concerning Apollo's origins. In either case, after being purified, Apollo returned to Delphi, where he persuaded Pan, the goat-footed god of wild places and evocative music, to reveal the art of prophecy. Inherent in this aspect of the myth is a reconciliation between Apollo and Dionysos, that god and force of nature that makes itself felt in orgiastic music and dance.

The God of Music

Apollo's instrument is the seven-stringed lyre, a sacred instrument invented by Hermes and perfected by Apollo. As pictured often on pottery, the lyre was made from the large shell of a tortoise and the curved horns of a goat. Its rival instrument was the double flute, played in particular by Pan and associated with Dionysos. The flute was a seductive instrument that produced passion, excess, and forgetfulness. The lyre soothed the passions and promoted peace, moderation, lawful harmony, and spiritual awareness. In myth, the lyre defeats all rivals in music, particularly the flute.

What little we do know about ancient Greek music is supplemented by our knowledge of Pythagorean principles. The lyre must have been strung in such a way as to produce mathematically graduated tones. The resulting harmonies must have contrasted dramatically with the sliding, imprecise tones of the double flute. The myths tell of contests in which Apollo always wins the prize with his lyre in competition with flute players, such as Pan. These contests continued at Delphi in honor of Apollo, especially every four years during the Pythian games.

The God of Civilization

The musical victories also represent conquest by the sophisticated city-states over the more primitive territories, like Phrygia and Arkadia, where the flute remained popular with the peasants. Apollo's defeat of the Python and his victories in musical contests signal the triumph of civilization over the nomadic lifestyle of an earlier time. In spiritual terms the connection to music symbolizes control by higher orders of the mind over the lower rule of the emotions. Representing a more human consciousness than his father, Apollo embodies the human hope that divine consciousness will impose itself and rule human affairs. This is apparent not only in Apollo's function as the god of prophecy but also in his associations with music and light.

Although Helios is the sun god, Apollo is also associated with light. Apollo illuminates the arts of civilization and champions the victory of reason. He is the builder of temples, the father of sacred geometry and architecture. He represents the belief that the divine may be understood through the study of philosophy as opposed to the revelations of divine Dionysian frenzy. But reason triumphs only in a state of purity, free of pollution.

Because he is the pure god, Apollo is also the god of healing, and in that capacity is the father of Asklepios. But

Engraving of Pan with his pipes and a goat-footed satyr figure

there is a double edge to this healing sword. Apollo is also the bringer of plagues, which were always regarded as signs of spiritual pollution. One of the curses of civilization was the presence of plague in the crowded, infested streets, and Apollo brings with him this punishment.

The Distant God

The myths of Apollo as told by Homer in the *Iliad* describe a god distanced from the Greeks and often using his powers to oppose their aims. He was on the side of Troy in the great war, bringing death to Greek heroes. His oracle was also vague on the subject of Greek success in the Persian Wars. The god's distance and ambiguity reflect his Asian roots and the elusiveness of his word. Apollo's weapons are the bow and arrow, shot from a distance and striking suddenly, without warning.

This aura of distance removed Apollo from the daily lives of the people, and he became an elite god, known well only by artists, poets, and intellectuals. The gods of the people, Pan and Dionysos, Aphrodite and Artemis, continued to live in the wild places, clinging to the rocks and springs, murmuring their words of affection and devotion, meeting ordinary needs and soothing the troubled spirits of ordinary people. That is why Dionysos came to share the sanctuary of Delphi with Apollo, residing in the temple for the three winter months while Apollo went to the far north to dwell alone.

The myths of Delphi serve to describe the site's natural surroundings and to set forth the story of civilization. Apollo represents the imposition of order upon chaos. When the rocks of the Phaedriades break loose from the trembling earth and destroy the temple, the power of human consciousness imposes form once again on chaos and builds another geometric expression of devotion and sacrifice in order to control

such awesome power. Nowhere on earth is the tension between order and chaos so dramatically displayed, even now.

THE SITE OF DELPHI

Delphi is a clear spiritual statement. It sits precariously in
the lap of a nurturing power that opens out beneath the twin
peaks of Mount Parnassos. The sanctuary embodies the human aspiration to know and to become one with the ruling
gods. The site for the sanctuary is imposing. The cliffs of the
Phaedriades, the "brilliant ones," surround the small rock
plateau out of which has been carved enough level space to
establish a temple and its supporting buildings. The site opens
out to the south and is crossed all day by the sun and swept
by sea breezes. The valley of the Pleistos River below is fertile, planted with olive trees, and extends to the port town of
Itea and the Gulf of Corinth.

The altitude of the site is deceptive, seeming higher than
its 1,870 feet (570 m). The deception is caused by the steep-
ness of the ascent from the valley and the frame of the hills
across the way, sacred to Athena and her nearby site at
Marmaria. The site is also very small, only 6 acres, huddled
against the cliffs near the Kastalian Spring, which still rises
with fresh water from the cleft formed by the Phaedriades.

WHAT TO SEE AT DELPHI

Delphi offers four distinct areas to the visitor. The first is the
Sanctuary of Athena Pronaia at Marmaria. Pronaia means
"before the shrine" or "gate to the shrine," and Marmaria is
simply the small plateau near the road, half a mile (800 m)
from the main sanctuary. The second, just above Marmaria
and on the other side at the curve of the road is the Kastalian
Spring, where pilgrims and temple priests and priestesses
bathed before entering the temple grounds. Third is the main
sanctuary, including the theater and stadium. The fourth is
the Delphi Museum, which contains many of the valuable artifacts uncovered during excavations by the French School
of Archaeology.

ATHENA PRONAIA

Occupying a narrow strip of land on the southern slope of
Parnassos and facing the twin mounds across the valley is
the Sanctuary of Athena Pronaia (see Fig. 27). This site is very

ancient, having been occupied during the Neolithic Period (5000-3000 BC) and later by the Mycenaeans. The site was dedicated to the Olympian deities, Athena in particular, but it belonged earlier to an ancient cult of the Earth Mother, whose form in the hills opposite is a powerful presence. The remains, consisting of pottery, ashes, tools, and figurines, suggest an area devoted to sacrifice. Later Athena, guardian of wisdom and consciousness, assumed her place on this sacred site, taking over its functions and bringing the devotion to the Earth Mother into the Classical Age.

This site remains a puzzle. It seems unlikely that it was established only as a gateway to the main sanctuary or as a secondary gift to a goddess in the aftermath of Apollo's usurpation of the oracle from the earlier Earth Mother cult. The answer to why this narrow strip of land was sacred for so many years may lie in its surroundings. A spring, farther to the east from Kastalia, emerged above the plateau and served the ritual needs of the site. Its waters may have sprung from the earth below the cliffs and produced an area of abundant growth, sacred to the Earth Mother in her role as nurturer. Second, the landscape across the valley stands in contrast to the threatening, more ominous twin peaks to the north.

THE ARCHAIC TEMPLE

There are two important structures on this narrow site. The Archaic Temple of Athena, the first version of which was built in the middle of the seventh century BC, was one of the earliest major temples in Greece. This early temple was no doubt destroyed by earthquake or rockfalls. Rebuilt in 500 BC, the temple was again destroyed, this time perhaps by Persians, or else by earthquakes. The Archaic temple was actually restored somewhat at the beginning of our own twentieth century only to be destroyed once again by a rockfall in 1905.

Capitals from the Archaic temple may be found at the site. These early Doric designs featured a thick *echinus* (molding above the column shaft), which gives the suggestion of a great weight flattening the column supports. The design of the temple itself was also unusual. Six columns fronted the temple and twelve formed the sides, making the length of the platform or stylobate exactly twice the width, rather than slightly longer according to the later pattern of six and thirteen. The reason for this unusual pattern may be the narrow and thus limited space of the site.

Some might argue that the temple should have been situated in the more customary east-west orientation. However, here in Marmaria the temple had to face the double-mounded hills and cleft across the valley, no doubt to conform to the orientation of an earlier Mycenaean-Minoan shrine to the goddess located at the same spot. Here among the ruins of at least three versions of the temple—Archaic, Classical, and Hellenistic—and in the presence of impressive sacred landscape one is able to sense the splendid continuity of ancient

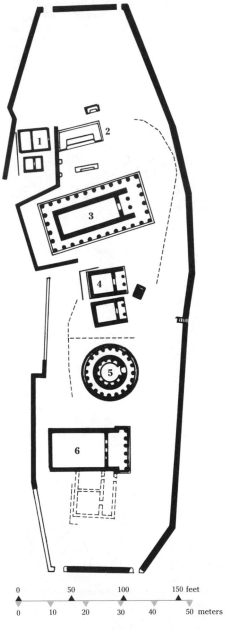

Fig. 27. *The Sanctuary of Athena Pronaia*
1. Treasuries or Early Temples
2. Altar

3. Temple of Athena
4. Treasuries
5. Tholos
6. Later Temple of Athena

Greek religious ritual. From the Neolithic figurines found here to Roman restoration and embellishment, a long and deeply held tradition was made manifest over a period of three thousand years.

THE THOLOS

The second important structure at Marmaria is the famous Tholos Temple, three columns of which have been restored to support a section of entablature. Built in the early fourth century BC, this temple, too, was constructed on a site sacred to the goddess. Like other *tholoi*, such as the one at Epidauros, these round temples may have been closely related to Mycenaean sacrificial pits, which in turn probably reflected Neolithic rites for the goddess. This Tholos was erected on a triple platform and was 45 feet in diameter (13.5 m). Its twenty outside columns were Doric in order, but very slim and graceful. They supported an entablature that featured sculptures depicting the War of the Amazons. The inner colonnade was constructed of ten Corinthian columns, one of the earliest examples of the order. The floor, seen more clearly from the bluff above the ruins, was set in geometric patterns of Pentellic and Eleusinian marble.

The Tholos sits in this landscape as an ordering principle. Its round, graceful shape gathers the conflicting elements into coherence. Because it is round, there is no orientation to a particular feature; instead, the wild gorge, deep valley, and distant sea are harmonized through the use of the circle within which smaller circles emanate. From this circle, so carefully crafted, the circle of the world takes shape, and from that circle the goddess who resides here is made manifest.

The Tholos Temple at Marmaria, shown in its wild landscape setting, Delphi

OTHER STRUCTURES

To the west of the Tholos are the remains of the later Temple of Athena, built in 370 BC to replace the earthquake-damaged main temple. This small prostyle building, fashioned of local limestone, had a simple Doric facade of six columns. Next to it was a small square building probably devoted to administration of the shrine. The other buildings on the site, to the east of the Tholos, were treasuries and were also oriented to the south in line with the hills opposite.

A path at the western edge of the sanctuary leads down to another plateau where the remains of the gymnasium are found. There is an ancient *palaestra*, or public building, a pool and Roman bathhouse, and, finally, the stadium. This area may be seen to better advantage from above at the theater in the main sanctuary.

THE KASTALIAN SPRING

Along the road to the west, where it curves as one approaches the main sanctuary of Apollo, lie the remains of the two sacred springs of Kastalia. Here, where the great cliffs form a steep chasm, both pilgrims and the priesthood gathered to purify themselves in preparation for entering the great temple. The spring closest to the road is the older shrine, built in the Archaic Period and not rediscovered until 1958. Stone ducts carried the water into a rectangular basin, walled in and fitted with stone benches. On the western wall four lion-head spouts fed the basin while gates on the eastern end regulated the flow of water.

The older, Archaic Kastalian Spring. Delphi

The later spring, farther into the gorge, was carved out of the cliff and constructed in Hellenistic times. It was provided with votive niches in honor of Kastalia, nymph of the sacred waters. The construction of this spring made it impossible to bathe in the spring itself. Instead, the source of water was covered and seven bronze spouts provided water for the purifying rites. In later years, Christian traditions added a shrine to John the Baptist, a column of which can still be seen in the large niche to the right.

The Hellenistic Kastalian Spring, with votive niches from later times, Delphi

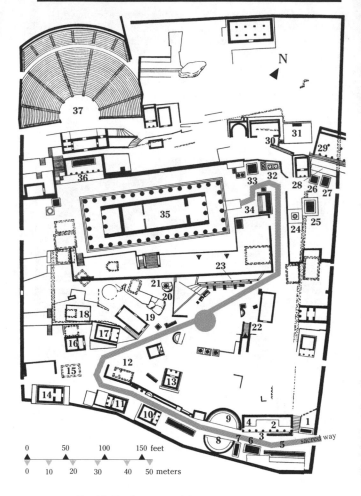

Fig. 28. The Sanctuary of Apollo at Delphi
 1. Bull of the Korcyrans
 2. Arkadian Statues
 3. Statue of Philopoimen
 4. Spartan Stoa
 5. Spartan Naval Monument
 6. Bronze Horse
 7. Marathon Memorial
 8. The Seven against Thebes
 9. The Kings of Argos
10. Sikyonian Treasury
11. Siphnian Treasury
12. Megarian Treasury
13. Aeolian Treasury
14. Theban Treasury
15. Boeotian Treasury

THE SANCTUARY OF APOLLO

Archaeologists owe much of their knowledge of the exact placement of the hundreds of statues and buildings contained within the main sanctuary at Delphi to the visit of Pausanius in the second century AD (see Fig. 28). Pausanius began his tour just as any modern visitor would, at the eastern corner where now the modern gatehouse is located, most fittingly at the site of the Roman *agora*, where pilgrims purchased offerings to the god and other trinkets.

The general shape of the sanctuary—a rectangle bounded by retaining walls at top and bottom and on the sides stepping down the natural slope—was established in the sixth century BC and maintained throughout its active history. The limited and fixed size of the site made it difficult to include all the offerings desired by various cities and individuals, the result being a crowded collection of monuments along the Sacred Way, but only up to a point. On sacred ground, such as near the Rock of the Sibyl and the circular terrace of the Halos, no new monuments were added. Thus there is a sense, even now, of the integrity of the Sacred Way leading to the entrance of the temple.

THE SACRED WAY

The Sacred Way begins at the four steps leading up from the courtyard of the Roman *agora*. The paving visitors tread upon today was laid down during late Roman times, when the sanctuary was in decline. The original lies several inches lower. The route of the Sacred Way leads first to the west and passes by a succession of monuments and important treasuries before it turns due north and angles up the slope. This portion of the sacred route brings the massive cliffs of the Phaedriades into view, a sight that was once unrestricted by the presence of any monument. The route passes northward through the most sacred ground of the sanctuary and then turns northwest for the final approach to the temple entrance. These

*The Sacred Way within
the sanctuary, Delphi*

final steps bring the focus of attention back to the immediate
surroundings and prepare the suppliant for the encounter
with the oracle.

The Lower Monuments of the Sacred Way

The first section of the Sacred Way was devoted throughout
most of its active history after 490 BC to various monuments
honoring military victories or special offerings to Apollo. The
first monument (#1), on the right at the top of the stairs, was
the Bull of the Korcyrans, a huge bronze erected in the 490s
BC. Pausanius tells the story of this extraordinary gift to
Apollo. It seems that on the island of Corfu a bull daily left its
grazing and went down to the sea and bellowed, until one
day the people saw that a huge school of tuna had appeared.
After trying unsuccessfully to catch the fish, help was sought
from the oracle. The people were told to sacrifice the bull to
Poseidon. This done, the tuna were caught easily. In gratitude a portion of the profit from the great catch was used to
erect this bronze in honor of the god.

Next (#2), also to the right on the long, narrow slab
(nearly 31 feet or 9.4 m), stood nine bronze statues erected
by the Arkadians for their victory over the Lakonians in 369
BC. The statues represented the ancestral line of the Arkadians,
beginning with Apollo, then Nike, and followed by the
founders of the state down to the then-living generation. Next
to this grouping is a statue base (#3) on which stood the figure of Philopoimen of Megalopolis, a leader and general who
defeated Sparta in battle in 207 BC. The large cleared area (#4)
behind the statue base contained a stoa with twelve columns.
It is of uncertain origin, but may have been erected by the

Spartans.

On the left side of the Sacred Way just at the top of the stairs is an area (#5) that most likely contained a large grouping of statues, thirty-seven in number, in honor of the decisive naval victory of Sparta over Athens in 404 BC. The statues included both gods and generals and reflected Spartan arrogance at the defeat of Athens in the Peloponnesian War. Next to the Spartan display is a base (#6) for a monumental bronze horse, perhaps meant to be the famous Trojan Horse, erected by the Arory in 414 BC.

In front of the horse and occupying a narrow base (#7) was the Athenian memorial to the Battle of Marathon, which in 490 BC delayed Persian adventurism in Greece for a decade. The memorial was designed to include thirteen bronze statues, including Athena and Apollo, the general Miltiades, whose military victory at Marathon was one of Greek history's greatest, and ten more heroes of Athenian legend. The group was an early work by Phidias, sculptor of the Parthenon, and was set in place around 450 BC. Today, little remains of the base, and its location is only suggested beside the pavement of the Sacred Way.

We now come to two semicircular niches, facing one another and both carved out of the rock of the hillside. Both were Argive offerings. On the left (#8) stood seven bronze statues representing the sons of the famous Seven against Thebes. The legend begins with Oedipus, the most miserable of men, whose crimes banished him from nearby Thebes. The original Seven Argives (celebrated in a play by Aeschylus) failed in their attempt to conquer Thebes, but their sons were victorious, and these two offerings celebrate that final victory.

The second niche (#9) was erected by the Argives after 369 BC and the founding of the colony at Messene. The grouping was of at least ten bronze statues, including the legendary Kings of Argos, of which Herakles was one. These two groupings must have made an impressive showing for the Argives here at the beginning of the Sacred Way, an indication of their long history and power in Greece. The contents of the next three niches on the right are unknown.

The Important Treasuries

A treasury was a small prostyle or *in antis* temple erected by a city-state in honor of the god and used to contain and display wealth. The sanctuary depended upon the generous contributions of the rich states, who in turn depended for their welfare upon the kind oracles of the god. Several of the treasuries here at Delphi were of exquisite design and featured fine sculptures, many of which have been preserved in the Delphi Museum. As Pausanius tells us, by the time he made his trip to Delphi, the treasuries were monuments only and did not hold any gold or silver.

The first of the fine treasuries (#10) is the Sikyonian Treasury, built in the early fifth century BC, the foundation of which remains on the left of the path. As its foundation indicates, the last of several small buildings built on this site was a simple temple *in antis* with two Doric columns before the entrance. Close examination of the foundation stones indicates that at least two other buildings were built on or near this site. One of these structures was a *tholos,* indicating the presence of an ancient sacrificial pit, perhaps an altar to Gaea, Mother Earth.

The next treasury (#11) belonged to the Siphnians, whose gold and silver mines produced such wealth that the island kingdom gave a tenth of the yield—a tithe—for the construction of a magnificent Ionic treasury. Completed around 525 BC, the treasury was without equal in the sanctuary, and fortunately for us, many of the fine marble sculptures were found and are preserved in the museum. As the plan reveals, the building faced west, and the porch was framed by two Karyatides, one of which was found nearby.

At least five other treasuries crowded the curve of the Sacred Way at this point. Across the way was located the Megarian Treasury (#12), and just above it the Aeolian Treasury (#13). To the west, along the huge retaining wall, was the Theban Treasury (#14), and just above it the Boeotian Treasury (#15) and above that the Poteidaian Treasury (#16).

As the Sacred Way turns north the famous Athenian Treasury (#17) comes into full view. It is a reflection of the modern importance of Athens that this treasury has been reconstructed, using most of the original blocks. The restoration was undertaken in 1906 by Replat, a French architect. The building is Doric, *in antis*, with two fluted columns supporting the porch. Thirty *metopes* pictured typical Athenian legends: the labors of Herakles, the battle against the Amazons, and the adventures of Theseus. The *metopes* currently on the building are plaster casts of the originals, which are displayed in the museum.

The Athenian Treasury, restored, Delphi

The dating of the building is in doubt. Pausanius suggests that the treasury was erected after the Battle of Marathon in 490 BC. But most scholars agree that the building is older than that and place it instead around 500 BC at the end of the Archaic Period. Pausanius may have been mislead by an inscription below the building on the narrow terrace upon which the Athenians erected a tripod in honor of the Marathon victory. The many inscriptions covering the walls of the treasury honor various Athenians. Late additions (138–128 BC) on the south wall are ancient musical notations that represent Delphic hymns to Apollo. The museum now holds most of these valuable inscriptions.

The Asklepieion

Just behind the Athenian Treasury are the remains of a small Asklepieion (#18), the precinct at Delphi dedicated to the man-god Asklepios and the healing arts. It was quite natural for Delphi to have an Asklepieion, since Apollo was the father of Asklepios and through Chiron taught his son the art of healing. Certain elements were always included in such a healing center: a source of pure water; an *abaton*, where patients slept under the care of priests and met the god in dreams; and a temple dedicated to Asklepios.

In Delphi, the evidence suggests a minimal facility. There was a fountain house, which provided a source of water from a spring located at the western end of the Temple of Apollo. Stone ducts have been uncovered that brought the water down the hill. The one building that occupies the space seems more like a temple than an *abaton*, which leads to the conclusion that this sanctuary may have been less a curative site than a devotional one.

The Precinct of the Goddess

Ahead on the left, roped off to prevent further damage to vegetation and erosion of the hillside, is the sacred precinct of the early goddesses of the shrine. Here, since long before the first temple was erected, stands the Rock of the Sibyl (#19). Legend has it that Herophile sang her oracles upon this rock. Herophile, whose father was Zeus and mother was Lamia, the first sibyl, sang of the Trojan War and foretold the fate of Helen. Greek history, philosophy, and religion give numerous accounts of various gifted prophetesses who sang "the will of god," which is the derivation of the word *sibyl* (the Doric *sio-bolla* or *theou-boule*). Herophile was the most famous of these gifted women. She is usually associated with the Temple of Apollo at Cumae (Italy), where she lived for many years in the crypts and gave oracle.

It is here, at this rock, that the Greek relationship with deity has its foundation. Although the oracle at Dodona is thought to be older and is probably more primitive in its form, here at Delphi, within this one sanctuary, is the major history of the Greek search for divine revelation. Ge, or Gaea, the Earth, spoke here, uttering her wisdom to those who came

The Rock of the Sibyl, first place of prophecy at Delphi

trembling to her rock, genuinely seeking to know. The rock itself may be part of the cliff, fallen in prehistoric times to its present place, or it may jut from the hill itself, marking a small crevice in the hillside. It rests close to a natural spring called the Sacred Fountain, which emerges from under the temple and appears to return to the earth behind the prophetic rock. A young olive tree sacred to Athena drinks today at this fountain.

Next to the Rock of the Sibyl is the Rock of Leto (#20) where in myth Leto, mother of Apollo, came with her baby boy and sat with him, instructing him in the art of dragon slaying. From this rock Apollo took up his bow and arrows and slew Python to become Lord of the Word of Zeus. Behind the Rock of Leto is the foundation stone of the Sphinx of the Naxians (#21). This masterpiece of mythical vision stood on an Ionic column well above the height of the temple retaining wall. The sphinx, now in the museum, was erected in the mid-sixth century BC and had the head of a woman, the breast and wings of a bird of prey, and the lower body of a lion. Her eyes are closed as she sleeps, guarding the entrance to the temple and the precinct of Gaea.

The image of the dragon Python, killed by the infant Apollo, represents the lower self, the unconscious, the powers of the underworld that must be conquered. The sphinx asked Oedipus the famous riddle: "What is it that goes on four legs in the morning, two at noon, and three at evening?" The answer Oedipus gave was "man." His answer was a vision of himself revealed by an introspective question but only partly understood by the sighted but wisdom-blind Oedipus. The Naxian Sphinx was Archaic: still, majestic, haunting, and powerful, but also very Egyptian, suggesting the close connection of the Naxian island culture to the more ancient religious imagery of its southern neighbor.

Stairs leading to the halos, used for the ceremony of Stepteria, Delphi

The Halos

Just beyond the sacred precinct of the goddess and on the other side of the Sacred Way was located a circular dancing floor or threshing floor called a Halos. The area is now cluttered with stone fragments, but was once an important place in the sanctuary. On this spot, every eight years, a drama called the Stepteria was performed in honor of Apollo. A hut, or *skene,* was constructed, within which was a table laden with religious objects. A young boy, chosen from among those whose parents were still living, was joined by other youths who raced up the stairs (#22) into the hut, upset the table, and then set fire to the hut. Without looking back, the boys then fled on foot, leaving the sanctuary, and went on a pilgrimage to the Vale of Tempe, to the north near Mount Olympus, where in one myth Apollo had gone to be purified after killing the Python. Some time later they returned to Delphi, bearing laurel leaves as a symbol of purification.

Most scholars agree that this ceremony was but a dim reflection of the myth of Apollo and the killing of the Python and more clearly involves the purification of the shrine every eight years, making pure what in the intervening years had become polluted by the temptations of office or the violence of greed and hatred among the competing states and individuals. There was always the danger that the oracle would be polluted by bribery or temptation. Thus, purification was mandatory if the sanctuary was to achieve its sacred purpose, the true word of Zeus, given freely to those who desired to know it.

Temple of Apollo from the Sacred Way, with cyclopean walls; columns of the Athenian stoa in foreground, Delphi.

Approaching the Temple

On the left of the path as it continues north are the remains of the Stoa of the Athenians (#23). This simple open colonnade was made of wood and supported by seven marble Ionic columns, three of which are standing in place. The capital of one rests on the right side of the path and shows the fine detail of this order. The stoa was erected by the Athenians around 478 BC to display images of naval victories.

The Sacred Way now turns left, forms broad steps up the hillside, passes by three more treasuries, and enters an area once again devoted to monuments, most of which were placed on high bases overlooking the temple entrance. The first important monument (#24) was mounted on the extant circular base. Called the Serpent Column of Plataea, this monument celebrated the Greek victory over the Persians in 479 BC. Three coiled serpents cast in bronze formed a high column, on top of which was mounted a golden tripod, the symbol of prophecy. In the third century AD, Constantine the Great of Byzantium stripped Delphi of many of its monuments, including the coiled snakes. The head of one is now located in a museum in Istanbul.

Farther to the right is the large base for a gilded chariot erected around 304 BC by the Rhodians (#25). Next (#26 and 27) are bases for statues of two kings of Pergamon, Attalus I and Eumenes II. The long, narrow base to the rear (#28) was an image of King Attalus I, who also built a large stoa (#29) in 220 BC. In the Roman era the stoa was destroyed in order to provide a water supply to the baths off to the right beyond the retaining wall of the sanctuary.

A small base (#30) on the upper level of the hillside held the famous Acanthus Column, an exquisite sculpture of dancing girls erected by the Athenians in the middle of the fourth century BC. The column was 36 feet (11 m) high, ending in a curl of acanthus leaves. Three girls in flowing dresses *(poloi)* dance while supporting a sacred tripod on their heads. The statue, without the tripod, has been preserved and is on display in the museum.

Next to the acanthus column was the Sanctuary of Neoptolemos (#31)—also called Pyrrhos—a place sacred to the Greeks. A supporting wall sheltered an altar and the grave of the hero, the son of famed Achilles. The legends of the death of this heroic figure reflect various interpretations of the rituals of Delphi. In general, the legends agree that Pyrrhos was killed by temple priests during a sacrifice at the temple hearth. Some understand the death to have been a just result of the hero's attempt to seize control of the sanctuary, or at least to seize some degree of power from the priests. Others, of a more philosophical bent, see the killing as a ritual slaying in the mode of true sacrifice at Delphi.

Ritual slaying at Delphi was particularly violent, involving a sudden and furious wielding of the sacred knife, the death of a hero or scapegoat whose life and actions exceeded human limits and whose death was necessary to expiate the crimes of the community. Thus, Neoptolemos, the son of the greatest hero in Homeric legend, was sacrificed in order to renew life and to atone for human excess. As such, his death was sacred and his grave a place of due reverence. Interestingly, excavation has not revealed a grave on the site, but instead a Mycenaean sacrificial pit, a place revered by later Greeks wherever they were found. It was understood that the Mycenaeans knew and understood ritual sacrifice, and honoring these sites may have been the function of the round temples, or *tholoi*, found in major sanctuaries.

The Temple Terrace

As the pilgrim approached the temple terrace, a series of monuments caught the eye and were quite splendid in their effect. To the right were three Golden Tripods (#32) which were dedicated some time after 480 BC by the kings of Sicily. The tripods were of great value and were stolen during the Third Sacred War in the fourth century BC by the Phokians. Engraved *stele* or marble slabs replaced the tripods, one of which remains.

On the large square base (#33) stood a massive statue of Apollo in his aspect as protector of the harvest. The statue was erected by the Amphiktyonic Council sometime during the fourth century BC and stood over 50 feet high (16 m), dominating the entrance to the temple. The final major feature of the terrace during the Archaic and through the Classical periods was the Great Altar (#34), dedicated by the citizens of Chios, who were privileged in their relations with Delphi, being first in line when the oracle spoke. As the foundation suggests, the altar was quite large, measuring 28 feet by 17 feet (8.6 m x 5.1 m). The dark marble of the body of the altar was quarried on the island of Chios. White marble made up the base and top.

As in most approaches to temples in Greece, the Sacred Way delivered the pilgrim to the gate of sacred experience as though through a labyrinth, in this case a labyrinth that began down in the depths of the valley and wound upward through the Gate of Athena at Marmaria, through the underworld of the Kastalian Spring, and then into a sculpted and golden world of manifest divinity. The Sacred Way led the aspirant up through visions of order in the form of small temple buildings and human and divine forms in marble, bronze, and gold. The labyrinth passed by the awesome precinct of the Mother Goddess and directed the gaze to the cliffs rising almost directly overhead, pressing down and yet opening out to the sky. The final approach, through close walls and broad steps, shielded the temple from view until the pilgrim turned to face the massive statue of Apollo gazing out over the valley. Here was the goal of the journey, the figure of the god before his temple, within which could be gleaned some measure of understanding, should the heart be open to the experience.

THE TEMPLE OF APOLLO

The six temple columns that have been reconstructed to suggest their position in antiquity represent the last temple to occupy this sacred site. Out of the legends of the past have come the stories of six temples, only three of which can be confirmed by physical evidence. However, the legends of the first three have the evidence of poetic power and a certain historical logic.

The location of the various temples depends upon two factors: the ancient belief and testimony that a cleft in the earth from which vapors arose was the source of Delphi's oracular power, and the demands of building a major temple on this particular hillside as close as possible to a specific oracular source. The myth of the cleft has to be related to the origins of oracular power in the time when the deities of the underworld spoke to human beings through natural sounds: the babbling of springs and the rustle of wind in sacred trees.

From caves and crevices came utterings as well, and the area around Delphi was rich with such openings in the earth. The precinct of the Goddess below the temple site shows geological evidence of fissure, permitting water to rise to the surface in several places beneath the temple site. There is no specific evidence below the foundation of the present temple of a geological fault from which volcanic vapors might arise. However, major shifting due to earthquakes may have obliterated evidence of such a cleft well before the stone temples were erected and the area was prepared for their construction.

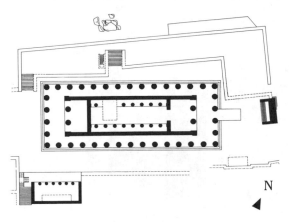

Fig. 29. The Temple of Apollo, Delphi

The Legends of Early Temples

Pausanius provides the legendary context for the history of temples on this site. He says that Earth gave her share of the oracular site to Themis in her aspect as protector of natural law. Themis in turn gave Apollo her share as a gift. Mankind discovered the oracle when shepherds stumbled upon the cleft and were possessed by the vapors in the name of Apollo.

Legend says that the first "temple" was a rude hut fashioned by laurel leaves imported from the Vale of Tempe—brought, it must be assumed, as a reenactment of the rites of purification in the original myth of Apollo's occupation of the site. The second temple was made of feathers and beeswax; in fact, the temple was made by bees sent by Apollo from the north. The bee in Greek myth was a sacred creature, a manifestation of pure spirit. The third temple was made of bronze, which Pausanius asserts was not an uncommon material in early architecture. It may have been a Mycenaean structure erected during the Heroic Age, when the sibyl Herophile gave oracle from the site.

The Early Archaic Temple

Temple number four was built around 650 BC, perhaps as late as 600 BC. Its construction was attributed to legendary priest-architects Trophonios and Agamedes, who followed sacred inspiration in building a temple that reflected the attributes of Apollo. It is said that Apollo granted them a peaceful death at a young age as a reward for their dedication to him.

Constructed on a *poros*-stone base, a conglomerate commonly used in temple building, this temple was smaller than the two later temples, measuring only 140 feet (43 m) long and 52 feet (16 m) wide. Very little is known of its appearance. The few remains indicate that it probably had a wooden roof and columns, with mud bricks used for its interior walls. The temple burned in 548 BC.

The Temple of Apollo from above, showing the valley of the Pleistos River, Delphi

The Late Archaic Temple

By that time Delphi was controlled by the council, which sought funds from all city-states in Greece for a new temple. The sum of 300 talents was acquired and the work began. By 515 BC the Alkmaeonid family of Athens, exiled for their attempts to overthrow the oligarchy then in power, undertook the completion of the work. Their contribution was to complete the pediments of the temple in Parian marble, no doubt in the tradition of the fine work done on the Acropolis in Athens.

In order to prepare the site for this more massive temple, the builders first had to construct a polygonal retaining wall in order to establish a firm, flat area. This impressive wall, still standing, along with the resulting terrace area it created, destroyed the evidence of several earlier buildings, including, it is thought, a temple to Ge and most of the evidence of the earlier temple to Apollo. The new temple measured 195 feet (59.5 m) in length and 78 feet (23.8 m)in width. There is some speculation that it was built without a roof over the *naos*, or central hall.

The Doric columns for the exterior numbered thirty-eight—six on the facades and fifteen on the sides. The interior columns were of the Ionic order. The combination of six columns on the facade and fifteen on the long side was abnormal, the usual pattern being six and thirteen. The extra length and hence two additional columns were the result of the special requirements of the building. In the usual temple the *naos* was the only space within the temple after the *pronaos,* or outer chamber. In Apollo's temple, however, additional space was required for the inner sanctum, or *adyton,* where the oracles were given and where the other sacred items of the temple were kept. This sanctum had to be separate, and adequate security was needed in the form of walls or screens to separate the pilgrim from the prophetess and priests.

Earthquake and Reconstruction

In 373 BC this fifth temple was destroyed by an earthquake, which also damaged other buildings and monuments. Because Sparta was then the dominant power in Greece, the Spartans took the lead in raising funds for the reconstruction. A new, sixth temple was to be built on the same site, with similar dimensions.

The Third Sacred War deflected attention away from temple building and work was delayed. In 350 BC work resumed, only to be delayed again by the Fourth Sacred War. The temple was finally completed and dedicated in 330 BC. The dimensions of this sixth temple turned out to be very nearly the same as those of the previous one. The materials were also the same: *poros* stone for the foundation, columns, and entablature, and Parian marble for the pediments.

The Inner Life of the Temple

The contents of the *naos* and the *adyton* of this temple have been described by various writers through the ages, allowing a tentative reconstruction of the way in which oracles were given. Sayings from the Seven Wise Ones were inscribed in gold on the walls of the *naos.* Speaking of the later temple, Pausanius mentions these seven, among whom were the famous Ionian Thales and the Athenian lawgiver Solon. It was from these philosophers that the phrases "Know Thyself" and "Nothing to Excess" came to be associated with Delphi.

Also in the *naos* were the golden statue of Apollo and the so-called eternal hearth. The petitioner waiting in the outer chamber was exposed, then, to several divine admonitions. The sayings of the Seven Wise Ones were designed to bring the mind to a proper appreciation of the moment. "Know Thyself" the inscription said. The Greek knew that this admonition meant two things: first, be aware of the human condition, of proper place and humility before the god; second, from the teachings of Orpheus, Pythagoras, and Plato, know that the god resides within and can be heard through the *psyche.* It was Thales, one of the Wise Seven and a teacher of Pythagoras, who said, "All things are full of gods."

The other famous inscription, "Nothing to Excess," was a prescription for harmony in every aspect of human life. Apollo was the god of harmony, the god whose likeness and aspect harmonized the extremes. Human happiness depended upon the individual's ability to harmonize the demands of the *psyche* with the demands of the mind and body. Harmony was the key to success and Apollo showed the way. Harmony also meant the proper alignment of the elements of *psyche,* mind, and body—in that order—with the god-centered *psyche* in control. Here in the Temple of Apollo, after purification in the sacred waters and at the end of the labyrinth of the Sacred Way, an individual had a good chance of achieving such an alignment.

The Events in the Adyton

The inner sanctum or *adyton* was a sunken area of the temple, surrounded by Ionic columns and approached by steps leading down to the place of prophecy. The Pythia, or prophetess, having bathed in the sacred Kastalian Spring and dressed in the robes of a young maiden, entered the *naos* and passed through the smoke and incense of the sacred hearth, or *hestia,* in which laurel leaves and barley burned. Again, whether or not entheogens in the form of ergot, mushroom, or other ingested drugs were involved is not known. Generally, among scholars there is a bias against such an influence, although the experience of native peoples throughout the ages argues in favor of such revelatory assistance.

Accompanied by priests whose task it was to record the utterings, the Pythia took her place upon the tripod, the seat of prophecy. The tripod was similar to a caldron, a large covered kettle in which were kept sacred objects. Myth held that the tripod contained the bones of the slaughtered Python, or perhaps even the bones of the slain god Dionysos. Next to the tripod was the *omphalos,* the round stone covered with a net of woven fillets, which was known to be the center of the world and also marked the grave of Dionysos.

Thus seated, waving a branch of laurel, with vapors arising from the chasm beneath, the Pythia entered a state of prophetic madness known by the Greeks as *enthousiasmos.* The utterings, sometimes barely grasped by the attending priests, were recorded and "translated" into Homeric hexameters. This shaping of the utterances into poetic form was one of the earliest forms of Greek writing, an art that was naturally enough associated with Apollo and connected more generally with the arts of civilization.

THE THEATER

The singing of hymns to Apollo was an ancient tradition at Delphi, and the area occupied by the present theater most likely served as the place where these musical competitions were traditionally held. Some slight evidence suggests that an older, perhaps Classical, theater with wooden seats and scene building preceded the stone structure.

The stone structure was built in the late fourth and early third centuries BC but was replaced—no doubt because of earthquake damage—several times. A major renovation was undertaken by Eumenes II, king of Pergamon, in the second century BC, to be followed by the present construction during the Roman Imperial Period.

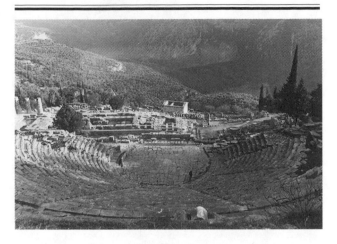

The Theater at Delphi, Roman Imperial Period; Athenian Treasury seen below

The present theater, which seats 5,000 persons, has thirty-five rows of seats with a diazoma after row twenty-eight. The orchestra, in its typical Roman horseshoe shape, has a diameter of 60 feet (18.5 m). A stone scene building rose behind the orchestra and provided a raised stage. This late construction provided for the presentation of plays as well as musical performance during various festivals, including the Pythian Games.

THE STADIUM

Nestled among the pines farther up the hillside are the remains of the stadium. Along the way the visitor passes several votive niches and fountains where natural springs provided water. Evidence suggests that the hillside now occupied by the stadium was first dug out in Classical times, sometime around 450 BC. Before that time the Pythian Games were primarily musical contests in honor of Apollo. Later, athletic contests were added and they eventually overshadowed the artistic competitions.

The present appearance of the stadium is attributed to Herod Atticus, the wealthy Athenian whose works in Athens include the Odeion near the Acropolis. His contributions to the stadium include the monumental entrance, the remains of which are still evident, and the stone seating. At the entrance the four limestone posts, two with votive niches, were the supports for three Roman arches through which the athletes entered the arena.

Runners took their positions at the marble slab, which was provided with indentations—the Roman equivalent of starting blocks. Holes in the slab indicate the positions for posts that marked the running lanes. Roughly twenty lanes

The Stadium at Delphi

were available. The course was 195 yards (178.3 m) long, which equaled one Pythian *stadion*. Some races were two lengths of the stadium, and some involved horses and chariots.

The Roman Imperial stadium of Atticus was provided with stone seating for 7,000 spectators. Included in the center were backed seats for the judges. The seating was arranged in a series of twelve sections, each with twelve rows, except at the rounded end, or *sphendone*, where there were only six rows. Recent excavation has revealed the remains of an Archaic fountain at the rounded end of the stadium, suggesting something of the ritual history associated with the Pythian Games.

THE MUSEUM

Because the museum reflects the cooperation throughout the excavations between the French School of Archaeology and the Greek government, all the accompanying inscriptions for the collection are written in Greek and French only. Those wishing a comprehensive description of the collection and an English translation of the inscriptions will find at the desk several fine full-color guides with adequate descriptions. This guide will highlight select items from this extraordinary collection in an effort to emphasize its high quality and sacred content.

THE OMPHALOS

At the top of the stairs on the main level of the museum is the marble *omphalos* that was found at the entrance to the temple.

The Kouroi—Archaic figures from Argos

This Hellenistic copy of the original, which stood in the Classical *adyton*, reflects the general design of such symbols throughout ancient history. The *omphalos* was both a grave marker and an image of a matrix; it was a point of origin and a tomb. Some have speculated that its shape also imitates the mound of white ash that was built up into this shape around a core of hot coals to keep a source of fire safe when not in use. The carving on the marble represents the covering of wool fillets woven like a net over the stone.

Of interest nearby are an Archaic tripod and an example of a bronze caldron. These two particular pieces would not have been seen or used together, but they illustrate the principle of the tripod and caldron upon which the prophetess sat when giving oracle. These examples are votive offerings.

THE KOUROI

In the Hall of the Kouroi stand two magnificent figures from Argos, sculpted by Polymedes, whose name appears on the base. The *kouroi* date from around 600 BC and represent the sacred principles of form so evident in the early Archaic Period. The symmetry of the pair reflects the ancient concept of the human form as an expression of the ideal. The symmetry is not a reflection of awkwardness or a primitive conception on the part of the artist or his culture, but an expression of perfection rather than appearance: Here is a human being, a manifestation of the creation in perfect form.

These two figures were inspired by the myth of Cleobis and Biton, two youths from Argos whose mother was a priestess in the Temple of Hera in the Argolid. The two youths yoked themselves to a chariot in order to take their mother to the temple, a distance of 5 miles (8 km). Once there, the mother-priestess prayed to the goddess to reward her sons for their devotion and service. The goddess responded to the prayer by taking life from the youths while they slept in the temple, thus giving them the reward of a peaceful death without suffering.

THE SILVER BULL AND GOLD TREASURES

In Room #5, a relatively new addition, the museum has displayed a valuable collection of silver, gold, and ivory treasures, all discovered in 1939 by the French archaeologist Amandry. Central to this display is the head of a bull of Ionian design from the Archaic Period. The bull was fashioned from thin silver sheets fixed onto a wooden framework. As was the custom from earlier times, the horns, ears, hooves, and genitals of the bull were gilded, indicating its sacred function and purpose as a sacrificial animal.

Also noteworthy in the room are several gold sheets with hammered panels depicting sacred animals. These Archaic panels formed part of the garment of a large statue and reflected the interest during Archaic times in connecting the images of the gods with animal attributes, both real and imagined. Pictured are griffins, bulls, lions, goats, an antelope, and a sphinx.

THE NAXIAN SPHINX

The contents of this room illustrate the Archaic vision of two prominent Aegean islands, Naxos and Siphnos. The Naxian Sphinx has already been described (see p. 280). What becomes evident in its presence is the remarkable fusion of the disparate elements. Here, after all, is a woman, very much like a *kore*—in other words, poised and enigmatic—who also has the wings of a bird and the body of a lion. The body, which is slim and graceful, seems to support the mythic wings and head so naturally that one might suppose such a creature to exist. The secret of this synthesis lies in the expression. The eyes are closed. The lips betray a smile expressing secret knowledge, both dangerous and personal.

The rest of this room contains elements from the famed

Treasury of the Siphnians. Of particular interest are the Archaic frieze sculptures. These are very rare because in most cases Archaic pieces from temples throughout Greece were destroyed or lost in the process of Classical and Hellenistic reconstruction. The subject matter here is the Trojan War. The gods pictured are Ares, with a shield, and Aphrodite, who is leaning over the back of Artemis, both of whom appear to be talking to Apollo, presumably pleading with him for the cause of the Greeks. Zeus the Father sits (headless) to the right.

To the Greeks such representations were full of mythical and sacred meaning. This was a harmonizing scene. Ares, god of war, sits at one end, poised and awesome in his strength. At the other end Zeus sits with one arm held in the same gesture. In between are the goddesses whose love and lawful order attempt to balance the wrath of Ares and Zeus, while Apollo turns to receive their pleas. Such balance and structure in Archaic sculpture were typical and illustrate the means by which myths were transmitted and meaning established through the plastic arts.

THE HYMNS TO APOLLO

In Room #6, dedicated to the Athenian Treasury, are the inscriptions from the Treasury that contain the Greek musical notation for two hymns to Apollo. These two hymns date from 128 BC and were inscribed at that time in honor of the Pythias, the religious festival celebrated by the Athenians. Two German scholars deciphered the notations, which use letters and dots in various positions to signify notes on the scale and finger positions on the lyre.

The Delphic Hymn A says in part:

Listen, pale-skinned daughters of thundering Zeus,
Maidens who dwell on forested Helicon,
Come sing and dance in honor of your kinsman Phoibos,
He who shall come to the twin-peaked cliff of Parnassos
And the rushing waters of Kastalia with the famed
Maidens of Delphi, to visit the oracular hill of Delphi.

THE DANCING MAIDENS AND DIONYSOS

In the large room (#11) dedicated to Classical sculpture, two important works are displayed. The first is the Acanthus Column of the dancing girls (see p. 282). Here again are the balance and symmetry so typical of the themes of Delphi. The three maidens emerge from the natural fecundity of the acanthus-leaf column to swirl in frozen dance, while holding the sacred tripod upon their heads. The design speaks of the human connection to oracular power and of feminine beauty as the image of the harmony and grace in such power. The column combines the ornamentation of the Corinthian column with the beauty of the Karyatides in a single expression of the sacred attributes of the Mother Goddess.

The second statue of great interest in the room is the figure of Dionysos, one of the monumental sculptures that decorated the southwestern pediment of the last Temple of Apollo. This piece, executed by Androsthenes of Athens around 340 BC, was accompanied on the pediment by the Maenads, the female celebrants who performed the orgiastic rites in honor of the god. This statue shows the almost feminine grace and beauty of the god, in dramatic contrast to the figures of Ares, Zeus, and Poseidon, the powerful, masculine gods of the pantheon.

This Late Classical image of Dionysos has another sort of power. The fleshy quality of the image and the artist's touch reflect the style of that period, but the characterization remains the same as earlier conceptions. Dionysus is the product of the union between the demi-goddess Semele and Zeus. Semele in turn came from the union between Harmonia, the daughter of Aphrodite and Ares, and the hero Kadmos, a mortal. To the Greeks, Dionysos was a sympathetic and accessible god, but also one who was dangerous when crossed. This statue is one of the finest extant depictions of him.

THE BRONZE CHARIOTEER

The final room of the museum houses its greatest treasure, the bronze Charioteer, whose grace and poise represent the best of human achievement and spiritual aspiration. There is an interesting legend about the Charioteer, which is often told by guides to the visitors to Delphi.

It seems that during the 1890s before the start of excavations, when the French were in the process of clearing the town of Kastri off the site of the sanctuary, one matriarch in particular would not leave her little house to relocate to the new town then under construction. Her refusal was holding up the whole relocation project. One morning she arrived at the house where the archaeologists were gathered and announced that she was ready to leave her house. When asked why she had so suddenly changed her mind, she reported a dream from the previous night. In her dream a boy who seemed to be trapped beneath the green sea called to her, "Set me free! Set me free!" The dream frightened her and she thought it was an omen. When the excavations began, the Charioteer was discovered beneath the old woman's house.

This magnificent bronze was produced in 470 BC as a monument to a victory in the Pythian Games. The group included four horses and a chariot. A separate group in front pictured a groom leading a single horse. The intent was to honor the victor and to demonstrate Plato's definition of mastery: control of four horses running in perfect synchrony drawing a chariot.

This figure depicts the exquisite control under pressure and the human achievement and perfection that were the Greek ideal of human life. The style is early Classical, sometimes referred to as the Severe Style. Still evident is the idealized form of the Archaic Period, which we see in the *kouroi*. What is yet to come is the so-called naturalism of the later Classical style and the still later decadence of the Hellenistic. Here is the human being inspired by spiritual attributes pictured in the moment of victory in one of life's most demanding exercises. Surely it is how the Greeks envisioned Apollo arriving at his sanctuary, drawn by four of Poseidon's finest horses.

The Charioteer, fifth century BC, Delphi Museum

OLYMPIA

*When, towards the fair flowering of his growing age,
the down began to shade his darkening cheek,
Pelops turned his thoughts to a marriage that lay
ready for him—to win from her father of Pisa famed
Hippodameia.*

— Pindar, *Olympion*

The journey across the rugged Peloponnese to the famous
site of the ancient Olympic Games is an arduous one. The
roads across the peninsula from Athens through Tripolis and
then onto the narrow, winding road (E 19) through the center
of the peninsula twist and turn, rise and fall, and the modern
visitor must wonder how the journey was made in ancient
times. Another option is to take the same numbered road
along its northern route within sight of the Gulf of Corinth,
through Egion and Patrai. In either case, the trip takes well
over five hours.

The rewards of the journey, however, are many. The
Peloponnese is beautiful, isolated by its geography from the
crowded, exhaust-filled world of Athens. It hangs on to the
tip of the greater Balkan peninsula like a leaf on the branch of
a plane tree and embodies in its rich, wooded landscape the
strength of the mix of people who settled here.

The aim of our particular journey is Olympia, which is
located in the prefecture of Elis in the northwest of the peninsula. The land occupied by the sanctuary of Olympia is
typical of the Earth Mother sites throughout the Mediterranean. Two rivers, one the Eurotas from the Parrasian Range,
descend from the central mountains and merge into the
Alpheos, and where its fresh waters slow in the plain to meet
the sea, the Earth Mother has her sacred precinct.

HISTORY

The descendants of the prehistoric people who originally
settled the peninsula prior to 3000 BC were gradually forced
into the central mountains by the Indo-European migrations
of 2000 BC. These original people, named by some historians
the Pelasgians, fought the new arrivals and were never com-

pletely conquered. In the area of Elis, where Olympia is situated, they worshiped the Earth Mother as the nurturing power of Nature and the chthonic power of the underworld.

Eventually these people merged with the new arrivals, the Mycenaeans, who built their fortresses and gradually moved out to conquer the rest of what is present-day Greece. In turn, the Achaean invasions of about 1250 BC threatened and eventually destroyed the great Mycenaean fortresses and imposed the Olympian sky gods upon the existing population. The characteristically rounded hill of the Earth Mother was renamed Mt. Kronos in honor of the father of Zeus, marking the tension that arose between the masculine dominion of the sky gods and the feminine dominion of the Earth Mother. As we shall see, this tension informs the history of the Olympic Games as well as the patterns of worship in the sanctuary at Olympia, which is the only one in the ancient world to hold major temples to both Hera and Zeus.

The formal history of Greece begins in 776 BC with the recording of the first winners of the Games. So also, the formal history of the site is really the history of the Olympic Games themselves. We can actually date the opening of the Games on our modern calendar to August 22 of that year. Moreover, from the history of the Games we learn that in order to effect a marriage of the masculine and feminine deities, exemplified as they were by the movements of the sun and the moon, a monumental compromise between competing religious calendars was required. In effect, the Olympic Games became the means through which some degree of unity was finally established among the various warring parties in what would eventually become modern Greece.

Although still a matter of some conjecture, it is highly probable that the Games originated in the annual race of young girls in honor of Hera Parthenos, Hera the Virgin. (Part of the ancient Goddess tradition was that the virginity of the Earth Mother was perpetually renewed after her marriage to the sky god—in this case, Hera's marriage to Zeus.) The various races of the virgins in honor of Hera took place in the ancient stadium at a distance of about 600 feet. The girls ran in order of age, with the youngest group running first. The winners were crowned with olive leaves in honor of Hera. It is probable that the races took place at the new moon in the summer month of Parthenios, which was named after the races.

In the Archaic year of 776 the men's games began, but the priests of the Temple of Zeus who organized them had to take the women's races into consideration when they scheduled the men's. As a compromise, the Games were scheduled by alternating the sun calendar of 50 months and the moon calendar of 49 months, in other words every four years on an alternating basis. This meant that if the first Olympics took place at full moon on 22 August 776 BC, the next took place 50 months later at full moon on 6 September 772, and so on every four years. In this way the moon calendar of the goddess and the sun calendar of the god were reconciled.

We owe much of this information to research done by Greek scholar F. M. Cornford and reported in his important essay, "The Origin of the Olympic Games." Cornford goes on to say that the Games were no doubt scheduled to reconcile the Hellenic moon year of 354 days with the solar year of 365-and-a-fraction days. In effect what we have here is the marriage of two traditions and, as the myths attest, two distinct forces in the history of Greece.

THE OLYMPIC GAMES

In the original men's games that started in 776 BC the events were sacred in intent. The purpose of the competition was to celebrate the ideal of human achievement in both form and content. Feats of speed, strength, agility, and control were featured. The aim was to win glory for one's *polis*, and all the city-states in Hellas sent participants. So celebrated were the victors that when they returned to their home cities, portions of the defensive walls were torn down to permit them to ride through the breach in a chariot.

A wide range of sports were included in the Games, most of which related to skills necessary in war. There were wrestling matches, swimming, bareback riding, dodging spears while riding, games of ball resembling lacrosse, field hockey, even handball. But the most important events, the ones attracting the greatest athletes and the largest crowds, were grouped together as the pentathelon. Each athlete had to compete in all five events, and the victor had to win three of the five.

The first event was the broad jump. Unlike the modern broad jumper, the athlete held a weight in each hand and, by thrusting his arms out as he jumped, was able to cover a great distance through the air. The second event, the discus throw, was very much like the modern event. The stone or metal disk weighed about twelve pounds. The third event was the javelin. Unlike the modern spear, the ancient javelin was thrown with the aid of a leather thong attached to the middle of the javelin, which added thrust to the throw. The fourth event was the sprint, a run of about 200 yards. The last event was wrestling, which is still a very popular sport in Greece. Often these matches were very violent and the athletes were severely injured.

Other bloody contests included boxing, in which the athletes wore soft leather gloves and blows were restricted to the head. Often quite brutal, the matches lasted until one of the participants either was knocked out or gave up. In addition to the 200-yard dash there were other foot races of varying distances, including an armed sprint in which participants had to carry heavy shields.

The culminating events of the Games were the highly popular chariot races. Set for both two- and four-horse chariots, these races often ended in terrible accidents. History records that at one Games, out of a field of forty chariots only one finished the race. The famous statue of the Charioteer at Delphi is an example of the high regard in which these athletes were held. One needed extraordinary skill to control the movements of four highly spirited horses around a narrow course in which up to forty other chariots were vying for victory. Indeed, as we shall see, the chariot race is central to the mythology of Olympia.

In 393 AD a decree from the Roman Emperor Theodocius the Great brought an official end to the ancient Games, which during Roman times had declined into commercialism and professionalism—two factors we also see today. The Games were not to begin again until 1896. Visitors may visit the Olympic Stadium in Athens that was built for the occasion. At that first revival of the Games a Greek won the marathon. This long-distance run of twenty-six miles commemorates the legendary run of the messenger who brought news of the Greek victory at Marathon over the Persian forces under Darius. He arrived in Athens declaring "Rejoice! We conquer!" and dropped dead. Some stories identify the runner Pheidippides as the messenger, but history records only that Pheidippides covered a distance of 140 miles in two days trying to reach Sparta in time to gather reinforcements for the Persian invasion. However his mission failed because the Spartans were engaged in the worship of Apollo and could not take up arms.

Given the history of the Games, it is highly significant that 2004 will see the return of the summer Olympics to Greece. Regardless of the commercialism and even corruption symptomatic of the modern Games, their return to Greece will renew something of their sacred history and may well rekindle a measure of the Archaic idealism in which they were founded.

MYTHOLOGY

The mythology of Olympia begins with the story of Pelops, son of Tantalus, whose sacrilege in the presence of the gods established for the Greeks important metaphors of death and resurrection. The terrible feast of Tantalus was a primitive saga of sacrilege as Tantalus sought to please (or offend) the gods by carving up his son Pelops and boiling up the parts in a horrible stew. Only Demeter ate of the flesh—a piece of shoulder—before the nature of the meal was discovered. Zeus ordered the pieces placed back into the cauldron, whereupon he restored Pelops to life and punished Tantalus for eternity.

The story of Pelops is related to the Olympic Games in that we witness in the competition the regeneration of youth in new victors as well as the celebration of fecundity. Here on the Alpheus Plain the profusion of trees, the luxuriant flowering of grain, the merging of two rivers with the sea speak eloquently of the gifts of Demeter, whose ancestor was Gaea. Pelops embodies the religious vision of immortality, and those pilgrims who came to his altar in the sanctuary made sacrifices to this miracle.

In his *Olympion* Pindar minimizes the story of the terrible meal and instead tells the heroic story of the marriage of Pelops to the beautiful Hippodameia and the young hero's victory over her father, King Oinomaos. Pelops knew the history of suitors who tried to win the hand of the young and beautiful Hippodameia. Her father Oinomaos was famous for making sure that no suitor survived the chariot race that was held to choose a worthy husband. The king used any means necessary to defeat attempts to win his daughter, and his spear found the backs of any who raced in their chariots towards Corinth and freedom. Thirteen suitors had died in this way, and their heads decorated the palace walls.

According to Pindar, Pelops came to vie for the hand of Hippodameia with support from Poseidon. Pelops prayed to the god after landing at Elis, saying, "Come now, Poseidon . . . do thou trammel the bronze spear of Oinomaos, speed me on swiftest chariot to Elis, and bring victory to my embrace." Poseidon granted the young hero's wish and gave him swift horses. Meanwhile, after thirteen failures, Hippodameia left nothing to chance. She arranged that the linchpins were removed from her father's chariot, which then crashed at a crucial moment, and Oinomaos was killed by Pelops with his own spear. Pelops married Hippodameia and she bore him six warrior sons.

This theme, the death of the old king and rise of the new, is typical of New Year mythology, as we know when we bid farewell each year to old Father Time and welcome the New Year Babe. In this case, Pelops dedicated his victory to Poseidon and to Zeus, whose father, Kronos, became the resident deity on the hill outside the sacred precinct, supplanting the Earth Mother. This sacrilege was atoned for each year by sacrifices to the goddess and was partly mitigated by the sacred marriage between Zeus and Hera within the sanctuary, which gave the Olympic Games its four-year cycle.

Implicit also in this story is the ancient conflict between Kronos and his son Zeus for ultimate control of the eternal ground. Zeus prevails and establishes his kingdom on Mt. Olympus. He rules with the thunderbolt, which he wields like a javelin to establish justice among mortals and immortals. His one concession is to his virgin bride Hera, whose sanctuary exists side by side with his own in the famed *altis* at Olympia.

THE SITE

The site of the famed Olympic sanctuary, or *altis* as it is called, lies in a peaceful plain near the sea. The Kladeos River flows in graceful curves nearby, feeding the fertile valley and creat-

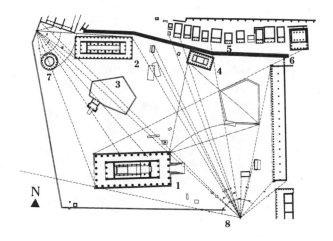

Fig. 30. *Olympia*

1. *Temple of Zeus*
2. *Temple of Hera*
3. *Pelopion*
4. *Metroon*
5. *Row of Treasures*
6. *Entrance to Stadium*
7. *Philippeion*
8. *South Entrance*

ing an atmosphere of tranquility. The hill of Kronos, once sacred to the Earth Mother, is the only dominant feature, and the sacred precinct is laid out in relation to it. The earliest remains in the area are the foundations of a Mycenaean *megaron* oriented to the hill. The stones are found between the Temple of Hera and the Metroon, a small Archaic temple devoted to the Earth Mother, Gaea.

The *altis* was surrounded by a protective wall, constructed not for defense but to mark off the sacred precinct. One of three entrances—perhaps the main one—was from the south at a point a few yards from the eastern edge of the Leonidaion, a large square Hellenistic guest house with a round center (see Fig. 30). This entrance appears to have been the one mentioned by Pausanius in his description of the site. The pilgrim passed through the four-columned Propylon and walked east along the sacred way, both sides of which were lined with offerings and statues of past winners at the Games.

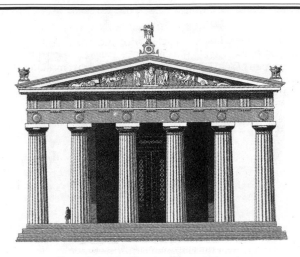

Engraving of the Temple of Zeus at Olympia

On the left was the famed Temple of Zeus, a Doric temple built in 472 BC. The temple dominated the *altis*. It sat in the landscape as a dominating presence. The statue of Zeus, sculpted by Phidias as a huge sitting figure, must have overwhelmed the other elements of the sanctuary. Its role was to shift power away from the Hill of Kronos and the temple of Hera and center attention on the undisputed ruler of Olympus. When the great doors were open, Zeus looked out on the stadium in the distance, a figure of authority and fatherly pride. If we think in terms of the myth of the site, we can see how this image portrays Zeus as the son who kills the father and seizes control, establishing his dominance over the culture and bringing order and justice to his people.

As we come through the trees around to the front of the Temple of Zeus, we see the central elements of the *altis*: the Pelopion and the Temple of Hera. The Pelopion was thought at one time to be the grave of Pelops, but excavation revealed nothing of a grave site. Instead, it was a sacred precinct, entrance to which was gained through a *propylon* of four columns on each side. The altar appears to have been a raised rectangle of sacred trees, emblematic of the rebirth of the hero. Such precincts traditionally were specially marked-off spaces with naturally occurring trees and flowers and may well, in this case, have included an olive tree, often sacred to Hera.

Flanking the Pelopion was the temple of Hera, in the Doric style and built around 600 BC. According to Pausanius, a statue of a seated Hera was accompanied by a standing Zeus, wearing a helmet. The temple rests in the shadow of the Kronos Hill, and we are reminded of its earliest associations with the Earth Mother.

The presence of both these temples, each facing east but at slightly different angles with the Pelopion between, suggests a special relationship of the gods to the mortals who worshiped here. The athletes came to take part in games that not only honored gods and heroes, but also reaffirmed on each occasion the lawful marriage of masculine and feminine powers. This affirmation was the foundation of the culture. To celebrate it every four years, with participants coming from every corner of Hellas, was crucial to the survival of Greek values.

Visitors can now turn to the east and pass through the Vaulted Tunnel to the Stadium. Only athletes and officials passed through this tunnel on their way to the competition. The stadium was moved out of the *altis* during Archaic times, and the present Stadium was constructed in the fourth century BC. The track is 212 meters long, and the original starting blocks are still embedded in the clay. To the right, toward the river and over the embankment, is the Hippodrome, where the horse and chariot races were held. One record indicates that the chariots did twelve laps around the track, symbolic of the sun passing through the twelve signs of the zodiac.

The remaining ruins outside the *altis* include the Gymnasium; the Palestra, where the athletes rested, dressed and prepared; and, most interesting for us, the workshop of the sculptor Phidias, which later became part of a Christian basilica. Excavation of the site indicates that this area was used by craftsmen during temple construction, and since Phidias was in charge of the work, the area has become associated with him.

THE MUSEUM

This brief section will highlight some of the treasures to be seen in the newly completed museum. The most important pieces are reliefs from the Temple of Zeus, including the magnificent Apollo and the central figures of Zeus, Oinomaos, and Hippodameia. The temple contained forty-two figures and twelve *metopes*, and the museum collection at Olympia represents the finest temple collection in Greece.

The Hellenistic figure of Hermes with the baby Dionysos by Praxiteles is indicative of the shift to naturalistic sculpting after the Classical Period. The developments from the idealized Archaic vision to the severe style of the Classical to this naturalism illustrate the changing vision of the human being from the high point of Archaic culture down to the realism of the pre-Roman period.

Other important items include the terra-cotta statue of Zeus with Gannymede from 480 BC; the helmet of the Athenian general Miltiades, which he wore at the Battle of Marathon and dedicated to Zeus after the victory; and the collection of paraphernalia from the Games.

4

THE LESSER PALACE AND TEMPLE SITES

Dotted throughout the mainland and islands of Greece are other sites where ancient sanctuaries of Minoan, Mycenaean, or Neolithic origins were celebrated, palaces were constructed, and temples were placed in honor of the gods. Such sites range in magnitude and importance from the oracle of Zeus at Dodona in the north to the barren remains of Delos in the Aegean.

These pages list several of the more important sites not given full treatment in this book. Those travelers interested in greater detail will usually find materials at the sites; some are full-color guides at reasonable prices. However, the traveler should also be forewarned that locally produced pamphlets tend to be carelessly translated and edited.

BASSAE

Also spelled "Bassai," "Vassae," and "Vasses"—the Greek *beta* being pronounced as *v*—"Bassae" means glens or ravines. The site of the Temple of Apollo Epikourios (the Helper) at Bassae sits in dramatic isolation among mountains and gorges in Elis, the Western Peloponnese. The drive alone is worth the trip, particularly the last 9 miles (15 km) from Andritsena. The road winds through the hills, moving up to an altitude of 3,700 feet (1,127 m), where the temple rests on the slope of Mount Kotilion.

The area surrounding the temple was sacred to Artemis in her aspect as goddess of wild things and places, and to Aphrodite, the remains of whose temple has been found higher on Mount Kotilion. Preserved here is the landscape of Greece as it was two thousand years ago. Even the spring mentioned by Pausanius still runs, at least in the winter.

The archaeological evidence tells us that an earlier Archaic temple of the seventh century BC stood on this site and could have been dedicated to Artemis—likely enough in light of the landscape elements. The temple to Apollo is the result of a dedication by the people of Phigalia, who during the Peloponnesian War in the fifth century BC were spared the ravages of the plague and in gratitude built the temple.

The great attraction of this temple is its design. Attributed to Iktinos, architect of the Parthenon, it was probably completed between 420 and 417 BC, although some scholars argue for an earlier date of 450 BC, which would make the use of Corinthian columns in the interior here the earliest on record.

The temple's excellent state of preservation is a testament to its isolation. Most of its columns are now standing, having been restored to their proper places early in this century. Of especial interest are the ten engaged columns—half-round columns connected to the walls—two of which at the southern end were Corinthian. Also of note is the eastern door, located so that the cult statue of Apollo would catch the first rays of the morning sun—no doubt lined up exactly on festival days.

BRAURON

Also spelled "Vravron," the sanctuary of Brauron is located 15 miles (24 km) east of Athens. Sacred to Artemis, the site rests at the foot of the Agios Georgias Hill. Its use dates well back into Mycenaean times, and it was continuously occupied throughout the Classical Period.

The site is neatly laid out and has been well excavated, revealing a Classical temple of Artemis—a peristyle court around which a dozen columns are standing—numerous small rooms for the priestesses of Artemis, and a sacred spring. This sanctuary was important to the life of young girls, who served the goddess and experienced the initiations of maidenhood in her precinct.

CORINTH

Also spelled "Korinthos," Corinth sits at the entrance to the Peloponnese, a location that gave the city much power in ancient times but also made it the target of frequent invasion and destruction. The present ruins are nearly all Roman, with evidence of Archaic and Classical stonework used in the later buildings and monuments.

Central to the present ruins is the ancient spring, regarded as sacred from the time of the Bronze Age. For most of its history Corinth was regarded as a place of pure waters and healing baths.

The sanctuary of Apollo is an Archaic temple to the god

Temple of Apollo at Corinth, with Acrocorinth in background

that has been partly restored. Nearby was also an Asklepieion, second only in fame to the sanctuary at Epidauros.

The imposing acropolis of Acrocorinth rises above the site and contains ruins of fortresses from Byzantine through Venetian times. Hearty souls may wish to scale these heights and explore the ruins, but little from ancient times remains.

DELOS

The island of Delos, also "Dilos," is the smallest of the Cyclades but is central in the group. Occupied from Neolithic times, Delos was of strategic importance during the period of Athenian domination in the fifth century BC. Now abandoned except by archaeologists, staff, and visitors, the island is accessible from Mykonos by small boats, which make daily visits during most of the year.

Delos is the most sacred island in the Aegean. Its history suggests that it was sacred to the Earth Mother Goddess from earliest times, and in the Olympian tradition that devotion was carried on by Artemis, whose temples and sanctuaries on the island were really more important than Apollo's. The stark isolation of the island made it ideal as a site sacred to the virgin goddess of wild places and windswept bluffs.

On Delos were celebrated the cycles of the sun (Apollo) and the moon (Artemis) in yearly festivals and sacrifices. Near the ancient sacred harbor lie the remains of the major sanctuaries. Mycenaean remains have been found amidst the Archaic and Classical temples erected to both gods.

To the north of the harbor lies the Sacred Lake, the entranceway to which is marked by the famous Archaic

Naxian lions. Highly stylized and roaring, these beasts guarded the sacred precinct of the lake and were emblematic of the birthplace of Apollo.

DODONA

Far to the north, near the Albanian border and some 12 miles (19 km) from Ioannina, lies the famed sanctuary of Dodona, the first oracular site in Greece and sacred to Zeus the Father. Dodona was home to the *selloi,* priests of Zeus famous for their habit of sleeping on the snow-covered earth and for their special gifts of prophecy.

The priests of Dodona were devoted to nature's revelations—the prophetic utterances provided by the voices of streams and the language of leaves stirred by the wind in the sacred oak trees. The legends of the sanctuary held that a pigeon had flown from Thebes in Egypt and landed in an oak tree, from which it declared that an oracle of Zeus himself should be established at the site.

The main sights at Dodona are the impressive Hellenistic theater, which holds 18,000 spectators for modern productions of Classical plays, and the Zeus sanctuary, within which the sacred oak tree was preserved for many years.

PYLOS

Beyond the Argolid, far to the west in Messenia on the other side of the Peloponnese, lie the ruins of the Palace of Nestor at Pylos. This storied palace, so brilliantly pictured in the *Odyssey*, was uncovered in 1939 and contains the remains of a Bronze Age *megaron* second to none in Greece. Those with the time to explore the Western Peloponnese will want to include Pylos in their itinerary.

The location of the Palace, just over 9 miles (15 km) from Pylos on the hill called Ano Englianos, is a truly beautiful site. One is reminded more of Knossos than of Mycenae, in that Pylos appears not to have been fortified. Like Knossos, the citadel depended more on sea power for protection than upon monumental walls to withstand siege.

The palace is well preserved and offers a clear understanding of Mycenaean construction. The main complex of the palace is of major interest. The *propylon* reminds us of similar main entrances at Mycenae and Knossos. A single column, the base of which remains, supported the porch and yielded to a second single column in the vestibule. Before the main portico of the palace is an open court where visitors awaited entrance before the king.

The visitor gains a sense of the majesty of this palace from the good state of preservation of the vestibule and cen-

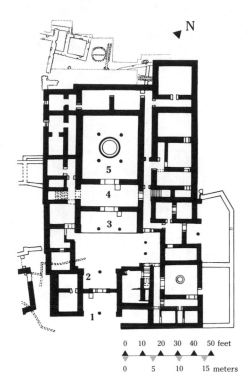

Fig. 31. Pylos
1. Propylon
2. Outer Court
3. Porch
4. Lobby
5. Megaron

tral *megaron*. The hearth, which was the heart of the palace, demonstrates the history of the circular offering pits and their importance to Mycenaean culture. We are able to trace circular pits and hearths of this type and size from Neolithic times through the Mycenaean into the Classical in the form of the *tholos* temples. As at Knossos and Mycenae, the wood-and-ivory throne was placed on the right-hand wall and was framed by griffin frescoes, symbols of wisdom and power.

SUNIUM

One of the most beautiful places in Greece was chosen as a sanctuary of both Zeus and Poseidon. On a bluff 200 feet (60 m) above the Aegean on the southernmost tip of Attica sits the famed Temple of Poseidon. Built in 440 BC, its very thin Doric columns of pure white marble seem to allow the entablature to float above the sea. The first glimpse of it told returning sailors that home was in sight.

One of the legends of Sunium (or Sounion) is that King Aegeus waited here for his son Theseus to return from Crete. Aegeus saw the black sail in the distance and, thinking his son dead, threw himself from the cliff into the sea that bears his name.

TIRYNS

Excavations beginning in 1887 and continuing to the present have uncovered numerous ancient sites in the Argive Plain, although none are so impressive or important as Mycenae. The Bronze Age citadel of Tiryns offers a glimpse of another fortress along the lines of Mycenae and contains examples of monumental stonework of the highest order.

Those who find accommodation in Nauplia or who merely wish to visit this beautiful seaside town and sample some of the best seafood in Greece, will want to stop briefly at the citadel of Tiryns, which is no more than 50 yards (46 m) off the main road. Because Tiryns is not a major site, its open hours are confined to the middle of the day. Visitors need to plan accordingly.

The first and major impression of Tiryns is that it sits very low in the landscape, only 60 feet (18 m) higher than the alluvial plain. Indeed, many scholars who have worked extensively in this plain have commented that when Tiryns was occupied and was an important extension of the power of Mycenae, the citadel was very close to the water and functioned as a port. In other words, the Gulf of Argolis extended further into the Argive Plain than it now does.

Most of the remains at Tiryns date from 1250 BC, the last period of construction for this fortress. The outstanding features include the long ramp leading to the entrance, the main gate which lies within the major fortress walls, the double walls with corridors leading throughout the citadel, the corbel gateway in the west wall, and the corbel-shaped passages built within the thickness of the main walls.

After the Dark Age, in the early Geometric Period, a temple dedicated to Hera was built over the ruins of the old *megaron*. Inscriptions indicate that during later periods both Zeus and Athena were also worshiped here. This evidence of cult activity suggests a continuity of worship that establishes Tiryns as a sacred place, one devoted particularly to the goddesses of the pantheon.

GLOSSARY

abaton	sleeping quarters for patients
adyton	inner sanctum
aegis	shield
agon	conflict
agora	marketplace
agrymos	the gathering
anaktoron	small building within *telesterion*
ananke	necessity
antae	extended walls
arche	head, leader
archons	officials
arete	excellence
aristoi	the few, aristocracy
arrheton	ineffable
basileus	king
cella	inner room (*naos*)
daemon	spirit, genius
deme	district, town
diazoma	inner circle
dike	justice
dromos	entry to tomb
echinus	molding above column
ekkyklema	rolling platform
en theos	with the god
enkoimisis	sleep cure
entasis	bulge in column
enthousiasmos	prophetic madness
epoptai	those gone before
eschara	underground altar
eurhythmia	rhythm
eurharmostia	harmony
gephyrismoi	"bridge jests" or hazing of initiates
guttae	decorative temple elements shaped as drops
halos	circular terrace; threshing ground
hecatomb	100, or a large number
heiron	sanctuary
hestia	sacred hearth
hexastyle	6-column front of temple
hoi polloi	the many, people
hubris	arrogance
in antis	projection of temple walls beyond enclosing walls
karyatid	column in the form of a maiden
kernos	offering table
kiste	basket

Kore	name of Persephone
kore	figure of a young woman
kouros, kouroi	idealized male youth(s)
labrys	double ax (source of *labyrinth*)
mechane	crane
megaron	great central room of early palaces; area in temple where only priests can enter
metope	sculpted panel
moira	fate, portion
myesis	beginning of initiation
mystai	worshipers
naos	inner room of temple
nomoi	laws, customs
nomos	law
nous	universal mind
omphalos	world navel
orchestra	circle in theater
ostrakon	pottery shard used for voting for banishment
palestra	public building
paradoi	entrance ways to *orchestra*
parthenos	maiden, virgin
peplos	robe for a goddess
peripatos	encircling road
physis	Nature
pithoi	large storage jars
polis	city-state
poloi	flowing dresses
pronaos	porch, entrance way to *naos*
propylaia	buildings forming entrance way
propylon	formal entrance to sanctuary
proskenion	Roman theater facade
psyche	soul
sekos	inner temple chamber
skene	scene building
stele	relief sculpture
stoa	covered colonnade
techne	skilled artisan
tholos	round temple
wanax, wa-na-ka	Mycenaean priest-king
xenon	guest room
xoanon	ancient cult statue

FURTHER READING

The authors represented here are those whose views and insights into the vitality of the Greek experience informed much of this book. Added to this list would also be the original documents of the time, the plays of the great dramatic poets, the dialogues of Plato, the histories of Herodotos and Thucydides, the poetry of Pindar and Hesiod, the philosophies of Heraclitus and Parmenides, and, of course, the great epics of Homer, the *Iliad* and the *Odyssey*.

Burkert, Walter. *Greek Religion*. Cambridge, Mass.: Harvard University Press, 1985.

Brunes, Tons. *The Secrets of Ancient Geometry*. Copenhagen: Rhodos, 1967.

Diel, Paul. *Symbolism in Greek Mythology*. Boulder and London: Shambhala, 1980.

Doczi, G. *The Power of Limits*. Boulder and London: Shambhala, 1981.

Dodds, E. R. *The Greeks and the Irrational*. Berkeley: University of California Press, 1951.

Graves, Robert. *The White Goddess*. New York: Farrar, Straus, and Giroux, 1948.

_____. *The Greek Myths*, vols. 1, 2. Middlesex: Penguin, 1960.

Harrison, J. *Epilegomena and Themis*. New York: University Books, 1962.

James, E. O. *The Ancient Gods*. New York: G. P. Putnam's Sons, 1960.

Lawlor, R. *Sacred Geometry*. New York: Crossroad Publishing Co., 1982.

Miller, H. *The Colossus of Maroussi*. New York: New Directions, 1941.

Neumann, E. *The Great Mother*. Princeton, N.J.: Bollingen Foundation, 1963.

Scully, V. *The Earth, the Temple, and the Gods*. New Haven, Conn.: Yale University Press, 1962.

Vernant, J. *The Origins of Greek Thought*. Ithaca, N.Y.: Cornell University Press, 1982.

Wasson, Kramrisch et al. *Persephone's Quest*. New Haven, Conn.: Yale University Press, 1986.

INDEX

NOTES

NOTES

NOTES

NOTES

NOTES

QUEST BOOKS
are published by
The Theosophical Society in America,
Wheaton, Illinois 60189-0270,
a branch of a world fellowship,
a membership organization
dedicated to the promotion of the unity of
humanity and the encouragement of the study of
religion, philosophy, and science to the end that
we may better understand ourselves and our place in
the universe. The Society stands for complete
freedom of individual search and belief.
For further information about its activities,
write, call 1-800-669-1571, e-mail olcott@theosophia.org,
or consult its Web page: http://www.theosophical.org

The Theosophical Publishing House
is aided by the generous support of
THE KERN FOUNDATION
a trust established by Herbert A. Kern
and dedicated to Theosophical education.